MANAGING HOTEL AND TOURISM OPERATIONS

MANAGING HOTEL AND TOURISM OPERATIONS

SUNIL SHARMA

AKANSHA PUBLISHING HOUSE
NEW DELHI-110059 (INDIA)

AKANSHA PUBLISHING HOUSE
R 37-B, Vani Vihar, Uttam Nagar
New Delhi-110059
Email: ektabooks@yahoo.com

Showroom
4649/21B, Ansari Road
Darya Ganj
New Delhi - 110 002
Ph.: 23269193 / 9811582579

Managing Hotel and Tourism Operations

First Edition 2005
ISBN 81-8370-021-7

PRINTED IN INDIA

Published by M.P. Misra for Akansha Publishing House, New Delhi and *Printed at* : Mehra Offset Press, New Delhi.

Contents

Preface

The hospitality and tourism industry is one of the leading global economic activities, because it brings in dollars from outside the community. It is a motor for employment and income creation and, especially in poor countries, a vehicle for development. Today, the industry is in the unenviable position of having to meet guest needs, owner/franchise demands and employee expectations —all in the face of threats of terrorism, war and economic uncertainties. A growing number of organisations, including the hospitality and tourism industry leadership, are increasingly conscious of the risks and are adopting a more responsible attitude in managing hospitality and tourism operations.

This book is a comprehensive tour of the fascinating and challenging fields of the hospitality and tourism industry: travel and tourism, lodging, food service, leisure and recreation. It offers a comprehensive treatment of all aspects regarding the management of hotels, food service and travel and tourism operations. It is designed for professionals, students and teachers of hospitality and tourism management. Through case studies and examples, readers are exposed to and encouraged to develop an appreciation for the diverse segments of and career opportunities in hospitality and tourism industry.

Editor

1

Event Assessment

Event coordination is all about "the list"-what goes on the list and why. Event coordination is the visualization, organization, and synchronization of the event elements and the tasks required to implement them. To create that list, you, as the professional event coordinator, must define the purpose of the event and analyse all the desires, demands, assumptions, and constraints involved to determine the products, materials, services, activities, and suppliers to be included in the event project.

Think of the event element assessment in terms of three "tents"-the intent (purpose), the extent (scope), and the content (program). In the world of project management, conducting the needs assessment is part of Project Scope Management. The event scope definition is derived from the identified need, request, or requirement for the event (purpose of the event and outcome/benefit expectations), the product description (type of event), the product analysis (event components), and the feasibility analysis (balance of resources), resulting in a Work Breakdown Structure and Activity Schedule.

Needs Assessment

Need is a complex term. People do not buy an airline ticket because they need an airline ticket-what they need is to be in Pittsburgh on Friday or in Paris on Tuesday. You must remember that you are not just taking an order. You are crafting a solution to what the client truly needs. Defining needs is a critical component of the ability to deliver a successful event. Needs, however, are not always apparent or fully considered. "I need a wedding reception" is certainly not enough to direct your design and delivery of a reception event for this client. It is definitely not enough to ensure that the event you coordinate will be a success, even if you have coordinated hundreds of other wedding receptions.

Marketing consultant Robert Middleton advises, "You cannot assume what success would look like. You have to ask. You have to get specific answers. " A needs assessment should provide these answers. A feasibility study then shows the viability of achieving success-the outcome envisioned by the client-by defining the event elements and requirements and putting them into the context of reality. Answers to Rudyard Kipling's "six honest serving men"-why, who where, when, what, and how-provide the information needed.

— *WHY*: the purpose of the event is the foundation that drives all other decisions about its scope and the event elements to be included.

— *WHO*: provides the audience or guest profile.

— *WHERE and WHEN*: provide the logistical parameters as well as creative opportunities.

— *WHAT*: determines the event context, content, and mandate.

— *HOW determines HOW MUCH*: how much in the way of resources will be required.

— *HOW MUCH determines HOW*: how the resources will be allocated.

Impact on Event Element

The marketing mantra "know your customer" is as applicable in event design and coordination as in any marketing realm. There are, however, many different customers you must serve during an event. There will be clients, users (guests and attendees), and numerous other stakeholders and influencers to consider.

Customers

Create a customer profile for each constituency you will need to serve, including demographics, lifestyle and life stage, purchase stimulus, and benefits sought. The profile of each of these customer groups will reveal needs and desires that should be factored into the event element analysis and plan. For example, you might use a generational marketing consumer profile. When determining the features and activities for a tourism festival or convention program. The Travel Industry Association of America (TIA) and the National Geographic Traveller sponsored a large-scale national study of the current and potential consumer market for geotourism, defined as "tourism that sustains or enhances the geographical character of the place being visited its environment, culture, aesthetics, heritage, and the well-being of its residents". The results indicate that traditionalists are conservative in their travel choices, looking for predictability and high levels of cleanliness, safety, and security. Baby Boomers show a distinct preference for culturally and socially related travel, and many are looking specifically for upscale travel experiences.

Capabilities

The capabilities you must consider include your ability to handle the event in its proposed scope and context, the availability of products and services, and the features of the event site. Although the core processes remain the same, coordinating a large festival for a civic celebration is different from producing a multicity product launch for a major corporation or the perfect wedding celebration. Each event context will have its own set of parameters and a specialized body of knowledge. You need to be completely honest with yourself and your client about your ability to deliver the event required and desired.

The world has gotten much smaller through the various forms of new communications technology, and vendors and suppliers to the event industry have embraced this opportunity by expanding their geographic markets. However, not all products and services are available or affordably accessible in all parts of the world. You must know what you can and cannot reasonably obtain in your area and through your supplier resources. The site selected for the event also involves capabilities that must be examined. These present a set of constraints, as well as creative possibilities, to be incorporated into your event design and implementation strategy. The event site and/ or venue is a key component of a needs assessment, and in determining the elements that must, should, and could be included in the event.

Competition

Considering the competition includes a determination of what will be competing with your event for the time, money, and emotional investment of the attendees or guests. If you are coordinating a fund-raising event, you will want to ensure that it is not scheduled at the same time as other charity functions competing for the same patrons. If you are coordinating a festival designed to increase tourism to your area, you will need to evaluate the assets of other tourism destinations and events. If you are coordinating an incentive event for General Motors at an exotic destination, you can be assured that the company does not want it in the same place and at the same time when Toyota is there.

You may also need to consider the situation of a single event within an entire event program. What else will be happening before, concurrently, and after the event? If the event you are coordinating is a hospitality reception in conjunction with a conference or convention, you will want to know what other receptions will be taking place and when, as well as where this reception fits into the overall agenda. You may be responsible for only this one reception, but you want it to become part of the overall event experience, as well as achieve the attendance expectations of the host client.

Prioritized Goals and objectives

A needs assessment helps you determine expectations so that you can define the scope and the specifications that result in an event that satisfies the customer's needs and desires the project deliverables. It is critical that you work with your client to specify the goals and objectives for the event and to put them in a prioritized hierarchy. You must clarify what the client is trying to attain, achieve, or accomplish. The client may not be able to articulate this immediately or succinctly. You may need to probe for the stated objectives, the unstated objectives, the hard objectives, and the soft objectives.

Unfortunately, this is not usually the case. More often the task is to help clients put their needs and desires into words, probing to determine what they mean by what they say. Return On Investment (ROI) applies to the corporate world as well as to associations, governments, charitable organizations, leisure and entertainment organizations, and private individuals. You must seek a definitive description of the return expected for the investment made.

To put this in perspective, suppose you are coordinating a conference for your professional association.

The costs to a delegate may include a registration fee of $600, an airline ticket at $500, a hotel room at $600 (4 nights _ $150/night), and meals, business center services, and other incidentals may add up to $400. Add to that $900 for a week away from work, and the cost to the delegate is $3000. To achieve a positive ROI, the delegate will have to come away from that conference with a $3000 idea. Goals and objectives must not only be defined, they must be measurable.

Specific Must be specific in targeting an objective Measurable Must have a measurable indicator(s) of progress/ success Assignable Must be capable of being assigned to someone to accomplish Realistic Must be realistic within allotted resources Time-related Must have a specified duration Without the goals and objectives specified, you will not be able to describe the results expected. You will not be able to define the scope of the project, specify the scope of your responsibilities, control the extent of your obligations, nor evaluate your success.

Event coordinators invariably encounter the "could-you-just" syndrome -"Could you just add candles to the centerpieces?" "Could you just have your people put up these flags behind the dais?" "Could you just change those table linens from red to blue?" The client keeps adding or changing one more thing, and one more thing, and one more thing, expecting there to be no change in the resources provided. In project management this is called scope creep-the scope of the project keeps creeping outward. Without establishing clear parameters and objectives, you will not be able to identify the appropriate event elements, sequence the tasks efficiently, or effectively manage the resources for the event.

How do you determine the prioritized goals and objectives? You ask. You probe. You listen. Using a comprehensive Client Interview Form and a consultative selling process, you keep challenging the client, in a nice way, to define the guest reaction and/or results expected.

Once the list of goals and objectives is established, you must work with the client to rank them in order of precedence and preference. You need to determine which event elements are absolutely necessary, which will enhance the event significantly, and which would simply be nice to have. This information will be critical when you begin to analyse feasibility and find that you must ask the client, who wants the sun, the moon, and the stars, to decide whether he or she wants the sun, the moon, or the stars.

Feasibility, Priority and Impact

Once needs are identified and the prioritized goals and objectives established, you must blend creativity with practicality. You must identify the resources and any obstacles to determine the practicality of the project and the potential for success. Resources include time, money, humanpower, information, space, and service availability. Each one of these can be an advantage or become an obstacle. You must make sure that you have a reasonable balance of resources to allocate to achieve the event requirements.

Michael C. Thomsett, author of The Little Black Book of Project Management, states, "True creativity demands a methodical, organized approach, " and recommends getting the answers to these questions:

— What is the purpose of this project [event]?

— What will the outcome look like?

— What is my responsibility?

— What is my authority?

— What is my budget?

As noted earlier, the event must meet the prioritized needs and goals and objectives of the client and other constituents. Therefore, another set of questions you should ask that will help to prioritize the event elements to be included might be the following:

— What must be done? Is it doable?

— What should be done? Is it affordable?

— What can be done? Is it meaningful?

It is critical to remember that in considering each potential event element, there are conditions and consequences that come with each choice. Each element has or can have an impact on virtually every other element. As when pebbles are dropped into a still pool of water, there are ripples that expand out in all directions. Selecting a theme for a party will drive decisions about the invitations, site selection, décor, food and beverages, entertainment, and party favours. Selecting pin spots to highlight the centerpieces on the banquet tables will affect the timing of when the tables can and must be positioned and dressed.

Perspective

The event experience must be considered from threshold to threshold and considered from the guests' point of view. Drawing on your experience with previous and similar events, as well as the history of this or comparable events, you identify the event elements that will deliver the required results to the client and the desired benefits to the attendee. You then examine the implications of each element within the overall plan. An event does not happen in a vacuum. You must include a comprehensive perspective of your different customers, plus the internal and external stakeholders, in analysing their needs, wants, and mandates.

Depending on the event type, the stakeholders or influencers you can be dealing with may include corporate executives, boards of directors, sponsors, family members, public bureaucrats, or regulatory officials. You must conduct a situational assessment of the macro and micro environments in which the event takes place. Macroenvironments include the economy, community and constituent sociocultural demographics, and governmental influence. Micro environments include industry-specific factors, competitive forces, and supply and demand. Failure to scan these environments and identify the needs of internal and external stakeholders can cause problems when it comes time move in and set up, not to mention contributing significantly to scope creep.

Resources Analysis

Management is allocating, directing, and controlling resources to achieve objectives, and resources, by definition, are limited. The professional event coordinator must balance the "need" with the "have, " making sure that what must be done can be done with the resources available for the event project. (Figure.1)

Resource		Project Management Process		Event Output
Time	➡	Time Management	➡	Schedules
Money	➡	Financial Management	➡	Budget
Humanpower	➡	Human Resources Management	➡	Organizational Chart
Information	➡	Communications Management	➡	Production Book
Space	➡	Site Management	➡	Site Plan
Suppliers	➡	Procurement Management	➡	Requests for Proposal and Bid Specifications

Figure 1. Controlling Resources through Event Project Management

Time, Money, And Humanpower

Of all the resources at your disposal, time is the one resource that is finite. When clients really want something that is not included in the budget, there are usually ways to find more money to make it happen. When money is short, volunteer humanpower can often fill in the gap. When space is limited, creative options such as adding a tented area are often possible. But when you have run out of time, you have run out of time. You cannot beg, borrow, or steal more. This is the primary difference between event project management and other realms of project management. The event's date, which is virtually always fixed, not flexible, is the starting point of project time management, rather than the project management process determining the completion date.

Time restrictions will determine the tempo of the event project. Monetary resources must be allocated carefully. It is important to remember that everything will cost something. Goods and services require labour and raw materials. Volunteers and donated items will incur administrative and hospitality costs. Securing more money through sponsorships, gifts, and grants will have costs attached. Even assessing needs and analysing event resources take time, and time is money. Nothing is free. The more limited the budget, the more focused you must be on the event goals, but a quality event does not depend on a large budget. Your humanpower resources may include part-time or full-time paid staff, casual or temporary labour, or a volunteer corps.

Depending on the type of event, these human resources may be secured through recruitment, hired through various agencies, or provided by the sponsoring organization. Your human resources must be assessed based on experience and expertise, as well as their availability within the schedule requirements.

Quantity and Quality of the Resources

You must be brutally realistic about the quantity and quality of the resources committed to the event project. Insufficient resources in one area may be mitigated by additional resources of another type-for example, less time _ more humanpower, insufficient number of volunteers _ more money for support staffing. However, if there are insufficient resources all around, the scope of the event may have to be reduced. You must validate the budget and the availability of additional money if required. You must specify the Work Breakdown Structure and analyse the schedule to be certain that what needs to be accomplished can be accomplished within the time constraints. You must assess the capabilities and availability of volunteers and vendors. You must verify the facilities and capabilities of the site selected. And you must calculate the realistic likelihood of achieving the level of success expected.

Direction

The professional event coordinator must always work within a team, even if he or she is a sole, independent practitioner. There are always vendors, suppliers, support staff, and volunteers or helpers involved in an event project. Their numbers can range from a few family members and a couple of suppliers to the hundreds of vendors and 26, 000_ volunteers and staff included for the 2002 Winter Olympic Games in Salt Lake City, Utah. Big jobs are accomplished by completing small tasks.

Utilizing these humanpower and vendor resources requires delegation and proper direction. The professional event coordinator maintains the focus on the big picture and delegates the task assignments. Project management consultant James P. Lewis, author of Fundamentals of Project Management, notes, however, that "delegation does not mean abdication. " Well-trained, experienced personnel may be utilized because they are usually more cost-effective, yet everyone, including professionals, will need direction. There will be lots of pieces to the puzzle, and the event coordinator is the one who knows what the final picture should look like.

Logistics and Logical sequences

Two of Stephen Covey's Seven Habits of Highly Effective People are to "begin with the end in mind" and to "put first things first. " These could arguably be the essence of the logistics and logical sequences of the event elements. There will be a natural order and a necessary order in which the various event elements (and the tasks associated with them) will have to be chronologically organized. Certain event elements and tasks will have to be sequential and others may be simultaneous, and many of the controlling and monitoring processes of event coordination are iterative.

Logical sequencing follows a critical path, meaning that some tasks will be dependent on other tasks having already been completed, and some tasks will be affected by the way in which others have been done. Developing the logical sequencing for an event depends on sound reasoning, collecting the specifications, and understanding the interdependencies. In project management, this is Activity Sequencing, which will depend on the activity list, mandatory dependencies, external dependencies, and milestones.

Components

The components of an event project will, of course, depend on the type and scope of the event. Each dimension, each feature, each product or service will indicate certain characteristics and options, as well as additional operational requirements. For example, if you decide to include colourful fabrics, spandex, or vinyl stretched from a high ceiling to the centers of the buffet displays to indicate their positioning within a cavernous space, you will probably need to secure a scissor lift or high jacker to install them. You will also have to ensure that the material used complies with the fire codes of the particular jurisdiction. In certain jurisdictions (e. g. , Las Vegas, Nevada), you must have the installation done by a professional rigger from a specific labour union.

As you visualize the event experience, from threshold to threshold, itemize the elements that will or should be included. Then analyse each of these elements to determine the products and/or services that will be required for implementation, as well as the likely impact they will have on the other elements. You will also have to consider the administrative issues, marketing implications, and risk management ramifications.

Flowcharts, Outlines, and Storyboards

A time line can serve as your event flowchart, illustrating the flow of the tasks necessary to produce the event. In project management, this begins with the Work Breakdown Structure (decomposing the event into its elements and components), which facilitates creating the Activity List (the tasks associated with each element). You then identify the interdependencies to create the Activity Sequencing and estimate the duration of each activity flowchart rules are:

— Always use the precedence method; what fits where and when according to what precedes it and what follows it.

— Make sure the path of activities and events makes sense; the path works when it is arranged logically.

— An activity cannot occur until a preceding activity or event has been completed; there will likely be numerous concurrent activities that must be precedence-connected.

— Carefully plot, explain, and control concurrent events; these concurrent activities may have individual flowcharts (and different team members) that must be supervised carefully.

— Exercise control over weak links; the flowchart helps you identify the weak links in the process that must be monitored.

The Work Breakdown Structure, Activity List, and Activity Sequencing may be composed in an outline form, either a Harvard or numerical outline, or can be generated via a mind-mapping technique or a scalar organization. Some find the storyboard method effective -creating a card for each task and arranging the cards in groups and chronological order. You should lock in the most important items first, incorporating the chronology, priority, and flexibility of each.

Collect Specifications

Once the list of event elements is prepared, the specifications must be determined. Consider the quality level or type of product or service that will be appropriate for the event style and context. For example, name badges can be handwritten on paper badges with sticky backs, printed on card stock and inserted in plastic holders, or embossed on plastic cards (like credit cards) with large amounts of data imbedded in a magnetic strip on the back, and can cost anywhere from a few cents apiece to double-digit dollar amounts each.

Ascertain the installation or implementation requirements for each element. You must thoroughly understand what resources (time, money, humanpower, and space) will be required for each product or service. For event elements, products, or services associated with disciplines with which you are unfamiliar, collect this information through research, your colleagues on the event team (i. e. , scenic designer, catering manager, or graphic designer), or directly from the vendors and suppliers you will be contracting (remember, they should also be practicing consultative selling). Include the following specifications.

— *Product*: quantity, quality, features, or brand specifications

— *Time*: fabrication/installation/removal duration; sequence restrictions; materials and/or information dependencies (what a vendor needs you to provide before it can begin)
— *Space*: dimensions; proximity requirements and/or restrictions
— *Humanpower*: number of people required to install/ operate/ remove (number to be included by provider and/or number to be provided by event organization)
— *Accessibility*: number and type of delivery vehicles; proximity requirements and/or restrictions
— *Other*: power requirements and other utility needs; installation equipment requirements; special permits, compliance instruments, and/or insurance requirements

Recognising Bottlenecks

You must understand what each provider will do, what equipment or materials each needs to be able to do it, how much time is needed to do it, and what impact that may have on other providers. Of particular note, you will have to integrate and synchronize those tasks and those providers who will need to be occupying the same or contiguous space or time in the sequence in the schedule. When setting up an event on-site, the activity will be fast and furious and you must carefully choreograph this delicate dance of possibly hundreds of people coming together in the same space at the same time to create, operate, and participate in the event experience.

The event elements must be arranged in order of priority, logistics, and chronology. Tap into your own experience and the experience of others to recognize, anticipate, and alleviate potential congestion and conflict before it can result in financial or productivity problems. In project management this is called Project Integration

Management, which includes Project Plan Development, Project Plan Execution, and Integrated Change Control.

Progressive Experience

A progressive event experience is an event program that follows a natural or designed progression from start to finish or threshold to threshold. Not everything happens at once, at least for the individual at the event. At a public festival, for example, there may be different activities and amusements scheduled continuously throughout the day, and the visitor will be experiencing these attractions one after the other. At a conference or convention, there may be numerous concurrent sessions, but the delegate can attend only one at a time. During an incentive travel program, there will be a balance of sightseeing, social events, free time, and rest. This progression, or flow, of the event will indicate additional operational elements that must be sequenced logically as well.

The professional event coordinator must supervise vendors as they replenish supplies and materials, monitor volunteer arrivals and activities, and arrange everything performers or participants will need for their arrival, preparations, waiting, performance, and departure throughout the duration of the event program. This may necessitate dressing rooms, a green room, and/or break areas for staff, volunteers, cast, and crew. The months of preplanning culminate in an event that is often over in just a few hours. But the party does not end there. You must remember that the breakdown and move-out is an essential component of the event production. It must have sufficient resources allocated (i. e. , time, money, humanpower) and must be choreographed as carefully as the move-in and the event itself.

You have identified the event elements, collected the specifications for each product or provider, and identified the interdependencies. Now you must integrate this into a project schedule that includes tracking systems and control points to ensure that the schedule is effective. Timelines, production schedules, running orders, and scripts should reflect the necessary chronological sequence of the delivery and implementation of the goods, services, tasks, and performances required to produce the event experience.

Production Schedule

The project schedule or timeline should be presented in a chronological format, which may be a scroll list or a graphical or schematic chart. The scroll list format may be a simple numerical sequence by date. The graphical format may be a bar chart (often called a Gantt chart, named for Henry Gantt, who developed a complete notational system for showing progress with bar charts in the late 1950s) or a network diagram, often an arrow diagram. The graphical format may also simply be a calendar. To facilitate monitoring functions, either the scroll list or graphical format should include the name of the person, vendor, or team responsible for each task listed.

The style or format you use will depend on the complexity of the event project and what best communicates the schedule to your event project team. In many cases a combination of formats will be needed for different event elements, such as printing, catering, décor and entertainment. The key for any of these formats is to ensure that Task A is done before Task B as needed, and that it is clear which tasks must be sequential, which are simultaneous, which are conditional, and which are iterative.

As the day of the event nears, the project schedule will shift from the broader calendar perspective to a daily and hourly (or even minute-byminute) version. This agenda is called a production schedule and is most often presented in the scroll list format, arranged in a table displayed in columns. The number of columns will depend on the type or scope of the event and the information necessary to monitor the schedule. Each column will include a qualifying factor such as starting and ending times, event element or activity, location, person responsible (with contact numbers), and other specifications or notes as required.

For multiday, complex, or mega-events, the production schedule may be dozens or hundreds of pages long and/or require versions specific to individual vendors or event team members. You may create customized schedules that include only the information required by each vendor or group. You might wish to print daily versions for each day of a multiday festival, or you might omit certain elements, such as the arrival time of a specific dignitary that should be confidential for security reasons. However, as changes are made to the master schedule, these updates must be included in the customized versions as well. Also remember that you want your entire team to have a clear understanding of the event as a whole.

The schedule may be printed a variety of ways. It can be printed horizontally or vertically on standard stationery, which would facilitate inclusion in the Production Book and/or on a clipboard at the receiving dock or registration table. It can be enlarged to poster size and mounted on the wall in the on-site headquarters office. It can be downloaded into a PDA (personal digital assistant) or posted on a company intranet. Again, form follows function; the format should facilitate effective communications.

Achieve Realistic Scheduling

Professional event coordinators learn to plan backward. You collect the specifications data and duration estimations for all the event elements, integrate the critical path of interdependencies into the Activity Sequence, and establish a deadline for each task. With the deadline noted on the calendar or schedule, you move backward on the schedule the amount of time it will take to accomplish a particular task to establish the start date or time.

When estimating the time required for each task defined, you must consider all constraints, assumptions, capabilities, historical information, and mandatory dependencies (the tasks that must be completed before another task can begin). You need to determine, from your prior experience and a healthy measure of optimistic pessimism, how much time it will actually take to complete a task. Although the industry trend is shorter lead times for event preparation, try to build plenty of flexibility into your schedule. You should be very conservative when estimating productivity and very generous when anticipating problems. Once you have the initial drafts of both your timeline and production schedule, you should distribute these to your staff, vendors, and/or key stakeholders for review and comment. These draft schedules should be distributed as early as possible to allow time for any changes or concerns to be addressed and incorporated into the final version.

Schedule Control System

A carefully crafted schedule is a thing of beauty, but unless it incorporates tracking and control mechanisms, it is next to worthless. In project management you use the Project Schedule with Critical Path Milestones, Performance Reports, and Change Orders to develop the Schedule Control System. The timeline and production schedule should have the critical milestones and deadlines highlighted, including those tasks or activities that must be completed before another task may begin. With the responsibility for each task assigned to an individual, regular performance updates should be plotted into the schedule, including written reports and in-person meetings.

These reports and meetings must be scheduled to allot sufficient time to take corrective action if required. Incorporate a Tickler System (to "tickle" your memory) into your timeline, computer scheduler, and/or personal scheduler system. Change controls include the manner of and documentation required for making any changes to the project scope or the project schedule. The professional event coordinator should develop and utilize a Change Order Form for changes to the scope of the event project. Change notification protocols must be developed to ensure that schedule updates are communicated efficiently and effectively. Not only are these tracking and change control mechanisms important for keeping the event project on time and on track, they will provide valuable information when coordinating your next event project.

This is why you should analyse and document the causes of any variances, the reasons behind the corrective actions selected, and other lessons learned. You should be creating a historical database for this event as well as other event projects so that you may continuously improve your processes and procedures.

Contingency plans

There are never unlimited resources. There are no guarantees in life. The only constant is change. Stuff happens! Given all of these caveats, it is clear that there will always be a certain amount of risk associated with any event project. The professional event coordinator must carefully identify, analyse, plan for, and manage these risks by examining problem areas and available options to develop suitable contingency plans for identified risks. This task may include anything from an Event "Survival" Kit to a full-blown alternate production plan. Risk, as defined by the Project Management Institute, Inc. , is "an uncertain condition that, if it occurs, has a positive or negative effect on a project objective.

Each risk has a cause, and if it occurs, a consequence. " Note that risk is not exclusively negative. There may be a risk that your Concert in the Park fund-raiser is more popular than your wildest dreams and you are selling tickets at an unprecedented rate. At a certain point, you must implement your contingency plan to secure more portable toilet facilities or bring in several more food stalls. This risk can be a good thing. However, most risk management efforts are directed at the potential hazards associated with an event.

In testimony conducted at the Coronial Inquest in conjunction with the crowd collapse death during the Limp Bizkit performance at the Big Day Out 2001 festival in Sydney, Australia, it was determined that there are no international minimum standards for crowd safety or management, but there are numerous factors that have been identified as specific to special events that may increase the degree of risk but do not necessarily mean the event will be "risky. "

It is important to understand that risk management is an ongoing, integrated, and iterative process. Resources must be allocated, plans must be devised, and a commitment must be made to manage the uncertainties and vulnerabilities surrounding your event. You must examine the worst-case scenarios and the best-case scenarios in order to be prepared with the appropriate contingency plans.

Categories of Risk

There are several categories of risk the professional event coordinator should examine: safety, security, capability, internal, and external. Safety risks include physical harm, violence, sanitation issues, and health issues. Security risks include physical or intellectual property loss, property damage, theft, and fire. Capability risks include processes, technology, unrealistic goals, and unrealistic projections.

Internal risks include resource allocation, scope creep, and changing priorities. External risks include legal and/or regulatory environments, labour issues, weather, and competition.

Risks are identified by reviewing historical information and industry standards; interviewing subject matter experts; conducting brainstorming sessions with the event team, vendors, and key stakeholders; and sometimes through simulation and scenario forecasting. You should also conduct a SWOT (strengths, weaknesses, opportunities, and threats) analysis, as well as a gap analysis (identifying the gaps in the planning process) to mitigate exposure and any disparities between what the vision is and what will be deliverable.

The professional event coordinator should continuously be developing checklists to serve as the starting point for the risk identification sessions. As the coordinator goes through the event element list item by item, he or she should question all assumptions and consider options as they relate to the cost, schedule, scope, and quality of the activities, products, and services included in the event plan. The causal influences associated with each risk identified should also be considered to determine whether there will be several risks driven by a common cause.

Once the potential risks are identified, you must assess the likelihood and impact of each. Peter E. Tarlow, author of Event Risk Management and Safety, notes, "All event risk analyses should be based on the principle that there is no object, person, or reputation that cannot be stolen, damaged, or destroyed. " You must also prioritize risk based on the potential impact on the event as well as the impact on the resources for the event. Using an evaluation tool such as the Event Probability/Impact Risk Rating Matrix (Figure 2), determine which risks can and/or must be avoided and which may be mitigated with additional event elements such as redundant equipment or other contingency planning, based on your event organization's threshold of tolerance.

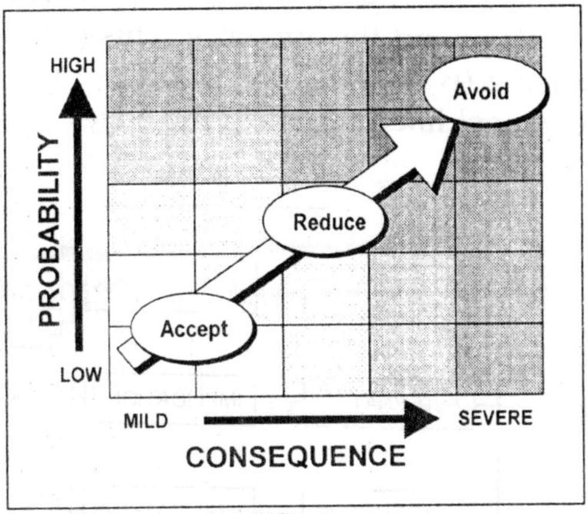

Figure 2. Event Probability / Risk Rating Matrix

As you are considering each identified risk, you must identify and evaluate the available options and their impact on the event's quality and resources. You must remember one of Norman R. Augustine's "Laws": No change is a small change. There will likely be a cost-in money, time, humanpower, or quality-for any contingency plan option selected. Reserving an indoor site or a tent for an outdoor wedding reception in case of inclement weather will likely require nonrefundable deposit money. Securing a portable generator as a backup power supply will incur rental costs, and the equipment must be plotted into the site plan.

Obtaining specialty insurance, such as in the case of the Albuquerque International Hot Air Balloon Fiesta, may be expensive or available through only one or two providers in the world. To create a list of potential responses, you might use a Decision Tree (Figure 3) to analyse your contingency plan options. There will often be more than one alternative to any contingency plan option, and each alternative will have its own set of implications, including costs, rewards, and potential residual risks. For example, if you are having a big-name rockand-roll band playing at a fund-raiser concert, you may need to construct a barrier between the stage and the audience. This barrier could be made of fencing (wire, mesh, or wood), or you could use security personnel lined up along the edge.

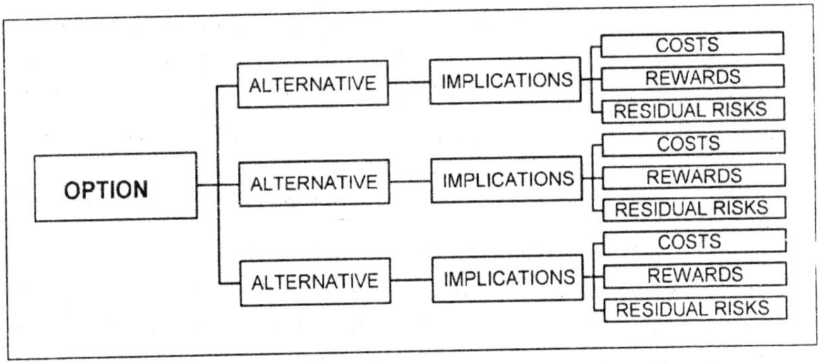

Figure 3. Event Decision Tree Analysis

The fencing option will have costs associated with fabrication and/or installation. It will have an impact on the look of the stage. It may have an impact on the event grounds, depending on the type of fencing and the installation procedures. The security guard option will have costs associated with it as well, either for hiring or subcontracting personnel or for T-shirts for the volunteers. Uniformed security or off-duty law enforcement personnel may create an offensive or militaristic feel to the event, yet untrained volunteers may not be sufficient if the audience is likely to be aggressive about approaching the stage. Clearly, each option and its alternatives must be considered from a variety of perspectives.

There are four ways to handle risk: avoidance, transference, mitigation, and acceptance. Avoidance means you do not take the risk at all. Transference means you transfer the risk through insurance, performance bonds, warranties, guarantees, or contractual liability. Mitigation includes incorporating redundancies into your plan and targeting the linkages or causes that control and prevent the potential severity of the impact. Acceptance includes your contingency plans. With your options identified, communication will be the foundation of the success of your contingency plans. You must specify your reporting format, including how and when decisions will be made to implement any portion of your plans and how this will be communicated to the event team.

The triggers, actions, and individuals involved must be determined. Your list of potential responses must be linked with the threshold of tolerance that will trigger the response. You must specify what action steps will be taken. You must also specify those individuals empowered to make the decision to implement a response. To eliminate any false alarms, only one person should be authorized to change, move, or cancel an event element, or the event itself.

These roles and responsibilities should be documented and communicated to the entire event team. You must verify and validate your contingency plans with the host organization or your client so that the resources required to implement a risk response or contingency plan are fully funded and supported. The host or client must be informed of the triggers, actions, and individuals involved and must be included in the communications surrounding response implementation.

Integrated Timeline

The contingency plans must be integrated into your timeline so that you will be able to monitor situations and/or conditions and act as required and appropriate. This will include periodic risk reviews, performance reviews, taking corrective action when necessary, implementing change controls, and continuously updating your plan. What happened, why it happened, and when it happened must be included in your documentation procedures. The professional event coordinator must be proactive rather than reactive. Decisions made in a panic are rarely cost-effective or efficient and often lead to more risk and unpleasant consequences.

If at all possible, incorporate a generous response time into your schedule so that your contingency plans may be integrated into the event plans and implemented smoothly if required. It is better to have the wedding reception weather tent installed and beautifully decorated, but not be required, than to have the bride's lasting memory be a muddy and miserable wedding day.

Insurance

As noted, there are four ways to handle risk, one of which is to transfer risk by purchasing insurance coverage. Of course, insurance will not prevent something from happening; it will only lessen the financial impact should it happen. An insurance policy is a legal agreement for transferring risk that defines what will be paid for, in the event of a defined loss, in exchange for a defined amount of money (the premium). The professional event coordinator will work with an insurance broker to identify and purchase the appropriate insurance coverage for the type and size of event that is being produced.

Most purpose-built and commercial venues will require specific levels of insurance coverage, primarily Commercial General Liability (CGL), also known in countries other than the United States as Public Liability Insurance, which usually protects your organization if a volunteer, employee, or other individual, supervised, directed, or whose duties are controlled by the organization, makes a mistake and a patron is injured or has his or her property damaged. This coverage is not universal, however, and you must always check the exclusions in your policy because not all persons injured and all property damaged may be covered. You should always secure Certificates of Insurance from your vendors, particularly those providing their goods and services on-site at the event.

Onetime and annual events often require Event Liability Insurance, often called Spectator Insurance, which will be priced according to the type of event and the capacity of the audience, and perhaps the event elements to be included. James N. Decoulos, a Massachusetts lawyer and insurance broker specializing in legal and insurance services for special events, explains that an event liability policy is really a CGL policy issued on an industry standard form, but rather than for the usual one-year term, it is issued for the duration of the event. Decoulos advises that there are basically four kinds of losses that should be addressed with the procurement of insurance coverage.

These products apply not so much to the type of event, but rather to the type of business that the event professional conducts. Also, the client bears potential loss and the planner may have a duty to advise the client about the risk of that loss and methods to reduce it. For example, if an outdoor event is being planned in the Southeast during hurricane season, a planner, being the professional and thus having certain higher standards of performance, may have a duty to advise the client to get weather insurance or to forgo the event altogether, especially if the client is not from the Southeast and is not aware of the hurricane season.

The weather insurance would likely be quite expensive or unavailable, but the risks should be discussed. Failure to discuss the risks could lead to a professional liability claim for which the planner may want insurance coverage to finance any liability that may arise due to damages incurred by the client if the event is cancelled or the risk is not otherwise properly managed.

The event professional must also become familiar with various insurance-related documents such as a certificate of insurance, declarations page, binder, policy, and endorsement, as well as the meaning of terms that appear in them such as additional named insured, policy limitations, exclusions, and duties in the event of loss. Insurance is a tool by which risk management is financed. An event professional shouldn't employ that tool without knowing what it does and doesn't do, any more than an audiovisual technician employs a soundboard, or a pyrotechnician employs a detonating device. Risk is an uncertainty about whether a loss will occur, what peril will cause that loss, and what damage may be done as a result. Once all the efforts have been exhausted at managing the risk by preventing it altogether, reducing the likelihood of its happening, and reducing the severity of it, one purchases insurance to finance it when it does happen.

Target competency

The professional event coordinator conducts an assessment to determine the purpose of and expectations for an event in order to be able to visualize, organize, and synchronize the elements and actions required to deliver the desired event experience. Using the principles and discipline of project management, the professional event coordinator will be able to identify, prioritize, and sequence event elements in a comprehensive and successful manner, as well as allocate and control resources to achieve the event objectives.

The professional event coordinator must create realistic time lines and production schedules that incorporate the interdependencies and critical path of activities, as well as manage the risks associated with them. These schedules must be validated and verified by the event stakeholders and then distributed to all appropriate personnel and providers. Timely and efficient communications are critical to the successful achievement of the event goals and objectives.

The professional event coordinator also performs risk assessment and analysis to identify problem areas, evaluate available options, and create contingency plans that will mitigate the consequences should an incident occur. These contingency plans should include the triggers to indicate implementation, the actions to be taken if implemented, and the individuals who will be responsible, as well as the procurement of the appropriate insurance coverage.

Professional Coordination

Determine the event elements and create a time line and production schedule for each of the following events. Be sure to include the research, design, planning, implementation, and evaluation phases.

— Your professional association will be holding its annual convention in your city two years from now. It will consist of four days, including 36 concurrent seminars, a trade show, a welcome reception, an awards banquet, and three days of leadership meetings before the convention begins.

— Your Convention and Visitors Bureau wants to hold a three-day Familiarization Tour for 50 meeting planners in conjunction with your city's famous cultural heritage festival six months from now.

— The city elections took place yesterday, and the newly elected mayor just called and wants to hold an impressive investiture ceremony and inaugural ball six weeks from now. The ceremony will be in the afternoon and the inaugural ball that evening, and both are to include elements that recall the campaign issues of supporting youth programs, strong law enforcement, and community pride.

2

Opportunities of Hotels in India

The year 2003 was an outstanding year in terms of inbound tourism, with tourist arrivals reaching 2.73 million. The strong growth in tourist arrivals in 2003 is partly attributable to the outbreak of SARS in east Asia, as well as the war on Iraq, which resulted in India being perceived as a safe region to visit. The more fundamental reason, however, relates to a strong sense of business and investment confidence in India: inspired by India's strong GDP performance, and initiatives taken by the erstwhile Prime Minister, to make peace with Pakistan, strengthen ties with the developed world and open sectors of the economy to private sector/foreign investment. Significantly, the bulk of international arrivals in India, both in 2003 and 2004, have been business travellers.

Domestic travel, both business and leisure, also benefited from a thriving economy. Prior to being voted out of power, the NDA government implemented certain important measures to provide a much-needed boost to travel & tourism. These included the abolishment of the inland air travel tax of 15%; reduction in excise duty on aviation turbine fuel to 8%; and removal of a number of restrictions on outbound chartered flights, including those relating to frequency and size of aircraft. The provision included allowing Indian charters to land at all airports in the country, and Indian passport holders to travel on inbound charters. The government also launched the Incredible India campaign, which has been successful in launching the `Brand India' image.

The new government, it appears, is taking active interest in developing tourism in India. The continued Incredible India campaign has had a strongly positive impact on tourist arrivals in 2004. Definite efforts are being made to communicate the Brand India message: India made its presence strongly felt at the WTTC-promoted Global Travel & Tourism Summit held in Doha, Qatar in May this year. India has also been selected to host the Summit next year.

An important new development is the government's recent decision to treat convention centres as part of core infrastructure, allowing the government to provide critical funding for the large capital investment that may be required. The government has identified Delhi, Mumbai and Goa as the markets to develop these convention centers, which is likely to further fuel demand for hotel rooms. Another effort is the decision to substantially upgrade 28 regional airports in smaller towns, slated to be completed by 2006. Expressions of interest have been received for the proposed privatisation (49% stake) of the Delhi and Mumbai international airports, but, as expected, the Left government has opposed the move.

Substantial investments in tourism infrastructure are, undoubtedly, essential for this industry to continue to evolve and grow, and ultimately achieve its potential. The upgrading of national highways connecting various parts of India has opened new avenues for the development of budget hotels alongside. Taking advantage of this and certain other key locations is the Tata group (owners of Indian Hotel - Taj) that has developed IndiOne, a 101-room economy hotel outside Bangalore; they hope to duplicate this across India in the next few years. Another hotel chain called `Homotel', being promoted by Sarovar Park Plaza group is also likely to compete in this new economy segment. International majors like Accor are also planning to bring in Ibis into India.

The year 2004 has been a record year in tourist arrivals, as is evident from data on foreign arrivals for the first eight months of the year. According to provisional estimates of the Ministry of Tourism, January to August 2004 saw approximately 2,093,600 visitors to India, 25.8% more than in the corresponding period of 2003. Growth has been spurred by large increases in airline passenger capacity: international airlines have added more than 4,000 seats a week on international routes to India in the last six months alone.

Increases in passenger capacity will play a significant role in fuelling growth in travel & tourism. British Airways has recently been permitted to triple its flights to India, and carriers from Australia are now allowed to offer 4,500 seats a week to India, more than double existing capacity. Moreover, Indian private carriers have recently commenced flights to the SAARC region, and have asked the government to be permitted to fly to East Asian countries. Capacity increases will not only bring in more international arrivals, but will, over a period, reduce airline fares to India, which are currently amongst the highest in the world.

Assuming a stable economic and political climate worldwide, the outlook for inbound tourism - both business and leisure - is strongly encouraging. Many international investors, particularly those who have invested heavily into China in the past few years, are now looking at India as the next opportunity. Conde Nast Traveller, in its readers' travel awards for 2004, has placed India at number six among the world's tourist destinations.

Domestic tourism will continue to develop rapidly and, according to HVS, will be the real driving force for this industry over the next decade or so. This segment will be helped by the growing wealth base of India's population and discounted fare options. A significant new development is the arrival of low-cost carriers, pioneered in India by Air Deccan, with other industry players such as Air India and Indian Airlines readying themselves to enter the low-cost market. According to recent estimates of the WTTC, Indian tourism will grow at 8.8 per cent over the next 10 years, which would place India among the most rapidly growing tourism markets in the world. A longer term, sustained growth of the industry depends on how successfully several issues are addressed - relating to old and poorly facilitated airports, inadequate hotels, poor road and transport infrastructure, high levels of taxation and a bureaucratic visa processing system. As of now, at least, India is clearly taking steps in the right direction.

Hotel Supply

In the recent past, we have been asked several times about the actual supply of hotel rooms in India. Taking into account all approved and un-approved hotels, we estimate this figure to be close to 90,000 rooms. This is an abysmal figure for a country of India's size and population. An increase in business sentiments, leading to higher business-related travel or increase in foreign tourist arrivals, causes occupancy in markets to go up dramatically.

Tourism Industry

The year 2003, as we all know, showed an especially strong performance of the tourism industry. While there has been much talk about foreign arrivals, very little has actually been said about domestic tourism, which has grown by about 40% in the last four to five years. Government statistics point to approximately 230 million domestic travellers in 2002 and indicate that this number has risen between 15-20% in 2003. Domestic tourism has, in fact, been the staple diet on which a number of domestic leisure destinations have sustained themselves - the hotel markets of Goa, Jaipur, Agra and various hill stations being among these.

With disposable incomes having risen significantly in the last five to seven years, across much of India's middle income and upper-middle income segments, families have been taking more holidays - and spending more on their vacations - than ever before. The concept of travelling for leisure has, in recent years, gained a more widespread appeal, not only with families, but also young adults, a segment that is earning far more than their parents did at that age. With a certain degree of social change taking place across India, domestic tourism is poised to grow rapidly in the coming years.

When will India actually touch the 'magic number' of 5 million tourist arrivals? This is a question that those involved in travel & tourism, or the hospitality industry, often ask. This year, for the first time ever, India is going to cross the three million mark. According to our estimates, India would witness nearly 3.5 million foreign tourist arrivals in 2004. The sharp rise in arrivals - as well as the increase in domestic travel - is already showing in the high occupancies of hotels across various cities. Demand for room nights grew at approximately 18% across the country in 2003/04 (according to HVS estimates) and is growing at 15-20% in the current fiscal.

Taking into account an estimated demand growth of approximately 18% over the next few years, we estimate that another 65,000-80,000 rooms will need to be added, across the country, in the next five years, to be able to meet the increase in demand. If this does not happen, room rates will rise dramatically, and, consequently, travel will come down, as people will find it too expensive to travel within India unless absolutely necessary. In addition to tourism infrastructure in India being woefully inadequate, the current supply of hotel rooms is much too small to meet the anticipated increases in demand. Our preliminary research indicates that, at best, there are currently only 35,000 - 40,000 rooms under different stages of planning and construction that are expected to enter the market in the next five years. The new supply will also include branded hotels in the budget segment being planned by some major hotel chains across the country.

Four years ago, the survey indicated that in the year 2000, 109 hotels were ready to open or were under construction. Last year, this number had declined to 63. This year, the number of new hotels under development has once again risen to 97. Moreover, an additional 100 economy hotels will also be developed in the economy segment. The maximum development is likely to be witnessed in the National Capital Region (NCR), particularly in Gurgaon. Bangalore and Mumbai are next in line, where at least 9-10 projects are currently under consideration. Hyderabad and Chennai are also likely to witness 5-6 new hotels. We expect the new economy hotels to be developed mostly in secondary and tertiary locations.

With regard to the expected increase in supply, it is entirely possible that a number of these projects will face financial difficulties while in progress. The blame for this lies with both the government agencies as well as the new developers. A classic example is that of the numerous developments in Gurgaon. The local government is auctioning land for commercial development (including hotels) at high prices, thus forcing new developers (bid winners) to build hotels that are luxury or upper mid-market in orientation, whereas the need of the hour is budget hotels or dedicated extended stay products. Many of the new developers do not want to be seen building budget hotels, as this does not fit in with the profile of their other businesses. Thus, several such developers are tending to partner with operators who are desperate to enter a particular market and will compromise their standards for location / partner and product just to plant a flag.

The recent success of some hotels in Gurgaon - which have done extremely well and beyond most expectations - has been the main motivator for these businessmen. These new owners, it seems, have failed to realize that when 7-9 hotels open at the same time (in the next three to four years), only those projects that have been careful planned and executed will survive the competition or the next phase of economic slowdown in the country. The NCR still remains the favourite destination, in terms of the number of new hotels slated to become operational in the next few years. Seventeen hotels are in various stages of planning and development in the NCR, of which eleven properties are expected to be located in Gurgaon. We understand that, apart from these, there may be a few additional properties under development in West Delhi as well.

The HVS International survey has been computed by dividing the respondent branded hotels into their respective classifications according to star grading. The performance of ten major cities across India, wherever a reasonable sample allowed. While most of the responses to the survey were given in Indian Rupees, we have presented some results in US Dollars as well. For the first time in six years, both occupancy and average room rates improved in 2003/04. The performance in US Dollar terms was even better due to the appreciation of the Indian Rupee.

The number of budget hotels in the branded segment in India has increased significantly over the past several years, and today represents approximately 35% of the total rooms in the survey. The increased representation of branded budget hotels has lowered the overall industry figure for average rate. However, it may be noted that, over a five-year period, the compounded growth has been the strongest in the budget segment. The RevPAR of the three-star hotel segment grew at 10.9%, followed by four-star at 8.7%. The slowest growth was, in fact, witnessed in the five-star deluxe segment, which grew marginally, at 1.2%.

For the second time in a row, there has been an across-the-board improvement in occupancy: average occupancy rose by 12.6% in 2003/04, compared to 10.9% the previous year. Demand for hotel room nights improved across all-star categories in 2003/04, with occupancy close to or higher than double digits, in each segment. The five-star category has witnessed the most growth (16.7%), followed by four-star (15.2%). The increase in occupancy levels this year was even stronger than in the previous year.

In terms of average rate, all star categories experienced healthy growth in 2003/04. The four-star segment experienced the most improvement (10.1%), while the five-star segment witnessed the least improvement (5.7%). In US Dollar terms the four-star segment grew at 15.4%, followed by three-star (12.1%) and five-star deluxe (12.0%). Average rate in Rupee terms increased at 8.3% (compared to a 5.7% decline in 2002/03), resulting in an overall improvement of 21.9% in RevPAR or a 27.6% RevPAR increase in US Dollar terms. Average rate in US Dollar terms showed a countrywide increase of, 13.4%.

Hotel Occupancy Rate

A new and interesting trend is that Agra and Jaipur have seen substantial improvement in their performance in terms of occupancy, growing at 53.1% and 29.8%, respectively. This is followed by Delhi, which is part of the 'Golden Triangle'. Bangalore and Hyderabad - the two IT giants - are clearly the star performers, recording occupancy of 79.6% and 75.8%, respectively. Significantly, Bangalore displaces Mumbai for the first time and has become the market average rate leader with a growth of 28.0%. This is an astonishing achievement for the city which, till four years ago, was ranked fifth (behind the four metros). Goa (19.6%) and Agra (17.0%) were the two cities that showed good improvement in average rate.

Hyderabad, which has generally been a very price sensitive market, also grew at 12.8%. Three large metros had modest increases in average rate, and that too for the first time in three years: these were Delhi (2.3%), Mumbai (2.2%) and Kolkata (2.0%). In 2003/04, only two cities exhibited a small decline in occupancy: these are Goa (6.3%) and Kolkata (4.6%). The decline may attributed to new supply entering these cities. Delhi grew at 19.9% and Chennai at 15.8%, followed by Ahmedabad (15.2%), Bangalore (10.6%), Hyderabad (10.0%) and Mumbai (8.0%).

In terms of RevPAR in 2003/04, Bangalore was in number one position, followed by Delhi, Mumbai and Chennai, with Mumbai having been relegated to third place for the first time. However, the biggest improvement during 2003/04 in terms of RevPAR was seen in Agra (79.1%), followed by Bangalore (41.5%) and Jaipur (39.1%). The only decline in RevPAR was seen in Kolkata (2.7%). All cities, with the exception of Mumbai and Kolkata, have experienced positive improvement in terms of compounded growth of RevPAR. Over a five-year compounded period, the two main centres of IT activity - Bangalore (18.3%) and Hyderabad (17.4%) - have grown the most. Negative growth was witnessed in Mumbai (–5.4%) and Kolkata (–1.2%) over the same period. This is much to do with a situation of oversupply in these markets.

The year 2003/04 saw significant supply additions to several cities, with the maximum growth witnessed in Goa, Mumbai and Kolkata. A huge surge in demand in Goa and North Mumbai has helped in absorbing this new supply. Goa may have experienced decline in occupancy, but its overall performance, in light of the supply increase, is commendable. With very little new supply expected in Bangalore, Hyderabad and Goa over the next two years, we expect these markets to improve significantly. In addition, in the medium term, even Delhi, Mumbai and Chennai are likely to improve. Average rates in cities like Bangalore and

Hyderabad are likely to be substantially higher, with Bangalore registering among the strongest growth worldwide. In the leisure segment, we expect Jaipur to see a slowdown, however, Goa remains a very strong prospect.

Future Trends

HVS has been conducting the survey for seven years, and, for, the first time, it appears that Indian hotel industry has completed a full cycle, experiencing both downswing and upswing periods. The industry is robust at present, and there are clear indications are that the next two to three years will be even stronger. Certain markets are already seeing huge un-accommodated demand during weekdays, with average rates in some of these markets witnessing unprecedented increases. All the ten cities we studied have seen a positive trend in both occupancy and average rate.

While all cities have seen increases in rooms occupied per day (over the previous year's corresponding period), Goa (28.7%) is the market leader, this is what has allowed this leisure destination to absorb the new supply increase of 23.8%. Mumbai (18.1%) has the second highest growth. In fact, of the seven cities studied by us, Hyderabad was the only city to have a single-digit growth (9.4%). Chennai (17.9%) Bangalore (15.9%), New Delhi (12.9%) were the other strong performers in the market.

In terms of average rate, Bangalore (58.4%), Hyderabad (21.2%), New Delhi (9.7%) and Chennai (9.2%) have all had increases. In fact Kolkata is the only market which saw average rates decline marginally. Year-to-date occupancy for Bangalore at 80% means that there is not much potential for further increase in occupancy, as weekdays are mostly sold out. Strongly escalating demand has caused hotels to push rates way beyond what they should be getting for the quality of product they offer. This is certainly true of some of the properties that never had a proper refurbishment and are now charging exorbitant rates.

We would expect operators to raise average rates strongly in Hyderabad as well. Recent indications are that the hotels in south Mumbai have also started to see improvements in performance. This effectively means that Mumbai is poised to see good growth in terms of both occupancy and room rate increases as demand outpaces supply. Goa and Delhi are also expected to see some rate increases. Traditionally, average rates rise in October, therefore, the data is not reflective of rate increases that are likely to take place shortly. Many of these rates are negotiated rates with corporates and travel agents which will come into effect as the peak season kicks in.

The most encouraging development during the first five months of the current year has been the healthy increase in RevPAR across all cities. Bangalore (61.2%), followed by Hyderabad (32.6%), have, for the second time in a row, witnessed the highest growth in terms of RevPAR. Chennai (27.4%), Goa (23.0%) and New Delhi (12.2%) have seen double-digit growths. Mumbai (9.9%) and Kolkata (9.5%) also witnessed single digit growth.

The Goa market has performed exceptionally well and in the years to come will be one of the best performing markets. The city over the past two years has seen substantial increases in rooms supply, despite this demand continues to outstrip supply, resulting in occupancies to go up marginally even in the current year. At present there is not much new hotel activity planned for Goa, making this one of the preferred location for investment. Another market performing extremely well is the Pune market.

The sharp upturn in Bangalore's performance is beyond what most hotel owners and developers had anticipated. Despite HVS having forecast the city's hotel market to do a sharp turnaround we, too, are taken by surprise by the extent of improvement. Existing hotel owners can expect a windfall gain this year as well as for the next few years, until new supply enters the market. The

Leela Bangalore is amongst the biggest beneficiaries; this hotel is already setting records for highest average rates in the country for a business hotel (US$275 - US$300). We understand that at least 9 hotels are planning to enter Bangalore. As a result, we can expect the market to slow down in two to three years with rates declining sharply.

The trends witnessed in Delhi in 2004 have been quite positive, reinforcing our faith in the city. Occupancies have picked up over the past few months, especially in hotels closer to Gurgaon. These hotels enjoy much healthier occupancies than city centre hotels which, in fact, are pulling down overall occupancy levels. Year-to-date average rate growth is only 3.2%, but is anticipated to increase further during the peak season. Also, with the proposed conversion of Kanishka to Shangri la and Ashok Yatri Nivas' re-development, we can expect further competition within Delhi's central business areas. The new Trident Hilton (in Gurgaon) has been an extremely good performer and is currently market leader in terms of RevPAR.

Opportunities

Opportunities for the Indian hotel sector continue to be in the budget and mid-market segment: we anticipate these segments to witness huge growth and expansion, in the next year or two. The luxury segment is set to perform extremely well over the next few years until the supply- demand gap is bridged. We expect average rates to grow in all major cities across India. New opportunities lie in the extended stay segment, which many potential developers are currently shying away from. Also, HVS has observed that owners interested in developing extended stay properties are keen to partner with existing branded chains already operating in India. This, according to us, is an area where specialized serviced apartment chains like Oakwood and Ascot have tremendous scope for involvement. This is particularly true in destinations that are near large concentrations of IT and related services development.

Medical tourism could also be the next big thing, and, while we are yet to see any development in this area, we consider that there could be some potential. If world class convention centres are indeed developed in Mumbai, Delhi and Goa, these cities are sure to benefit. Similarly the further liberalization of the aviation sector would mean additional tourists, and with supply unable to keep pace with demand, nearly all segments of the hotel industry would see improvement.

HVS is of the view that if you are not already building a hotel in India, then you are late. The present period of upswing however will last longer than the previous period of upturn. There are clear indications that travel & tourism in India will grow faster now than ever before this bodes well for the hotel industry. Agra and Jaipur were the weak links in the industry. But now, increase in both inbound and domestic tourism, the two cities have experienced the strongest recovery over the 12-month period. We expect this trend to persist into the current year as tourist arrivals continue to go up. Agra, while having seen highest improvement, has still a long way to go (citywide occupancy 47%). There also some unfinished hotel projects in Agra, which will continue to put pressure on the city's performance.

As regards Jaipur, the recent announcement by a major IT company to set up a base outside Jaipur, as well as the state government's initiative to promote IT-related activity in the city, means that Jaipur can look forward to some additional room night demand from the business segment. These developments in the leisure segment including the strong performance in Goa leads us to believe that the leisure segment is clearly benefiting from the increase in foreign tourist arrivals and growth in domestic travel. We also consider that in the future years new leisure destinations in Kerela and other coastal areas will also pick up. Recent announcements by the Government of India to promote tourism in the Andaman and Nicobar Islands could not therefore have come at a better time.

Hotels in metro cities, with an average rate of Rs 2,600-3,000, and hotels in non-metro cities, with an average rate of Rs 1,800-2,400, are likely to experience rapid growth in demand in the next year or two. Cities to watch out for, in terms of development opportunity, are Pune, Goa, and certain pockets in major cities like Delhi (west) and Mumbai (mill lands). We would however, like to caution investors to stay away from the current 'hotspots' of Hyderabad, Bangalore and Gurgaon, as large additions to supply have been planned here. The real opportunity, we believe, is in a good mid-market or budget hotel of international standards.

India's hotel industry has entered the global stage, supported by its growing economy and the development of the 'Incredible India' tourism brand. Previous security concerns due to the Kashmir situation have reduced due to improved relations with Pakistan. Meanwhile the cost of travel has fallen following the government's liberalisation of the airline industry. Given that these two main barriers to travel have been tackled, not surprisingly, hotel performance has benefited.

With India capturing the attention of the world, Deloitte has responded by dedicating the 18th edition of the HotelBenchmark Survey to report each month on the country's hotel performance. To put the size of India's gigantic domestic market into perspective, it equates to over one third of total international arrivals received by all markets globally. While current mid-market players like Choice Hospitality India, Best Western, Fortune Park and Sarovar Park Plaza have catered for domestic tourism for some time - this market has recently exploded and demand is growing. As the domestic market continues to expand, the escalating economy provides the rising middle classes with increased disposable income.

The arrival of low cost airlines and the associated price wars have given domestic tourists more options than ever before. The 'Incredible India' destination campaign has also helped the growth of many domestic markets including religious tourism. As a next step, the government has recently launched the 'Atithi Devo Bhavah' (ADB) campaign aimed at increasing awareness of tourism in India.

To respond to the needs of this growing giant, companies like Choice and Best Western plan to significantly increase their portfolio over the next two years, by 100% and 50% respectively. Other hotel companies have also taken steps to ensure they benefit from the country's huge domestic demand. Indian Hotels launched its IndiOne brand with huge success last June in Bangalore. Accor has entered into a joint venture with InterGlobe Enterprises to introduce 25 Ibis branded hotels, the first will arrive in 2006. InterContinental Hotels Group is also introducing their economy brand, Holiday Inn Express, with ten properties planned, starting later this year. Marriott has also announced plans to introduce the Courtyard brand in India.

Despite the international market being significantly smaller than India's domestic market, it also shows promising growth. The country's appeal to international visitors has previously been affected by the political situation in Kashmir as well as the global events of the past few years. However this has now improved due to relative geo-political stability and international economic growth. Tourism in India is also benefiting from the stronger economies of India's two major source markets, the United Kingdom and the United States. The peace talks with Pakistan have also improved the situation, with the ongoing cricket test series between the two countries further instilling confidence of future harmony.

Currently corporate travel dominates the international arena. The Indian subsidiary of Kuoni estimates that 80% of foreigners staying in their hotels are there on business. While corporate business will naturally continue to expand as the economy grows, there is enormous untapped potential in the country's leisure market. "Incredible India" has focused not only on promoting traditional holiday attractions and cultural experiences, but on defining unique markets from medical to religious tourism. In fact, India has already seen growing Japanese arrivals due to the promotion of Buddhist travel.

But India still faces many challenges in attracting the international traveller. This will continue whilst the government addresses the quality of India's infrastructure. Although the World Travel and Tourism Council rated India second in price competitiveness (after Brazil) there are many factors which need to be dealt with to encourage foreign visitors. Poor roads, overstretched railways and old airports discourage international travellers. Add to that hotel taxes higher than most Asian countries and a bureaucratic visa process - and you start to get a clear picture of the challenges facing India.

According to the new India edition of the HotelBenchmark Survey by Deloitte, the growth in hotel performance is impressive. As indicated in the graph below, all markets tracked by the survey reported double-digit growth in the twelve months to February 2005 compared to the same period the previous year. This is not surprising given the global economic growth in 2004, India's bustling domestic economy and reduced travel barriers.

Amongst the unique features of the hotel industry in India is the sheer volume of the domestic market. Hotels receive twice as many domestic guests as international guests. With most branded supply in India sitting in the top tier of the market, the hotel industry is currently very top heavy. While many companies are addressing the needs of the growing domestic market for more economical hotel products, most projects are still in development. Future growth of the hotel industry will not be helped by archaic land laws that make construction of new hotels time-consuming and expensive.

What is interesting to note, is that the demand for hotel rooms far exceeds the country's supply. While an opportunity exists to develop the hotel industry to meet this demand, India experiences large seasonal shifts in demand and corporate travellers currently represent the bulk of guests. Due to the lack of a widely distributed business mix, annual occupancies and average room rates in India did not rank very high in the 2004 HotelBenchmark Global Ranking Index. The industry must explore ways to seize untapped potential demand whilst addressing the down-time to maintain profitable operations. Developing a more diverse business mix is key.

Airline Industry

The opening up of the aviation industry in India brings exciting opportunities for hotels; as they rely on airlines to transport 80% of international arrivals. Increased airline activity has stimulated demand and has helped to improve India's troubled infrastructure. Increased competition will lead to the development of new and improved services. In addition to new aviation brands, many existing companies have ordered new planes. This is long overdue considering state-owned Indian Airlines has not purchased a new plane in 16 years.

The open skies policy has benefited both international and domestic travel. On the international front, the capacity and availability of destinations serving India continues to grow. In late 2004, India and the UK agreed to double (in phases) the number of direct flights per week. Earlier this year, Malaysia Airlines announced their plans to add 18 new routes in India within the next five years. Jet Airways and Air Sahara, two privately owned airlines have launched services to other South Asian destinations, and will shortly launch services to Singapore. The increasing competition in the domestic airline industry will continue to drive the growth of India's domestic market. In May, two new private domestic airlines are expected to enter the market.

The government has expanded the scope of airline liberalisation with its approval in January for private airlines to fly all international routes excluding the Gulf. To qualify the government requires a company to have a fleet of at least 20 planes and five years domestic experience. Jet Airways and Sahara will be able to benefit immediately. In three years time India's state-run carriers will also have to share their Gulf routes. These routes currently earn them most of their operational revenue and profit. The recent IPO (Initial Public Offering) by Jet Airways was over-subscribed several times - indicating the confidence this industry has gained over recent years.

The aviation industry in India will drive future tourism growth, with the continued increase of flights and options for travel. But the question remains, can the country's accommodation meet the increasing expectations of the global traveller? Hotel supply must catch up with demand whilst creating a healthier business mix. Mid-market properties especially need to respond to the growing middle class. But even as the hotel industry joins the airlines in responding to India's thriving economy and driving future tourism growth - infrastructure challenges could still prevent India from grasping its full tourism potential.

Encouragingly major government initiatives such as 'Incredible India' and tax policy revision are well underway. With the growth of the economy expected to continue, and considering the size and dynamics of the domestic market, Indian hotel performance will be exciting to watch over the coming years. Future performance should reflect a country of vast opportunities, especially as mid-market products develop to satisfy the country's thriving domestic market.

3

Tourism Marketing Strategies

Tourism is an interesting subject in worldwide because of its recent growth and current size; its potential for further growth; its economic contribution measured in terms of investment, employment and balance of payments; its effects on host communities; and its impact on the physical environment of visited destinations. Marketing is a crucial practice in the extremely "competitive and quickly changing environment" and should play a significant role in the entire process from product creation to product consumption and beyond. It can be used to "attract clients against competition from many providers; both of tourism and of other products or services, on which people can choose to spend their discretionary time and money."

Marketing is an important consideration in the selling or distribution of any product or service. "Marketing is the management function which organises and directs all those business activities involved in assessing customer needs and converting customer purchasing power into effective demand for a specific product or service, and in moving that product or service to the final consumer or user so as to achieve the profit target or other objective set by the company or other organisation."

The marketing system following the elements are given below:

— assessing the "external business environment";
— surveying the business' financial situation;
— "forecasting" or "predict[ing] the future business environment";
— determining the business' goals;
— performing a "SWOT analysis" (i.e., examining the business' Strengths, Weaknesses, Opportunities, and Threats);
— formulating the marketing goals and objectives;
— preparing the marketing budget;
— devising a "strategic marketing plan and marketing mix" (which consists of product, price, promotion, place);
— creating "strategies to achieve these objectives";
— "estimating the outcome of these strategies";
— "co-ordinating and executing" the marketing strategies;
— assessing the outcome by comparing results with goals;
— "taking corrective action";
— "re-establishing goals and objectives or re-formulating marketing mix and strategies."

Marketing has evolved from "an art practised by those with intuitive judgement or hunch," to a process governed solely by research and analysis to the more recent belief that: "a scientific approach in marketing can never be exact or precise and there is never a single right answer to a marketing problem. Marketing is comprehensive coordination, part science and part art; scientific yet creative and above all dynamic."

Marketing tourism must be considered some special characteristics. Firstly, tourism is a service, defined as "any task performed for another, or the provision of any facility or product or activity for another's use, not ownership which arises from an exchange transaction" and thus must be marketed accordingly. The "product" of tourism has been described as "a satisfying activity at a desired destination" a "bundle of benefits" and "an amalgam of attractions, transport, accommodation, and entertainment." Services, including tourism, have four special characteristics: "intangibility," "perishability," "inseparability," and "heterogeneity." Intangibility is the idea that a holiday cannot be "touched, tasted, seen, heard or smelt before it is bought." Thus tourism services are perishable, because they "cannot be stored and sold at a later date."

The tourism experience is "inseparable" from the people or products providing the service, and thus the tourist's perception of the quality and overall satisfaction is directly influenced by the attitudes and performance of the person, or condition of the product, which performed the service. Closely related to inseparability is the idea that each tourist's experience will be different because the moods, attitudes, and external forces influencing people's behaviours will continually vary. Tourism is undergoing dramatic changes due to the development of new technologies which provide a new means for competition. Tourism will continue to be a valuable industry the world over, and that "marketing within it will be a subject of growing significance and interest." Furthermore, travel marketers need to adopt a more professional attitude due to the increase "in consumer expectations and sophistication."

Role of Image Creation

An image is defined as a "mental conception, perception or idea" of something and is the product of the perception process. The personal image one has of the phenomenal environment is said to be one's perception of the environment. However, "the perceived environment or image is more than the sum of direct perceptual experiences" as additional, indirect, information about environments may come from "... simulative exploration, cinematic and photographic displays, sketches, drawings and replicas".

People travel for many reasons, such as:

- to experience change or
- to "see different places, things and people" or
- to "consume culture" to research ancestry
- to "recover...wholeness and structure"
- to learn or appreciate something
- for "self-actualization or self-realization"
- to be different;
- for rest and relaxation;
- for prestige or status
- to "escape personal problems"
- to experience "reduced constraints on behaviour"
- to play out a "fantasy"
- to get closer to relatives.

In order to better understand tourists' needs and motivations, researchers have developed various tourist typologies. Tourist typologies reflect the diversity of individual motivations, styles, interests and values, and the subsequent differences often correlate with specific disciplinary research interests. There is two typologies based on the type of travel undertaken. These included "sunlust" and "wanderlust," the first being travel undertaken for "rest and relaxation," the second being "motivated by the desire to learn."

Two groups of tourists are

1) institutionalized —"organized mass tourists" and "individual mass tourists"
2) non-institutionalized —"the explorer" and "the drifter."

Institutionalized tourists are those which desire comfort and safety and rely heavily upon the tourism industry, whereas non-institutionalized tourists are those which prefer to follow their own path and have little contact with the tourism industry. Pleasure-seeking tourists include the recreational tourist, who simply desires "entertainment and relaxation" and the diversionary tourist, who wishes to "escape the routine of everyday life."

Modern pilgrimage tourists encompass three different typologies: the experiential tourist who "seeks an authentic experience... but does not totally identify with the foreign culture;" the experimental tourist who wishes to "seek an alternative lifestyle but does not become totally immersed in a foreign culture;" and the existential tourist who becomes totally "immersed in the foreign culture." Another typology was created that there are seven types of tourists: charter tourists, mass tourists, incipient mass tourists, unusual tourists, off-beat tourists, elite tourists, and explorers. These typologies gradually progress from tourists who "arrive by the planeload in large numbers and are just there to enjoy their holiday" (charter tourists), to the few tourists who explore new areas and "fully accept local culture."

Regardless of the reason for travelling, the choice of a destination is dependent upon the potential tourist's perception of the ability of that destination to satisfy the reason, or "need" for travelling. The key word here is perception, which has been defined as "both the response of the senses to external stimuli and purposeful activity in which certain phenomena are clearly registered while others recede in the shade or are blocked out." The personal image one has of the phenomenal environment is said to be one's perception of the environment. From this it may be seen that image and perception are intricately linked, as an image is based upon and formed by one's perceptions.

An image is an "idea" or "conception" of something and is the "basis of the evaluation or selection process." Furthermore, perceptions, and thus images, are also dependent upon a number of influencing factors, such as age, sex, physical and mental ability, weather, time, political factors, money, fashion, social ambitions, personality, culture, and lifestyle. Other external influences include movies, books, and legends, and therefore images are not simply the result of promotions put forward by various companies or destinations.

The purpose of image creation within marketing is either to create, to confirm and enhance, to alter, or to completely recreate or change the existing image, thereby motivating the consumer to choose the product or service being marketed. The Internet can be of great assistance in this process, but the effectiveness of various elements, specifically maps, in the image creation process when marketing tourism destinations on the Internet is still unknown.

Role of Maps

A map is "a representation of things in space" and thus facilitates spatial visualization, perception, learning, and image creation. As a means of communicating spatial information, maps appear unsurpassed: "One has to regard cartography as visual communication of a special kind which, with regard to its two-dimensional and systematic information, is superior to all other means of communication as far as certain messages are concerned." Maps are an important part of most tourism experiences, and it makes intuitive sense that maps should be part of any marketing campaign promoting a travel destination.

Maps and tourism are inseparable. From early adventurers who used rudimentary maps and charts to explore "new" worlds, to the modern-day tourist who uses a travel map to navigate within a chosen destination, maps play a significant role in how we discover, learn, and communicate information about the world around us. Tourism involves travel to a place where the tourist normally does not work or live. Therefore, the traveller has limited spatial knowledge of the visited environment and maps perform an essential function in the acquisition of spatial information by tourists. Their importance is emphasized as:

> "Maps are indispensable to strangers orienting themselves to new places... Sightseeing rarely starts without... a map. Maps direct seeing, visualization serving to validate expectations predicated on map use."

Maps break down our inhibitions, stimulate our glands, stir our imagination, loosen our tongues. The map speaks across the barriers of language; it is sometimes claimed as the language of geography. Maps perform a valuable function throughout the entire tourism process. They are a source of inspiration and daydreaming about future travel destinations. Maps may be used by tourists in the decision-making stage in order to visualize and imagine potential destinations. They may be used in the trip-planning phase, to decide how to travel to, from, and within the selected destination, where to stay, which attractions to visit, and even which neighborhoods or regions to avoid. They are used during travel, to assist with navigation and orientation.

And maps may be used after traveling, to remember places visited, or to help with post-trip visualization and reminiscence. Since the "goal of map making is to communicate information and ideas about places" maps are fundamental vehicles for communicating spatial information and creating images of space and place. Just as a "picture is worth a thousand words," a well-designed map can speak volumes about a travel destination. Although maps have traditionally played a significant role in tourism marketing, and although the Web provides significant opportunities for the communication of spatial information and image creation, this area of tourism marketing is not being used to its full potential.

From a preliminary examination of the content and design of tourism web sites and maps, it appears that some tourism marketers overlook the importance of maps in the tourism marketing process. In other cases it seems that tourism marketers realize the importance of maps, but fail to use them effectively. Frequently, maps are underutilised, poor in quality or design, hard to find with the web site, unsuitable, illegible, or so complicated that they take a long time to load or crash the computer.

Destination of Marketing

Marketing is an important activity for any business that wishes to become and remain competitive and successful. This is certainly the case in the rapidly changing tourism industry, and therefore tourism destination marketers must constantly review and revise their marketing goals, images, strategies and plans. The tourism industry encompasses many businesses, such as accommodations, attractions, transportation, and restaurants, each of which may undertake marketing efforts. That is, there are different scales at which marketing can occur, from large-scale marketing of individual businesses or attractions to small-scale marketing of regions or entire countries.

Tourism is a very competitive industry with a highly volatile product. Destinations in vogue today often are out of fashion tomorrow. Marketing is one of the main ways for destinations to inform and entice potential tourists and to gain competitive advantage. However, many service industries such as tourism have traditionally used marketing less than manufacturing firms, as they felt it was too expensive, time-consuming, unnecessary, and unprofessional relying primarily on an established reputation to attract business. And there are still those who consider marketing unprofessional, particularly within the area of advertising.

Such detractors hold on to the belief that marketers will do anything to sell their products or services, with their number one goal being the making of a "quick buck." They are seen as having a complete lack of respect for customers' opinions, desires and intellects, and the environment or society as a whole. But this is an unfair view of many of today's marketers, because in a true marketing philosophy, customer satisfaction is key. Some have noted that marketing also can be used to protect the environment, improve quality of life, and help society as a whole. Marketers can use demand management to increase, decrease, or shift demand for a product or service either temporarily or permanently (Ibid).

In the case of tourism, demarketing can be particularly useful, as it can be used to even-out demand (i.e., increase off-season visits, and limit high-season visits, thus reducing congestion, crowding and environmental impacts), to restrict access to sensitive areas, and to inform and educate tourists about problems facing various areas. Tourism destinations that adopt a modern marketing philosophy "that focuses on the satisfaction of tourist needs and wants while respecting the long-term interests in the community" will benefit not only themselves, but consumers, the environment, and society.

Who believes that "new tourism can play a leading role in providing and promoting more sustainable patterns of development and in saving Planet Earth." Thus, tourism marketing can and should assume an important role in education and conservation, because in the tourism industry, there is much more to gain (or lose) than just profits. In these days of increased amounts of leisure time, higher standards of living, greater quality of life, higher expectations, and increasing choices (at least in so-called "developed countries"), tourism destination marketers must work harder to provide tourist satisfaction and to ensure they obtain and retain their share of the market. But tourism marketers should be sensitive to the new situation in which they are marketing.

They must realize that tourism can and does have a sizeable impact on the environment, and tourism should not be promoted without full knowledge and understanding of that fact. Certainly not all regions are ready or willing to accept and develop tourism. Nor should they, as tourism does not always have a positive effect. But in many areas, tourism marketing can make a significant contribution to the quality of life of residents and tourists alike.

Destinations that have chosen to embrace or at least accept tourism as a valuable industry must find a way to compete and succeed, and to protect the environment from the negative impacts of tourism. Adoption of a marketing philosophy is the key to success, and tourism marketers that adopt the societal marketing concept will be better off in the future, as consumers are becoming more educated and concerned about choosing products and services that benefit rather than harm the environment.

Promotional Materials

The most visible tourism marketing materials are those involved in the process of promotion, as its purpose is to create and increase awareness of a business' products or services and involves communicating with prospective clients. Promotion encompasses the areas of personal selling, direct marketing, sales promotion, public relations, and advertising and of these, advertising is usually the most obvious as it is conducted on a larger scale than the other four.

Personal selling consists of one-on-one interactions between a company's salespersons and their prospective clients, and is one form of direct marketing, which involves communicating with potential customers, usually by direct mail and telephone, and measuring the response. Public relations involves "building a good reputation and image" and "handling or heading off unfavourable rumours, stories, and events." Sales promotion includes "short-term incentives to encourage purchase or sales of a product or service" such as rebates, coupons, or contests. Advertising can occur through a number of different media, including print materials (such as brochures, magazines and newspapers), direct mail (flyers, announcements), television commercials, videos, radio advertisements, window displays, and through the newest communication channel: the Internet.

These advertisements usually consist of pictures, graphics, drawings, videos, maps, animation, and text, in varying amounts depending on the advertising channel employed. Consumers access marketing materials by either seeking them out, coming across them while pursuing other activities, or receiving them directly from the company undertaking the advertising effort. Once discovered, they can choose either to ignore the information, to express interest, to request further information, or to put the information to use. In addition, marketing may be either direct or indirect. Direct marketing is that which attempts to make a sale immediately, whereas indirect marketing is aimed at making a sale eventually.

Images of space and place play a prominent role in promotional materials, as their goal is the creation of a desirable image of the destination region, with the hope of causing consumers to seek further information and eventually select the destination as the site for future tourism experiences. Images are created through textual description, pictures, drawings, graphics, maps, music, audio, video, and animation. Even the overall "look and feel" of the promotional materials, the choice of promotional methods, and the communication channel used, may influence the image of a destination. However, there are other factors which may influence images of place. Indirect influences (both positive and negative) on place images include movies, television shows, web sites, books, magazines, clothing, sporting events, music, posters, myths, rumours, stories, legends, and word-of-mouth from family and friends.

Advertising Materials

Tourism advertising materials are used to communicate images of tourism destinations to potential tourists. As humans are mainly "visual beings" these materials usually contain many pictures, maps, animation, and video. Textual descriptions are rich in adjectives and adverbs, and sounds or music elements are used to complement the images created by the visual elements. Print advertisements include those in magazines and newspapers, and tourism brochures and flyers.

The "Official Vacation Planner [for] Victoria and the Islands" is a typical example of a tourism brochure. It is filled with pictures, maps, lists of, and advertisements for, attractions, accommodations, and restaurants, and rich textual descriptions of Victoria and the surrounding area. These elements, including design elements such as text font, page layout, and background colours all work together to create the overall image of the destination in the tourist's mind, as the following excerpt demonstrates: "With the mildest climate in the country, Victoria is perfect for visiting at any time of the year. Spring begins as early as February when residents count the number of blossoms in their gardens and a total for the city is tabulated. Summer, with its lush, vivid gardens, is warm and dry, never too hot to be out exploring. Fall begins in late September and is a lovely transition as deciduous trees change from green to gold."

Television commercials also endeavour to create desirable images, and due to television's visual nature are largely focussed on video images and pictures of the destination. Music is played, and while text is minimal, verbal descriptions and commentary are common. Most commercials provide a toll-free telephone number which you can call to obtain a brochure, and many recent commercials also refer watchers to their web site. Radio commercials for tourism are less common, mainly because radio is a "nonvisual" form of communication, thus making it harder to create an image of the destination. Radio advertisements are more commonly used to announce current specials or promotional offerings by various tourist agencies and transportation carriers, rather than to promote destination regions.

The Internet is the newest and perhaps most powerful tool available to tourism marketers. The World Wide Web, the graphical interface through which users may navigate the Internet, has multimedia capabilities and, therefore, is a valuable device for creating images of tourism destinations. Tourism destination web sites may consist of pictures, videos, sounds, animations, graphics, maps and interactive maps, charts, text, games, and even programs, such as distance calculators and currency converters.

Images of Space and Place in Tourism Marketing

The creation of a desirable place image, "the sum of beliefs, ideas, and impressions that a people have of a place" is an important concern for place marketers, as the ability to attract tourists spells success or failure for the destination. Tourism destination marketers must project the right image of their destination in order to entice the potential tourist to consider the site for a future vacation or business endeavour. The key here is the creation of a desirable place image of the tourism destination in the mind of the potential tourist. However, the mental images that tourists create are rarely, if ever, identical to the images projected by the destination as there are many other forces which influence images of space and place. Therefore, in order to understand why tourists select certain destinations it is necessary to identify the influencing factors, and examine how people perceive, and then create mental images of, space and place.

Environmental Perception

The process of perception has been defined as "both the response of the senses to external stimuli and purposeful activity in which certain phenomena are clearly registered while others recede in the shade or are blocked out." During interaction with the environment, the senses of sight, hearing, smell, taste, touch, and the sixth sense of "feel" constantly and selectively sense and collect information about that environment, in the process known as environmental perception. A concise explanation of the environmental perception process is provided as:

> "In operating within any environment, man [sic] is involved in the 'image system.' He [sic] perceives, selectively, certain information by means of his [sic] various senses and adds this information to his [sic] store of mental images. Images from other environments, as well as the image of the environment under consideration, will be 'consulted' before behaviour is decided upon. Behaviour itself will be varied by motivation and the play of social, political and economic factors, but when it does take place the environment itself will be affected and the

> individual's information on that environment will be supplemented. During and after activity within the environment, perception by the individual will continually change."

Perception is gradual and takes time—involves difficulty and effort —has emotional accompaniments— and can be rewarding and pleasurable. There are three different stages of perception: pre-visit perception, on-site perception, and post-visit perception. Pre-visit perception is that which occurs before direct, on-site perception has occurred, and is a result of information collected (both consciously and unconsciously) from sources other than the environment itself. On-site perception is perception that occurs during interaction with the environment, but is influenced by pre-visit perception. Post-visit perception occurs after interaction with the environment, and is influenced by various information sources. Post-visit perceptions may continue to change, as memory tends to be selective and may fail over time.

All three stages of perception, and therefore also the image an individual has of the environment, are influenced by numerous factors, including physical and mental ability, gender, age, familiarity with and affection towards the surroundings, socioeconomic status, religion, ambitions, education, time, weather, fashion, and the political situation. Images are influenced further by the media, television, radio, the Internet, movies, books, magazines, advertisements, stories, myths, legends, and rumours, and discussions with friends and family.

As individuals interact with the environment, the information they receive may be used for: classification and description; appraisals involving emotions, meanings and values; or "predictions and inference which give to the image a depth, continuity, pattern or meaning beyond that justified by experience of a particular scene alone." Once information about the environment has been collected, from both direct and indirect sources, and during all three stages of perception, the process of environmental cognition organizes, stores and recalls the information when necessary. Thus, personal perceptions, evaluations, preferences, attitudes, aesthetic judgments, appraisals and images of the environment are formed as a function of direct and indirect experiences, before, during, and after interaction with the environment

In order to understand how people make judgments about space and place, we must first examine the relationship between these two abstract terms. Here illustrates the link between them by explaining that: "what begins as undifferentiated space becomes place as we get to know it better and endow it with value —From the security and stability of place we are aware of the openness, freedom, and threat of space, and vice versa. Furthermore, if we think of space as that which allows movement, then place is pause; each pause in movement makes it possible for location to be transformed into place."

In terms of tourism destination selection, space and place always play a role because tourism is "the experience and consumption of place" but this role varies in significance. Often it is the specific place, such as a specific city which attracts tourists. However, in certain situations, the place is the deterring factor. These may be considered a "real place" typology. Alternatively, sometimes the specific place doesn't matter as much as the specific attribute(s) that the place possesses, such as the climate; recreational resources; status; special events; location relative to home; or even special pricing.These types of destinations are somewhat "interchangeable" because the desire for travelling could be satisfied by visiting any place that satisfies these criteria.

Judgments of environments are based on numerous criteria, both tangible and intangible. Tangible criteria involve such factors as air and water quality, noise pollution, recreation facilities, transportation systems, amount of green space, safety, crowding, remoteness, climate, natural resources, infrastructure, and tourist or recreation amenities. Intangible criteria upon which individuals form judgments of space and place include abstract concepts such as aesthetics, landscape quality, "style" or status, and the meanings or significance attached to place, such as biological, ecological, cultural, moral, economic, political, symbolic, and emotional.

Perceived Environment Quality Indices (PEQI) have been developed in order to assess environmental quality using measurements such as air and water quality, noise pollution, crowding, and even aesthetics. Traditionally, tangible criteria have been given more "weight" when judging space and place, as they are scientifically quantifiable, and therefore considered objective. Measurement of intangible elements is performed "indirectly, in terms of human experiences" and is therefore considered "subjective." All indices of the quality of environmental components, however concrete and tangible the components may be, are based upon human perception and judgment. The identification of a component as a determinant of environmental quality, and the determination of appropriate standards of quality for that component, rest upon human (subjective) judgments.

PEQIs have been used for decision-making by organizations rather than individuals. Personal judgments of space and place may be based on some of the same criteria as PEQIs, such as safety, climate, recreational amenities and aesthetics, but these judgments vary "with experience and perspective... novelty and familiarity... distance and memory," and are influenced by the intensity of feelings towards the environment, especially in crisis situations. Furthermore, environments that are valued today, may not be valued tomorrow, as "value is a dynamic concept."

PEQIs changes as a typology of place goes in or out of fashion. The media, societal trends, fashion and prestige change, as do variables such as safety. Recommendations and opinions from both formal and informal sources play a significant role in the formation of personal judgments of space and place, particularly in the selection of a holiday destination. Judgments and images of space and place depend on what individuals have done, are doing, or plan to do, in that space and place, their individual perceptions of that space and place, their experiences in and of that space or place, and the surrounding circumstances in which the judgments are formed. Therefore, it is obvious that images of space and place will affect decision-making, especially in the process of "holiday selection."

Holiday Selection Process

Individuals are constantly interacting with, and collecting information about, their immediate environment as well as distant places. When the decision is made to plan a holiday, individuals will consult their personal images and information in order to begin the process of "holiday selection". The first step is "problem recognition," and encompasses the factors motivating the individual to take a holiday. At that point, a "preferential image" is formed, based on the type of holiday the individual wishes to take and which he or she believes will best satisfy the reason for traveling. Obviously, this is subject to various constraints and outside influences, such as time, money, and peer pressure.

As an individual's information about the "total set" of holiday possibilities is limited, the individual undertakes an "information search." Information is gathered from both formal (e.g., travel agents, brochures, travel magazines, Internet sites) and informal (e.g., friends and family) sources, and may be promoted or unpromoted. Unpromoted, informal information usually is judged by potential tourists to be more credible, as these sources do not have a "vested interest" in promoting a certain destination. In addition, perceived destination image is influenced by the communications channel through which the information is received and the environment in which the information is received.

Individual has information on a number of different sites, forming the "awareness set" these are compared against the "evaluative image" that the potential tourist has created. The information gathered is used to form attitudes, preferences, and aesthetic judgments and these in turn are used to form "naive or factual images" of each of the destinations in the "consideration set." These images are continually compared against each other, the "evaluative image" and the reason for traveling, until the number of destinations under consideration is narrowed down to the "choice set" (Ibid). Other significant influences upon the consideration set include numerous trade-offs between, for example, time at the destination versus en-route travel time, destination versus cost, and cost versus length of holiday.

From the final choice set, the destination which is expected to "exceed the aspiration level by the greatest amount" is chosen, unless the decision to travel is aborted. Essential role of destination images in the holiday selection process:

> "... unless a given destination figures amongst a would-be tourist's current set of mental images it has no chance of being selected as the holiday base. [W]here it does figure in the tourist's image set a very positive image of that destination must be projected in the tourist's mind for it to be selected in preference to an alternative. [W]here the tourist is successfully enticed to a destination it is equally important that the satisfaction derived from the

holiday at least matches the expectations created by the image - otherwise the tourist will not wish to return and will not recommend that destination to friends (indeed, the dissatisfied tourist may be instrumental in implanting a negative image in the minds of friends)."

Destination marketers must be aware of their image as perceived by potential tourists. If this image is not positive, place marketers must attempt either to alter or to recreate their image. But this should be done in an ethical manner. With large amounts of money at stake, place marketers sometimes "stretch the truth" in order to persuade and attract tourists. Deceptive or unrealistic images can lead to tourist disappointment and dissatisfaction, loss of repeat business, bad "word-of-mouth" advertising, and a poor reputation.

Place Marketing

Contacts and communication are vital elements" of tourism. Within the tourism marketing process, communication refers to transferring an image of the tourism destination through various promotional channels to potential tourists. The purpose of this is "to create, maintain, or change attitudes or behaviour toward particular places" and: "to persuade the potential tourist to make a holiday purchase where none was made before: to induce a change in holiday behaviour by getting the tourist to purchase a different destination or type of holiday; or to reinforce the tourist's existing behaviour by maintaining the purchase of a given holiday 'brand'."

Destination marketers must first conduct research in order to determine how consumers view the destination. As different markets have different needs, wants and, therefore, different images of the destination, the consultation must be performed within the chosen "target markets," the groups of consumers sharing similar characteristics that the destination has decided to attract and "serve." If the image is unsatisfactory, destination marketers will have to determine why the projected image is inadequate.

Various strategies that may be adopted by tourism marketers in order to improve a destination's image. First, the actual, physical attributes of the destination may be improved, a process termed "real repositioning"; or tourism marketers may undertake "psychological repositioning" to influences people's beliefs about the destination. "Competitive depositioning" and the highlighting of "neglected attributes" of other destinations may be employed, in order to influence beliefs about competing destinations. Finally, they may change the "importance weights" by "persuad[ing] buyers to attach more importance to the attributes in which the place excels," or attempt to "shift the buyer's ideals". Selection of the appropriate positioning method is dependent upon the natural, competitive, social, cultural, political, technological, and economic environments in which the destination exists.

In order to be effective, projected place images must be simple, distinctive, appealing, believable, and valid. As tourism services are "interdependent" (i.e., they are made up of several services) the coordination of the images of these services is necessary for the creation of a simple and distinctive image. This prevents tourist "confusion" and aids in distinguishing the destination from competitors. The image must be appealing and believable in order to attract tourists, and then must be valid in order to avoid tourist dissatisfaction and disappointment (Ibid).

To achieve a simple, distinctive, and appealing image, tourism marketers may employ "slogans, themes and positions," "symbols and branding," or "events and deeds." Aesthetics play an essential role in the creation of a destination's identity, and its image as perceived by target markets. This argument is forwarded here:

> "Aesthetics is not esoteric. The vitality of aesthetics in customers' lives provides opportunities for organizations to appeal to customers through a variety of sensory experiences and thereby benefit both the customers and the organizations through customer satisfaction and loyalty. These opportunities are not limited... Any organization whatsoever, in any industry, for any customer base, for profit or not for profit, governmental or private, consumer, industrial or service can benefit from using aesthetics."

Projected images, including the aesthetic qualities of these images, may be considered important "pull factors" for tourism destinations. That is, they may attract or "pull" tourists toward a certain destination. Place marketers must understand the image formation process, and the role of aesthetics in this process. After tourism marketers have decided on the nature and design of the image they wish to project, they must decide how, and through which channels, this image will be projected or communicated to potential tourists.

An important concept regarding marketing communications, known as the "AIDA model," is identified in the literature. Before a tourist selects a destination, they must be aware of the destination and have the interest and desire to visit the destination. Interest and desire may be created through the design and delivery of a positive place image to potential tourists. At this point the tourist may choose to perform the required actions to visit the destination, but this will only happen after a desirable image has been formed in the mind of the potential tourist and that image has out-bid all other potential destination sites in the choice set.

No matter how good the marketing strategy, how low the price, how available the product, and how visible the advertising, if a consumer's image of the destination is not sufficient to make the choice set, nothing will convince them to choose the site as a tourism destination. This awareness, interest, desire, and action may be created through promotion of the destination region, but marketing and promotional efforts will differ depending upon which phase of the AIDA model the tourism marketer is trying to address.

Promotion encompasses personal selling, sales promotion, public relations and advertising. Each of these elements can influence perceived images of a tourism destination, however, advertising is the most visible factor as it is undertaken on a larger scale than the others. Both informative and persuasive advertising may be used to increase awareness of, and demand for, products and services, including tourism. Informative advertising is generally used to increase awareness of new products, features, or destinations, whereas persuasive advertising is an attempt to convince consumers that the destination will best satisfy their "need" for traveling.

Promotional materials and information about tourism destinations may reach consumers through a number of "communication channels" including television and radio, print ads in magazines and newspapers, brochures and flyers, and most recently, through the Internet. Although tourists may obtain a "virtual" tourism experience through videos and web sites, in reality the tourism product is 'intangible.' Therefore: "to reduce uncertainty [and increase tangibility], buyers look for 'signals' of service quality. They draw conclusions about quality from the place, people, price, equipment, and communication material that they can see."

It is essential for tourism marketers to realize that not only does the quality, design, and timing of these materials have an influence on tourists' images, but the communication channel itself can play a role. The Internet is the newest and most powerful communications and research tool available to tourism marketers. Use of the

Internet may make tourism information available to a larger audience, as the Internet is quickly spreading worldwide. Moreover, a well-designed, informative web site that provides information and value to potential tourists may help to create a positive and professional image of the destination.

Role of Internet on Marketing

Internet is one of the modern technologies affecting competition in the tourism industry, and is the newest and most powerful tool available to tourism marketers. Yet its history, composition, capabilities, limits, and potential for use within a marketing strategy must be fully understood in order for it to be successfully incorporated into an overall marketing plan. The Internet began as ARPAnet (Advanced Research Projects Agency Network), a computer network set up in the 1960s by the US Department of Defense, in order to provide secure communications "among various military facilities and educational research centers around the world." The intention of ARPAnet was to decentralize the storage of information and thus reduce information loss in the case of nuclear attack.

This network gradually evolved into what we now know as the Internet, a much larger and faster system of information storage, retrieval and communication. Internet has traditionally been used for research and communications, and this may explain the reluctance of people to accept it as a marketplace. Nevertheless this attitude is changing, and wise use of the Internet for marketing will help tourism destinations remain competitive in the rapidly evolving tourism industry. Internet's role in a marketing strategy is new, and rapidly evolving. Initially, much of the literature concerning marketing on the Internet was actually focussed on advertising and selling on the Internet rather than using the

Internet throughout the entire marketing process.

Marketing on the Internet is "affordable, dynamic [and] wide-reaching." It is an incredibly powerful communications and research tool, which can help the marketer effectively perform traditional marketing duties such as conducting market research, examining competitors, forecasting and advertising. However, it has some special attributes which must be taken into account. Due to the historically non-commercial nature of the Internet, it is necessary to adapt traditional marketing and promotion strategies in order to avoid creating an annoying, unprofessional image. On the Internet "customers come to you" and should experience your promotion and marketing as a result of their inquiries.

Travel is a trade in people, where contacts and communication are vital elements. The Internet is the newest and most powerful tool for creating contacts and for communication. With regard to tourism destination marketing on the Internet, the message to be communicated to potential customers is a desirable and realistic image of the destination, and so the image creation process must be understood by tourism marketers.

The evolution of the Internet, and its deregulation from a research tool into a free network that anyone may use, means that marketers are now free to adopt the Internet as a marketing tool. This has radically affected the ways in which marketers apply their skills, and has forced them to acquire new skills altogether. But these advances affect more than those involved with marketing. They affect consumers as well. Technology has advanced so much that consumers can do banking, order products, or plan for a trip from home! The Internet and the World Wide Web have made all of this, and much more, possible.

The technological pace has been so furious, however, that we have been falling behind in our efforts to learn how to use this technology to its full potential. The Internet has certain characteristics and limitations which must be understood before it can be integrated successfully into a marketing plan. Furthermore, despite the immensity of the Internet, and its continued rapid growth, only a relatively small portion of the world's population has access to it, and this access is concentrated in certain countries and socioeconomic groups. Therefore, when marketing on the Internet, there are several questions one must consider.

Internet and World Wide Web

In 1989, two significant events in the history of the Internet happened. The ARPANET was decommissioned and the World Wide Web (also referred to as the WWW or Web) was created at the European Laboratory for Particle Physics (CERN). By 1992, the Internet was so large that, despite opposition from many of the Internet's users, commercial activities were finally allowed to intrude. The first web browser to offer the entire hypertext package, Mosaic, was released to the public in 1993.

The World Wide Web is one of the many methods for travelling on the Internet. The key advantage is that the WWW has the ability to display information in multimedia format, including videos, interactive maps, and animation. Therefore, the Web is the Internet medium in which "creative talents are at their best." In addition, the Web uses hypertext links which allow users to jump to related topics within and between documents, and incorporates most aspects of other Internet services such as Electronic-mail, File Transfer Protocol, Telnet, and Mailing Lists. For these reasons the Web "has become more popular than non-Web functions, [attracting] millions of users."

Internet can improve a company's marketing activities. Relative to traditional marketing and promotion methods, it provides increased access to information which may be used to "keep a finger on the pulse of the marketplace." Furthermore, proponents of Internet marketing highlight the fact that organizations can use the Internet to obtain information about competitors, current customers, prospective customers, and even themselves. Another advantage that has been identified is that the Internet provides a channel for faster, easier, and more direct communication, both internally and externally and such improvements in internal communications can lead to greater "organizational cooperation" and integration.

In turn it is argued that enhanced external communications help to eliminate barriers between companies and their customers and can cause "disintermediation" which refers to the elimination of the need for "middlemen" [sic], such as travel agents, salespersons, etc. This brings the company and the consumer closer together enabling "better relationships" and greatly improving customer service. It may also "save time and cut steps from the marketing process." Plus, web sites are available to Internet users all day long, every day of the year.

By using the Internet, businesses can acquire new markets "that weren't being reached by the traditional marketing campaign." For example, a web site may attract different people than a print ad or television commercial, thereby increasing the business' exposure. A high-tech image created by a well-designed web site may cause customers to view the business in a whole different light. Furthermore, it has been asserted that the Internet also increases opportunities to develop new products and services or to offer them in a new way. It allows people to "do things that were not possible before" such as grocery shopping, paying bills, or researching a term paper without leaving home. This provides companies with the possibility of creating new products and services they had not imagined prior to the creation of the Internet.

Information on web sites can be constantly updated, providing customers with the most current products, the correct prices, or the most up-to-date facts and figures. In addition, the interactive capabilities of the Web mean that users can become involved, literally, with web sites, thus increasing their recall and interest in these sites. The growth in this new communications medium is happening faster than any other in history and this development is expected to continue. Coupled with advancements in hardware and software, and reductions in cost, it may even speed up. However, some of the recent literature suggests that growth rates have slowed in developed countries due to market saturation, from 7% in the first quarter of 2002, to 4% in the second quarter of 2002 but at the same time, e-commerce is "gaining strength" as users are beginning to feel more comfortable with the idea of shopping online.

Many business have already endeavoured to establish their "Net presence" and consumers are getting accustomed to using the Internet. Experts argue that companies that do not set up a web site, or fail to create an effective web site, risk the development of an unprofessional or out-of-date image, customer disappointment and dissatisfaction, and loss of business. In fact, it is recognized that consumers who fail to find information from one company probably will not hesitate to locate another to fulfill their needs and wants. Some supporters of Internet marketing rationalize that it is becoming "easier and more profitable" to use the Internet and that "there is no reason why anyone can not make a living marketing his products or services over the Internet." While this is probably not the case, as some businesses simply are not suited to the Internet, in situations where it is appropriate to market on the Internet there seem to be many reasons to create a web site.

Little literature exists at this point in time which takes a negative view of Internet marketing. The dearth of literature critical of marketing on the Web may be due to the fact that this is a relatively new marketing approach, or perhaps it truly has few drawbacks. Perhaps by embracing this new technology too quickly, without taking the time to examine and evaluate its impact, it will cause, or may have already caused, problems of which we are completely unaware. Perhaps we will see the emergence of a backlash against online marketing in the future, as we come to recognize more disadvantages and problems association with this new marketing tool. Hopefully we will be able to strike a healthy balance as we find our way.

Characteristics of Internet Marketing

In order to incorporate the Internet and Web into marketing strategies, the characteristics, possibilities, and limitations of these new technologies must be recognized. Firstly, the Internet and Web are different from all other types of media, and therefore may need to be implemented differently.

> "Warning! Just using multimedia technology to do business the old way is a direct route to failure. Many large companies are transferring traditional flat media (brochures, catalogues, etc.) to multimedia without reaping the benefits of the new technology." "The Web is not print. The Web is not television. The Web is not a CD-ROM...Although it has words like books, images like TV, and multimedia like CD-ROMs, the Web is singular."

This unique nature must be examined, understood, and respected when marketing on the Internet. And just as this media is different, so can be the experience provided by that media. There is a need "to make the viewer an active participant" in order to increase awareness of, interest in, and the desire for, the product or service. A new approach is required in order to convince users to actively participate. The Internet differs from other marketing media because it must "pull" or "attract" people. A television or radio commercial can force itself upon people (and therefore they are described as "push" media), while a web site cannot force itself upon people (unless they stumble upon it while surfing the Internet).

Therefore, web sites must be advertised through traditional advertising channels. People must be given a reason to visit a web site. And once they visit, the web site must "appeal more to reason than emotion" as Internet users "want information, not sales hype." As many people are still reluctant to accept the Internet as a marketplace, any intrusive marketing efforts will drive consumers away. For these reasons, the basis for competition on the Internet is also different. Once an Internet user is attracted to a site, it must offer them something of value.

In order for products and services to be successfully marketed on the Internet, they must be unique, or they must be offered in a unique way. But the Internet makes it easier for businesses to see how their competitors are implementing their marketing strategies, and thus makes it easier for ideas and innovations to be copied. Furthermore, Internet marketing practices must be monitored more closely, because "all the marketing stages happen at the same time" and the Internet provides a different market.

The market segment of people who are on the Web and who might also have an interest in your product is a special segment, and it deserves some special attention." Rather than a mass market, customers should be thought of as individuals, and Internet promotions should be created on a "one-on-one" basis. However, the Internet creates international markets, and thus businesses must decide which languages and customs will be observed on their web sites. Finally, there is the issue of security. Some people are still afraid to conduct banking online, or to make purchases through the Internet. However, advances in security are being made, and even though people may not feel comfortable making purchases over the Internet, a web site can still move customers toward making purchases through traditional channels.

With regard to web sites designed for marketing purposes, the first step is to create Awareness of the site, and then the products and/or services available on the site. This must be done by advertising through traditional channels, such as television and print ads, and by including the site address on all materials created by the company. While it is possible to advertise the site through mass e-mailings, this requires tactfulness, as many Internet users dislike unsolicited e-mail messages, and may form a negative impression of the company that sends such a message. Press releases sent to topical online discussion groups and forums may be well-received if presented in a non-aggressive format to an appropriate group.

Furthermore, "search engine optimization" may be used to increase the chances that your site will be listed at the top of the results when a user performs a search on a related topic. Basically, this involves "designing, writing and coding your entire web site" based on "keywords and key phrases." However, each search engine uses different criteria for finding, indexing, and listing results, so designing a site for optimization is quite involved. To create Interest in a web site, the site should be easy to use, fun, dynamic, memorable, interactive, and efficient. It should "present a professional corporate image" and that image should be valid, believable, simple, appealing, and distinctive.

The site should also "establish the business and products' benefits to customers early in their visit" so that their interest in the site will begin to develop right away (or so that it won't waste their time if they are not interested). Web sites can help to generate the Desire for a product or service, by providing accurate, "up-to-date" and honest information about the product or service. In addition, a well-designed web site with a high-tech look may help to create desire simply by appearing to be on the "leading-edge".

Customers' questions should be anticipated and they should be provided with easy access to "human contact" in case they "need attention". Customers should be provided with clear and easy calls to Action within web sites. They should have access to "a simple, secure ordering and billing procedure", or should be provided with contact information or a "link" in case they need more information about the product or services. There should also be an opportunity for customers to provide suggestions or "feedback" to allow for "continual...improve[ments] to site content and presentation." Marketers who are serious about providing a quality web site need to "be proactive...make a long-term commitment...develop a vision and have patience" then follow through by continually updating the site."

"The Web has its own language, aesthetic issues, and problems and yet represents a convergence of nearly all other media. Its content must be built to travel across vast networks to unknown devices and browsers—Making great Web sites forces you to take classic design principles and apply them in ways you'd never dream of if you were designing a poster or making a movie—The Web relies on the divine design commandment that form follows function—Being clear on where your project fits on the library-gallery continuum is the first step toward successfully navigating the maze of compromises and tough questions that working on the Web will demand of you. The goal is to balance pure information with an aesthetic that not only complements the message but also becomes part of the voice."

Destinations on the Internet

Internet users comprise a relatively small portion of the

world's population. Consequently, tourism destination marketers must ensure that it is appropriate to market their destination on the Internet, in order to reach the desired audience through their Web marketing efforts. While not all travellers or tourists have access to the Internet, there is most likely a large degree of overlap, at least in North America, between people with access to the Internet and those who have the leisure time and disposable income required for travel.

The United States has the largest overall number of Internet users, at 165.75 million (59.1%). The number of Internet users in Canada is currently estimated at 16.84 million (52.79%). In addition, a survey entitled "Using the Web for Travel Plans" found that "87% of online consumers use their computers to find travel destination information" and that "84% have visited travel Web sites." So the potential for marketing tourism destination regions on the Internet is huge, and constantly growing. In fact, in today's world, a tourism marketing strategy is not complete without incorporating the Internet.

As a communication tool the Internet makes it possible for potential customers around the world to access the marketing information from their own homes without the need for solicitation or a distribution campaign - one digital copy of the marketing brochure can be accessed by all, eliminating the need for costly duplication. Some argue that the Internet is so profound that "[i]n the 21st century, the Internet is going to be as important a business tool as the cash register and telephone have been throughout the 20th century."

Tourism marketers recognize the Internet's importance and its potential, as supported by the following quote: "To reach today's Internet users effectively, tourism businesses - whatever their size - must have an overall Internet strategy." Despite the Internet's potential as a communications technology and research tool which may be used by tourism marketers in order to gain a competitive advantage, "it is important for companies to realize that the Internet, by itself, is not a self-supporting mechanism." Internet marketing efforts are unavailable to a large percentage of the world's population, and it would be extremely foolish to market solely on the Internet.

Thus, "any Internet marketing activities...should provide additional exposure and should complement...traditional marketing efforts (and vice versa)." The Internet should become "an integrated and complementary element of the entire marketing mix." Internet advertising will not suddenly do away with traditional advertising, marketing and public relations. The traditional advertising and interactive advertising worlds will coexist for some time. The best values from Internet advertising will be realized by combining Internet advertising with traditional marketing.

In addition, "you must advertise that you're advertising." That is, online marketing efforts must be advertised using offline marketing channels. Potential tourists must be made aware of tourism destination web sites, and must be provided with a compelling reason to visit them. A central goal of tourism destination marketing is to create a desirable image of the destination in the mind of the potential tourist, in an effort to entice the tourist to select the destination for a future vacation or business endeavour. Thus, image plays a central role in tourism marketing.

And there is more to creating a desirable image of the tourism destination than simply presenting tourists with a tourism destination web site. This is made clear by the following statement:

> "Marketers must be aware that on the Internet, there is a distinct difference between communicating to customers and promoting to them. Internet marketers have to realize

> that communicating with Net surfers often has to be restricted to the informing aspect of advertising. Information, not a hard sell, is what Internet users want and respect"

Once a tourist makes the effort to visit a web site, he or she must find a site that provides them with value. It must be well-designed, up-to-date, and relevant. The elements used in tourism destination web sites, such as maps, pictures, graphics, and text should be well designed and integrated. The site should inform, educate, or entertain (and preferably combine all three). For example, tourism web sites can be used to educate visitors to the social, environmental, and economic impacts of tourism. Responsible site developers will alert visitors to these issues, and can use their Internet presence to "demarket" the destination, or to attempt to shift traffic to off-seasons.

The images and information presented must be valid, believable, simple, appealing and distinctive. This will get the tourist more involved with the destination, and it will give them the feeling of importance. Furthermore, a carefully-designed multimedia tourism web site may promote a positive image of the destination, and may help to increase the potential tourist's trust in, and desire to visit, the destination. A successful web site may cause the destination to enter a tourist's "awareness set," "consideration set," "choice set," "selection set," or even the "future holiday consideration set" as shown in the "destination selection process." The key in this process is, firstly, to make the potential tourist aware of the destination web site so that it may be included in the awareness set.

In order for the site to enter the consideration set, it is necessary to convince the potential tourist to visit the web site. In order for the destination to move into the choice set, the web site must be successful in creating a desirable image in the mind of the potential tourist. A destination may move into the selection set when the destination attributes such as the image, price, value for money, and so on, match what the tourist is looking for. A destination that satisfies the tourist by living up to expectations may move into the "future holiday consideration set." Tourism marketers who take the time thoughtfully to plan, implement, and update a destination web site may be successful in this process.

A well-designed destination web site may help alleviate a few of these problems. Firstly, the tangibility of tourism can be increased, as potential tourists can be presented with an interactive, multimedia site which helps them "experience" the destination. Although tourism services will always be perishable (i.e., "they cannot be stored and sold at a later date"), visitors to destination web sites can be made aware of special offers and seat sales in order to help reduce the amount of services which perish. Inseparability, the idea that the tourist's perception of the tourism service is intricately linked to the people and products providing the service, will not change. However, customer service can be improved with the use of web sites, and marketers can provide a feedback section.

Tourists can provide comments, suggestions and complaints, and tourism marketers can learn where they are succeeding, and where they are failing, as far as their tourists are concerned. Heterogeneity relates to the fact that each tourist's experience will be different. This is not necessarily a bad thing. Many people travel in order to be different, and tourism web sites are capable of providing a different interactive experience for each visitor. However, the integration of the Internet into a marketing plan can provide a more consistent level of service quality and can potentially increase customer satisfaction.

Although the Internet and the Web have caused a paradigm shift away from mass tourism towards a more individual tourism experience providing tourism services and communicating with potential tourists has become a more "one-on-one" procedure. This provides the customer with "greater control over the marketing process than ever before" and increases the need for attention to great customer service. Indeed:

> "Marketing is a learning process. It is not something that you do, it is not simply a transaction in which you're doing all the action, you're not marketing at people, it becomes a learning process so that [in] everything you do, you're gaining knowledge, in order to enhance, to build, to change, and to incrementally improve what you do. And everything in the future is going to be integrated with a service. Everything. Every product is going to become more servicelike. Because again, the way to differentiate yourself is no longer through the technology itself, but in the use of the technology to create a tool for improving service."

Because the user chooses which information to view, when he or she wishes to view it, this information may be more valuable than that provided by traditional advertising channels. Again, as the user must make the effort to seek out the information, once they find the destination's site, it must offer something valuable or the visitor will view their efforts as a waste of time, and possibly develop a negative image of the destination. And what is worse is that they may decide to communicate this negative image to other potential tourists. The communication and advertising roles of the Internet have been identified in the literature but it has the potential to assume a much wider role.

The Internet may be used in many more areas of the tourism marketing process, such as data collection, market research and positioning, analysis and examination of competition, and identification of target markets. And as the Internet is affordable and fast, these other roles may not weigh as heavily upon the marketing budget.

Some issues of concern when marketing tourism

destinations on the Internet. Firstly, "information overload and complexity may cause consumers to turn away from specific areas of the Web or to avoid the Internet altogether." This highlights the need to keep web pages simple, organized, and easy to use. Internet marketing efforts are more visible than traditional methods, and as a result are more susceptible to imitation by competitors. Furthermore, as the Internet is available worldwide, this competition is increasingly global.

This increased competition accentuates the need for constant research, analysis, monitoring, and innovation. The Internet, is not "just a cheap substitute for paper and ink marketing and advertisement." The Internet's history, characteristics, capabilities and limits must be fully understood before it may be incorporated successfully into any marketing plan. Effective marketing of a travel destination on the Internet, therefore, is not a trivial task. Indeed, the Internet has placed some daunting challenges before tourism marketers. Increased access to information and instantaneous communications have resulted in greater global competition.

A recognition of the Internet's potential combined with a fear of being 'left behind' has caused some tourism marketers to rush into establishing a presence on the Internet without taking the time to consider what is needed, wanted, appropriate, or effective. The resulting misdirected web-based marketing may do more damage than good. Many companies obviously feel they need a presence on the web to remain competitive. But they fail to recognize that a poor [web site] that delivers a poor experience does far more damage.

A poorly designed travel destination web site, or annoying Internet marketing practices may fail to attract visitors, and can lead to a loss of repeat business, bad 'word of mouth' advertising, or a poor reputation. In tourism marketing, the medium of communication may be as important as the message. Consequently, tourism marketers must realize that the quality of promotional materials has an influence on tourists' images of a destination. The Internet marketing literature stresses the need to "add value" to potential customers. That is, web sites must provide users with something of value, such as a novel experience, superior customer service, or new products or they will fail to entice sales.

The World Wide Web has incredible potential for use in image creation largely due to its multimedia capabilities. Web pages may include animation, pictures, graphics, music, text, videos, and even programs such as currency converters and distance calculators. The real strength of web-based travel destination marketing, therefore, is in image creation, and given arguments presented earlier, the map is an important component of such a multi-media image creation process. Web-based maps, which can be dynamic and interactive, will facilitate visual communication of the geography of a travel destination, attracting and retaining attention, increasing interest and curiosity, and possibly improving comprehension and recall of a travel destination web site.

Thus, tourism destination marketers should be taking advantage of maps when designing travel destination web sites, ensuring that the maps are useful and valuable to web site visitors. Given that maps are so fundamental to tourism and tourism marketing, the specific niche they can and should occupy in Internet-based tourism marketing must be researched. But to-date, no formal research has studied the role of maps in Internet-based tourism marketing, nor have the needs, wants, and preferences of Internet users with regard to travel maps been examined.

The future of Internet marketing is not clear, experts believe that Internet usage will continue to grow and that new markets will open up as access becomes cheaper and faster. The growth in some segments will slow as the market becomes saturated. Thus, the demographics of Internet usage will most likely shift. This will cause the technology to change, and possibly to improve, continuously. New products will be developed, new avenues to access the Internet and WWW will be invented, and these advances will be applied in new and innovative ways. This in turn will bring about changes in marketing methods and principles. Some experts point out that there may be increased "regulatory influences" and that security will improve both of which will exert an effect on Internet users and Internet usage.

One of the last challenges of Internet marketing is to develop tools to measure effectiveness...one of the current problems is that few measures have been developed that are specifically tailored to understanding Internet marketing effectiveness. However, such measures are essential since, in order to justify the investment of valuable resources (time, effort and money) in the Internet, companies will have to increasingly monitor the effect that their Internet presence has had on their business.

4

Revenue Management

Revenue Management (RM) is a set of revenue maximization strategies and techniques, which may improve the profitability of businesses which work in fixed capacity environments, face time-varied demand, their product (in hotels: room nights) has similarity and their cost structure reflects a high proportion of fixed and a low proportion of variable cost items. The commercial lodging industry fits the bill perfectly just like the airline and the cruise industry among others. REVPAR (Revanue per Available Room) would have been realized without RM.

— Hotels and hotels can be compared in a given comp set. That is: if they are considered competitors.

— A hotel can compare its performance indicators to industry averages or its own historical data.

What part of a percentage change can be attributed to a RM system and what positive or negative changes are the result of market trends, beyond the control of a given hotel.

Present Market Situation (PMS)

The current market situation can be described in a nutshell as a painfully slow recovery following an economic downturn, worsened by travel safety and security issues. A survey last fall commissioned by the Travel Industry

Association of the USA showed that only a small percentage of those, who choose not to travel, do it because of the 9/11 terrorist attacks. The majority of the guests who stay away from hotels would not travel because of the economy. If we reduce revenue management at the hotel operations level to manipulating only two key indicators: room rate and occupancy through rate control and duration control for the most part, chances are that we will be disappointed with the results.

Revenue management deserves a somewhat different and a more complex approach from hotel managers in order to unlock its full potential. Changes in market conditions must be clearly understood by management before applying revenue management solutions. If we don't know exactly the root cause behind changes, we may pull or push the wrong lever.

A strategy is a lot more than the application of certain techniques. Those techniques are important parts of a strategy. However, a revenue management strategy should include more elements than working with only two of our key indicators if we want our hotels ride out the economic downturns better than we did it in the early nineties. For hotel managers, the battle cry of the last decade was Yield Management! Through sophisticated computer models and highly trained sales, reservation, and front desk staff, most hotels were able to maximize the average rate achieved on a given night, week, month, and year.

Duration control techniques, especially stay restrictions, are most useful in periods of high demand. Hotels may require a minimum duration before accepting a reservation and that allows them to tell the higher yield (longer staying) guests apart from the one-nighters. However, looking at room revenue only may not provide us with the full picture in case of guests with a history. Hotels have data on average spending; to a Front Office, the comparison of a 3-night guest paying a premium rate, who spends on room only, and a one-night guest who spends heavily on meeting room rental, food and beverage, parking and internet access — should be a no-brainer. Provided, our system works with total revenue per stay.

The other most popular revenue management technique is rate control. It has always made to think, why would most front office managers reduce revenue management to a numbers game with room rates? One possible answer is that this is what they are evaluated on. Just compare your hotel's ADR (average daily rate) to your comp set and there you are... Another possible answer is that this is what they understand best and have the most control over.

Experience suggests that discounting our room rates is a natural first reaction to changes in demand. When experience low demand, discounting kicks in, if not for other reasons, just because our competitors may have already undercut our rates. Also use sophisticated software to help us doing the number crunching. True enough, computers are extremely useful when it comes to a quick and efficient way of performing complex calculations involving a lot of variables.

Artificial and Human Intelligence

Automated revenue management (RM) solutions provide hotels with sustainable competitive advantages to navigate through this period of uncertainty. These solutions provide quantifiable financial and operational benefits in all market conditions, critical to the success and longevity of hotel properties worldwide. There is some validity in that statement by Ideas, a leading provider of RM solutions. Hotel operators which go beyond the day-to-day room rate adjustments and put time and effort into strategy development, create well targeted value packages to cater to the needs of their clientele, will do better than those who only feed the data into their RM program and read their computer printouts. Revenue management strategies include market segmentation and packaging with the objective of creating revenue from those who are hesitant to buy at the price offered. The point is that we may but we don't have to. The emphasis is on creating perceived value.

A package that has an appeal in the eye of the customer may help a hotel sell room nights. This strategy is one of the most underutilized in the RM repertoire. Another strategy could be the differentiation through value added items. Some brands created theme hotels, others claim to offer the best mattress or stake house in their properties. There is no limitation what can be introduced, provided the hotel has a clear understanding what would do the job for their clientele; high speed wireless internet access, complimentary valet parking, a spa or heightened security with biometrics.

It seems that the current downturn will not have staying power. Those who go the extra mile and look beyond their front office, willing to use more elements from the RM repertoire than discounted room rates, will be better positioned to upgrade their products when guests return to fill our hotels.

Automated revenue management (RM) solutions provide hotels with sustainable competitive advantages to navigate through this period of uncertainty. These solutions provide quantifiable financial and operational benefits in all market conditions, critical to the success and longevity of hotel properties worldwide. Automated RM solutions successfully assist hotels in optimizing demand and increasing RevPAR. Booking controls such as rate availability, overbooking controls and length-of-stay restrictions are designed to accept the right mix of business, at the best rate, at the right time for the optimal length of stay. Revenue management results have been impressive;

occupancies have increased as well average daily rates with measurable RevPAR increases.

Quantifiable Benefits

Hotels with automated RM solutions continue to outperform other hotels in their markets, even in periods of declining demand. According Universal Orlando, "Universal has seen growth in a market that is down, some of it is certainly attributable to revenue management." The fact remains that the economy works in cycles – up and down and up and down again. Automated RM solutions do their best, most valuable work when demand is fluctuating between busy and not-so-busy nights, not just when hotels are sure to always fill up.

These solutions generally outperform manual environments, semi-automated tools and decision support systems by 4 to 12%. Detailed analytical processes, scientific forecasting, automated restrictions and constant monitoring, combine to ensure hotels receive unequalled benefits. In all market conditions, hotels with automated RM solutions will maintain significant advantages over their competition.

Fluctuating Demand

On a daily basis automated RM systems look far into the future...60 days, 90 days and further. They are designed as a strategic tool that prioritizes business-critical information and alerts users when bookings materialize greater or less than anticipated. By harnessing the power of the microchip these solutions efficiently analyze massive amounts of data picking up even slight changes in demand. In times of less than anticipated demand, this information becomes strategically important, enabling properties with information to deploy sales and marketing strategies to build demand. Mövenpick hotels attributes an automated RM solution with impressive results, "The average room rate at our hotel rose 21% from DM 137 to DM166 from last year to this year."

Optimized Occupancy

When demand fluctuates and is uncertain, automated RM solutions continue to deploy decisions to optimize both occupancy and rates. Even in environments of low demand where occupancy could be as low as 30%, there are often special events, holidays and perhaps trade events that present significant opportunities to increase revenue.

Take for example events such as ITB/Berlin, the London Trade Show, Paris Air Show, Comdex or the Bledisloe Cup Match and Communiqué Asia; each of these events presents an important opportunity to increase revenue. According to Vail Resorts, one of the largest resort operators in North America, "The most critical factors that contribute to successful room yielding are: maximizing occupancies; booking guests with the longer length of stays; managing the amount of overbooking we are willing to accept; and selling rooms at the best price based on demand. That's why we chose...a system with an automatic, integrated decision-making ability to consider those factors at the moment when reservations are made."

Increased Efficiency

Automated RM solutions represent a radical reduction in manual labor and an exponential improvement in reliability and results. These solutions tackle the complex task of analyzing vast amounts of data, save valuable time and provide better information, providing significant operational benefits. In all circumstances an automated RM solution is, "...the most effortless system to support," from the perspective of experienced hoteliers at the Orchard Hotel Singapore.

Revenue Management Culture

Hotels with automated RM benefit from a consistent deployment of RM practices from person-to-person, hotel-to-hotel and across large chains. Organizations that invest in building a RM culture around a highly sophisticated and integrated tool jeopardize both benefits and culture if they discontinue using that tool for any period of time. Some of the most respected hotel companies in the world, such as Hilton International, work hand-in-hand with solution providers to "develop and enhance integrated revenue systems, ensuring that Yield underpins our strategy."

The benefits of maintaining a consistent revenue management culture are tangible in the superior RevPAR and competitive set performance of hotels with automated RM solutions. In today's market, more pressure is put on properties to reduce rates and renegotiate group contracts. Automated solutions enable hotels to evaluate potential business that might be displaced by accepting a particular group, evaluating days prior to arrival and after departure. They provide comprehensive scenario evaluation and rapid response to group inquiries. Through automated solutions, properties now have access to tools that quantify the impact of making these types of strategic changes on group business, enabling them to evaluate and accept the right mix of groups versus transient business.

Contrast Revanue

Contract business builds a solid base business for hotels and may account for a significant amount of a hotel's business. A revolutionary new RM tool for contract evaluation provides properties with the ability to negotiate more profitable contracts. Automated solutions provide tools to objectively measure the financial impact of potential contracts and provides management with the ability to make more informed decisions about rates and access. Despite current market conditions, hotels are entering the important contract season and this capability is invaluable in maintaining inventory flexibility and maximizing revenue from contract business.

Managing Market Resurgence

Hotels worldwide will experience subtle increases in group inquiries, conversion rates and occupancy that automated systems are designed to detect. Each of these events represents critical revenue maximizing opportunities. Hotel properties with automated RM systems installed and operating will have competitive advantages in both short and long-term performance. In today's market, every opportunity to maximize revenue is critical to the success and longevity of hotel properties. As hotels worldwide anticipate recovery and the return of business, having the appropriate solutions in place is not only practical, it's imperative. Automated RM solutions provide strategic competitive advantages and quantifiable benefits.

Revenue Management Strategy

A revenue management strategy establishes "target" numbers to be achieved through a variety of ways; sales, manipulating the GDS, controlling the allocation and rate in the electronic distribution channels, etc. In other words, it is a pro-active rather than reactive function that simply turns the faucets on and off. A revenue management strategy incorporates all of the revenue drivers such as GDS, the web site and the electronic distribution channels is key. However, it requires the involvement of the sales department and all other profit centers of the hotel. This is unlike a budget in that a revenue strategy is renewable and adjustable where a budget is usually written in stone.

A sound revenue management strategy includes the optimum revenue mix and the tactics to achieve it -- this is where the marketing plan comes in! "Managing" revenue is just that — it assumes an element of control in the revenue that you accept from various sources based upon cost of reservation, commissions, etc. The sales strategies in the marketing plan flow from the revenue management strategy although sales is critical in developing it. The sales department is critical in that they have their fingers on the pulse of the market. They are responsible for assembling the economic information on market conditions and analyzing the potential threats to the market as well as identifying the opportunities.

The sales department knows the potential of each market segment and the rate that each one will bear. The development of the revenue management strategy allows sales to gage how many rooms in a given period they can book by market segment and at what rate. It also insures that existing and future group blocks won't be sabotaged by lower rates on the web site or distribution channels.

Process of Work

Gathering the info: Each member of the team, but especially sales, should have been keeping information in regard to the market such as trends indicated by the STR reports and other industry sources. Sales should take the temperature of top accounts to see what their forecasts for travel next year look like. The group logs pace reports for this year and next year should also be put into the file. Sales should also have the situation analysis completed as well as identified challenges and opportunities for the upcoming year.

Analyzing the Revenue Data: The revenue reports should be analyzed to indicate the percentages currently generated by all revenue drivers. This, of course assumes that the data is accurate. If anyone has any doubts about the importance of proper market segment coding by reservations and the front desk they should end here. It is "GIGO." (garbage in — garbage out)! If there aren't accurate numbers, you will be playing a SWAG game.

The Facilitation: This is the meeting of the minds, GM, sales, reservations and any other interested party such as the owner. They take a look at the budget, market conditions, all sources of revenue, etc. and begin projecting the revenue strategy by segment. This can be a contentious process as the sales department fights for accounts and room allocations by rate. However, as an associate once said, harmony is vastly overrated. This process can take several days as all of the evidence is presented and numbers are plugged into the model and adjusted — yada, yada. It never hurts to have an outside consultant facilitate this process to provide objective third party input.

The Final Product: The spreadsheet, created from compromise that fulfills the requirement of the budget, becomes the basis of the revenue strategy. Every revenue driver is identified and the ideal mix of revenue and rate is there to yield the targeted REVPAR. Every revenue driver in the revenue strategy should have its own strategy and tactics section in the marketing plan — including the web site, the GDS strategy and the electronic distribution channels.

The Review Process: The same fractious group that designed the strategy should meet periodically, it could be monthly or quarterly, to make adjustments based upon reality. In the initial development, "triggers" should have been identified that would automatically call for adjustments. Those triggers include unanticipated market changes, good or bad, changes in the economy and any national security breaches.

It's a "messy" process, but a necessary one for the marketing plan to be developed. It then becomes the road map for the coming year. The marketing plan is not just about sales but the revenue management strategy for the entire hotel.

Revenue Management : Challenge for Hotel Sales

The dilemma for hotel sales departments is to locate and manage group business to fill in the blanks mid-week and weekends, often from market segments and demand generators that press for lower rates. They also are dealing with third party meeting planners attempting to negotiate the best (read lowest) rates for their clients. The Revenue Manager is pressing for a higher rate, group booking contacts are pressing for lower rates and the sales person is under pressure to meet their booking goals — it is a stressful situation for the sales department!

In a typical urban/suburban mid level corporate transient property, the mid-week peaks are dominated by business travelers whose rate sensitivity is less as they, individually, are not paying the bill. While corporate travel departments are continuing to try and manage the cost of travel, the reality is that in prime locations, room rates are increasing and they find themselves negotiating higher rates in their RFPs than in previous years. Another factor to consider is that bookings from all electronic sources have increased another 30-40% from 2003. This includes all channels from the GDS systems, e-commerce channels and the franchise web site. These bookings are also driven by an increase in leisure travel that has been induced by the lowest airfares in a decade. While airfares remain low, this segment demonstrated in the summer of 2004 that they were willing to pay higher hotel rates than in past years.

The solutions are varied but hinge upon the ability of the sales person and department to understand and be able to measure the impact of potential bookings and rates upon the hotel's revenue management strategy. Once they understand those parameters, they can then align their new business development activities in relation to the client profiles that fit the revenue management model. It is both the lack of understanding and/or the inability to measure their potential contracts prior to negotiating and booking that provokes the criticism that "sales only wants to book the lowest rates." In other words, understand the difference between good business and bad. Ther are some suggestions given below:

The Revenue Management Strategy: Those who are involved in developing the strategy have "buy in" to its successful execution. The Revenue Manager is part of the sales team rather than a direct report to the Rooms Division.

Develop Client Profiles for Each Rate Period: Which types of groups in market segments and sub segments will fit within the rate and catering parameters that will align with the revenue management strategy. Attempting to meet these goals through only responding to telephone inquiries and working the trace files is insufficient to attain the goals. First of all, there is no control over the kind of prospects calling and the pressure builds to respond to their requests if this is your only means of prospecting. Secondly, the accounts in the trace files may or may not be in alignment with the new revenue goals in terms of rates and meeting configurations. A client profile should be driven by market segment, where the bookings are likely to originate, their rate sensitivity or history and their meeting configurations.

Develop a New Business Development Strategy: Once the client profiles are developed, it becomes a matter of developing a strategy to locate and qualify these prospects. Strategies might include using the Internet to locate certain organizations within a market segment from a specific geographic location or getting on an email distribution list or mailing list for organizations that have the potential to produce groups for the hotel is another one. There are web sites that specialize in producing leads for groups for hotels in various market segments. These can be sorted by geographic location and often give the rates, meeting specs and history of where the group last met.

Group Revenue Management Tool: A revenue management tool can be as simple as a spreadsheet of the group rooms budget by month into which the parameters of the group can be entered so that the sales person can see how the number of rooms at the proposed rate effects the room revenue of the entire hotel for the period. It can be as sophisticated as a computer program that measures the revenue of a group on all profit centers. These take various forms and often are included with the sales contact management system such as the ones offered by Delphi. Some of these products interface with the property's PMS and Revenue management systems.

Revenue Mannagement: Role of General Manager

Understand the Revenue Management Process: Many General Mangers are uncomfortable with the process because they simply do not fully understand it. The discipline of revenue management has morphed over time with many new systems and programs available. Take a course on up to date revenue management. There are many offered on the Internet that are both time and cost effective. You cannot manage the process unless you fully understand it.

Develop Electronic Distribution Channels: Back off, take a deep breath and consider the following:

— These are reservations that your front desk or reservations staff does not have to process,

— You have been paying a commission to Travel Agents since the beginning of time anyway and

— You don't have to offer them a dirt bag rate! While recently assisting a client in the development of the hotel's revenue management strategy, it became evident that the ADR for these channels in one high occupancy period exceeded the hotel's ADR by $5 (after commission). Because the hotel had let them pull the rate from the GDS during a period when all low rates were closed. By understanding this, you can make these electronic channels a valuable part of your revenue management strategy.

Establish a Revenue Management Strategy: Establishing room and rate allocations by market segment and opportunity dates and seasonality for the year, to be reviewed quarterly. This should be an essential part of the marketing plan developed in collaboration with the Revenue Manager, the sales department, front office and reservation managers and anyone else whose department is affected. Be prepared for heated discussions as everyone makes their case for their "pet" market segments. Make it clear that if sales or anyone else wants to give a lower rate to a group or segment in a given time period, the revenue must be made up in other segments:

Be prepared to take risks: Revenue Management is not an exact science. Be prepared to take risks yourself and encourage the "risk takers" on your staff, provided that they can provide valid reasons to take them. You will win sometimes and sometimes you will lose.

The "last to fill at the highest rate" strategy is always a risky one. A week prior to the group's arrival, they were sitting pretty much dead empty, the anticipated demand no where in sight and the GM was sweating bullets. At the end of the day, or night in this case, the hotel filled at a rate $25 higher than the rest of the market but it could have gone either way.

Integration of Revenue Drivers

Revenue drivers are defined as all areas of revenue generation within the organization. This includes central reservations, property-level reservations, the sales department,, the electronic distribution channels and the web site. While franchised properties have a higher level of consistency through the GDS, it still requires monitoring and management at the company or property levels.

At a sales seminar, participants expressed frustration that they are largely unaware of, nor are they consulted about the rates that are posted on the electronic distribution channels. One result is a very high attrition rate in meetings and conventions as attendees book their hotel at these lower rates and "fall" off the group block. Another consequence is when the rate posted is lower than what has been negotiated with third-party suppliers such as wholesalers. A coaching client of mine expressed frustration over his lack of consultation in the development of the new property web site and the rates that are being quoted through the site.

First of all, the content was skewed to a specific market segment that was not representative of the core business segment and secondly, the copy changes disrupted the optimization strategy. Secondly, the rates that were quoted were not at all aligned with the rates being quoted at the property level or through the central reservations agent and many room descriptions were inaccurate.

The end result was that not only was this hotel nowhere to be found on the key word searches in the major search engines — a potential disaster for this independent property, but fewer reservations were being made through the site. Collaboration across all departments that generate revenue is the only way to ensure continuity. This need not be a tedious process of endless meetings. A few things put into place and adjusted periodically, based on market conditions and forecasts, are sufficient:

Product/Rate Positioning: A plan for product/rate positioning is ideally developed as part of the Business/ Marketing plan process and includes consideration of the product/rate positioning of the competitive set, group bookings, rate resistance input from reservations and past history. Once the strategy is developed, it then only needs to be adjusted periodically. Don't forget to monitor the franchise yield management system in light of groups or events in previous years that may not be a factor in the present year.

Existing and Anticipated Contracts: These include group contracts, volume contracts with LNRs, wholesalers and any other rate commitments. Just as the sales department makes decisions based on the rate structure, so should consideration be given to any agreements made thorough sales. It is one thing to adjust rates on the web site or distribution channels to drive volume at a slow time but if it undermines the agreements above, it is counter productive.

Web Site Presence and Reservations: Many leisure customers locate the hotel through key word searches on the search engines. Others locate the hotel on the electronic distribution channels then access the hotel's proprietary web site. Still others will pick up the phone after visiting both and call reservations to see if they can cut a better deal. It is essential that the "message" of rate and offering be relatively consistent across all channels to be effective. The rates on the web site need to be adjusted in tandem with the electronic distribution channels and reservations needs to be aware of what's appearing on both.

Another consideration in web site development is the increased use of the site as a sales tool. It becomes the electronic brochure. The sales department's inclusion in its development is essential to the site's secondary role as the electronic brochure. Sales people should be accessing the site with their clients to moderate the virtual tour. If there is a special rate posted that is inconsistent with the rates sales are quoting, it blows them out of the water and appears to the client that the hotel doesn't know what it is doing.

The process of collecting the information is about communication and collaboration and can be accomplished through periodic updates from the revenue drivers to the revenue management team. This swings both ways as revenue management needs to keep the revenue drivers informed of their proposed tactics in order to solicit input and buy in.

Revenue Management Systems

In a nutshell, revenue management is the science of using past history and current levels of booking activity to forecast demand as accurately as possible to maximize revenue. Everyone attempts to even out the peaks and valleys of occupancy by increasing rates during times of high demand and discounting them when demand is low. Most properties break this approach into manageable chunks by applying different rates and booking constraints to different market segments, and make changes as necessary as bookings come in.

Too often, however, the trigger for action, especially discount action, is an emotional reaction to low levels of bookings for short-term arrivals, and not a reasoned decision based actual – but hard to see - trends. However, if a property has good historical data on its major market segments and their typical booking patterns, it might be less tempted to offer a discounted rate if it could reasonably expect that full-rate guests would, as they have done before, book only in the last thirty days before arrival. Equally, if it knew it had a pattern of medium-stay guests (say, four to five nights) at a particular point, it might be more confident about turning down a full-rate single-night stay in favor of the greater overall revenue available from the longer stay, even at a slightly lower rate.

And if it knew it had a small but reliable group of guests who regularly called for a room right at the last minute and were willing to pay a premium for that flexibility, perhaps it could increase its rate for those guests without driving them away. This approach to managing rates and length-of-stay restrictions to get the most income over any particular period isn't rocket science. Given appropriately-detailed records (enough market segment divisions to be useful, not too many to be monitored effectively) this level of Revenue Management is easily done in a manual environment, and falls under the general – but crucial –heading of knowledge-based decision-making.

Every room in a property on any night has a wide range of potential customers. For maximum profitability it's vital to know how much someone who really values that particular room on this date with this amount of lead time is willing to pay for it, and then to have the courage and confidence to hold out for that rate from that customer. From the knowledge that you have a firm bedrock of property history, coupled with your own assessment of how similar current circumstances are to those of the historical data, and a clear understanding of the purchasing patterns of your particular customer mix. In other words, your Revenue Management allowes you to make informed decisions, not just relying on gut feelings.

The constant re-calculation of the value of taking a particular booking, compared to all the other possible bookings you might expect to be requested for that room later, becomes an impossible mental task. But high-speed evaluation is where computer systems, RM systems in particular, excel. Far faster than even the most experienced director of sales, an RM system can take historical data, current booking levels and the forecasts of which market segments are expected to be looking for these rooms in the future, balance the various rate tolerances of these segments, and set minimum rate hurdles and length-of-stay constraints below which you should not accept a current booking request.

These forecasts are updated at least every night - some systems do it every hour - to make sure that there's no delay in deciding whether to take a booking; the criteria are always right there on the users' screens. They also refine their calculation formulae if the original assumptions don't seem to be working. The RM system can highlight potential problem areas that fall outside pre-set limits, allowing the managers to focus on these exceptions.

Some critical points are here; the systems don't make your marketing decisions for you, they just try to achieve the goals you've set in the context you've defined through experience. Humans can't calculate as well as computers; computers can't make expert evaluations of the effect of changes in their operating environment. Setting your marketing goals and strategy, and changing them if you're not reaching the right potential guests, is still something you have to do yourself. Setting these baselines is another area where automation can help out, of course.

Guest history and database analysis tools allow a far more detailed look at historic and potential customer base, and automated marketing plan development and tracking tools (such as those available from Driving Revenue) can make a really significant difference to setting your focus and goals. Identifying what's actually happening from your RM results can also provide valuable feedback. The most productive approach is to let humans and computers each do the work they do best.

Pretty much any property can benefit from a RM system. Size isn't so much a factor – successful implementations exist in properties from 40 rooms to 1,200 – but typically the more complex the environment, the more varied the mix of market segments, and the greater the peaks and valleys in current occupancy, the greater the benefit. A high percentage of transient guests also helps, since applying RM principles to group bookings is still a relatively young art. It's easier to say who wouldn't get much benefit. It's a short list:

— hotels with a very high percentage of group business at pre-negotiated rates with guaranteed last-room availability, i.e. if a single room is available at rack rate, a group member can take it at the discount. Even then, RM can help by shifting stay patterns, e.g. locking out that available room-night by imposing a minimum-length-of-stay at that point.

— a hotel which sells all its rooms, all the time, at rack rate – and they need a consultant to advise them on re-positioning their marketing strategy!

The price issue has a couple of aspects, one illusionary and one more real. The illusion is the belief, coming from most people's experience with RM coming from dealings with the airlines, that these systems only apply to hugely complex operations and must therefore be hugely expensive. Maybe that was true once, but now the programming expertise and the power of those mainframe systems has migrated down to PCs.

Hospitality-specific systems are available from XXX and YYY per room, or about $25,000 for a 200-room property. At least one vendor – IDeaS – offers a revenue-sharing approach: no revenue gain, no payment. While determining how much of that gain is directly attributable to its system pretty much has to be done with their own measurement tool – unless you're in an unchanging market and have kept your rates constant before and after RM installation - those hotels that have gone this route do seem to validate the systems value. The pricing issue that's real is the one of every property having multiple projects competing for the same capital dollars, and, as for all computer-based systems, it can be hard to see any immediate tangible benefit from investment in an RM system.

Some managers are more comfortable just working with the rate management functions built into many modern property management systems; sell only five of this package, cut off these rates if occupancy goes above 75% on these days, and so on. They understand exactly what the system's doing because they know what they told it and can see all the steps involved. With a full RM system, they have to trust that the "black-box" nature of its calculation engine is doing the right thing, a premise that can only be proven by checking the results.

This trust and confidence will only come in time, but it will come, as the accuracy of the forecasts is borne out. If you don't like the results, resist the temptation to blame the system; it's only doing what you told it. Re-examine your strategy, and see if it's still appropriate for what's actually happening in the real world. All the vendors agree that hotels of all sizes and types can benefit from their products (no surprise there), they also all agree that the criteria must be met for the systems to work effectively. These are:

— the right culture
— management commitment
— PMS interface
— good, plentiful historical data, and
— constant attention to relevancy and context.

Right Culture

Dropping a PMS into a disorganized rooms operation just gets you more disorganized faster. Dropping a RM system into a sales operation running on instinct and guesses will give you misleading results you'd rightfully have little confidence in. The most important requirements for a successful RM implementation are that the property must already believe in the operational importance of knowledge-based decision-making (or be willing and ready to embrace it), and must have a focus on maximizing revenue rather than minimizing cost.

One reflection of the culture would be the nature of any incentive plan for your reservations agents. The temptation to offer discounted rates during peak demand periods could be too high. A revenue-focused organization would lean more toward rewarding agents for closing increased RevPAR sales in high, medium and low demand periods. As a further benefit, encouraging awareness of the property's unique value and revenue potential rather than constantly reminding everyone how tightly costs must be controlled has an enormously energizing effect on morale and productivity, even before you leverage that energy with a RM system.

Management Commitment

The enthusiasm and direction must come from the top, and exist throughout the operation, to get the most benefit from the system. Everyone needs to accept that it's a tool to be used, kept sharp and its strengths and weaknesses understood and worked with. Ideally each property should have a RM champion, someone who focuses on keeping the systems parameters current and revenue flow maximized across the property. A lot of time and resources will be invested to set it up. Stay committed to making it work and understanding what it tells you, and you'll see results.

PMS Interface

This sounds as if it should come first; after all, the very basis of an effective system is the wealth of detailed reservations data captured by you're the PMS, and without an automated interface to transfer it to the RM system you'll never keep up. However, it's still essential that the property's culture accept the need for the concepts first, otherwise no RM system will have a chance of being used properly. The need for a PMS interface may place limitations on the options somewhat, since interfaces are produced according to customer demand. Most RM systems have interfaces with varying degrees of complexity to at least one of the major PMSs.

The accuracy of any RM systems forecast is directly related to the size and detail of the database it is working from, regardless of the specific mathematical approach it takes. Ideally, most vendors like to have at least a year's worth of complete, detailed property data to use as the forecasting basis, usually from the PMS' archived end-of-day back-ups and reports. Frequently, however, this amount of data isn't available, or isn't as complete as it could be.

Some PMSs don't track all changes to a group block along with the date and time they occurred, and it really helps to know what booking constraints were in effect when a reservation was taken. In such cases – and especially with newer properties – the available data has to be supplemented with general information from management experience, and with additional system detail captured on-site. Most vendors will record live data for three months before cutover to give a more accurate starting point. While systems' accuracy improves from day one as real-world data can be compared to predictions, it's important to have the baseline be as solid and complete as possible.

Measurement of Revenue Management System

Successful measurement can only occur when the hotel measures its performance working with the yield management system, and compare it to the revenue performance it would have received without the system, everything else being equal. Five of the more well-known measurement approaches.

Historical Revenues

Spikes from the statistical noise produced from seasonality and demand fluctuations are smoothed to determine stable patterns. The patterns are used as a basis for making future projections, which are expected to grow at a steady rate. By comparing the future projections with any deviation from the projections, the amount of deviation, in theory, may be tied to the system. However, this approach fails to account for the impact of new events that happened after the system was installed - new marketing campaigns or the introduction of a web site, for example - which were not done in the past. It still makes it impossible to see what revenue change is due to the system or to other factors.

"After the Fact" Review

The process considers demand "on the books" and, after there is no more hotel capacity, it attempts to figure the amount of demand turned down. With this information in hand, the hotelier speculates that, if he or she accepted the best business mix after the fact, how much revenue would have the property generated. That amount is compared to the actual amount of revenues. This difference or "gap" offers a possible measure for improvement. The "gap" before the system install is weighed against the "gap" after the system installation.

The difference perhaps illustrates the system's impact. Simply, this approach only teaches the hotelier how to be wiser after the event, instead of making the best decisions for future booking opportunities. If you made investment decisions, in the stock market, for example, solely after the fact, knowing how prices fluctuated, and realizing when would have been the best time to buy and sell, you still would not enjoy optimum return because the decisions did not factor future volatility and uncertainty. This approach can not separate what the system is doing and what is being affected by changing market conditions and other factors.

Comparison of Hotels Within Comptetitive Set

To consider the effect of extraneous factors on revenues, the comparison is tracked against any demand fluctuations from a similar hotel (without the yield management system) in the same competitive set, and/or with nearly the same demographics. Hotels and resorts pride themselves in their uniqueness. So it is impossible to imagine two hotels that would experience identical affects from the extraneous factors, and it is highly unlikely they would share the same pricing strategies directed or the same marketing mixes.

Computer Simulation in Controlled Environments

One of the first places where this type of system measurement with isolation was attempted was in a controlled environment, using computer simulation. In this case, a yield management practice with basic demand data is deployed. First, booking decisions from the yield management practice are based on simulated human decisions, which result in bookings accepted and not accepted. Next, the booking decisions are based on yield management system decisions. Again, bookings are accepted and not accepted.

Accepted bookings from both decision scenarios translate into revenue, and the compared revenues between the two illustrate how the yield management practice may deliver results.Humans are not efficient at executing on "first come and first served." Even if the measurement shows benefits in a controlled environment, how can the hotelier be assured that there will be benefits in the "real" world. It is impossible to predict in a controlled setting how the users would interact with the system.

True Scientific Measurement

If demand does increase due to marketing programs or an improvement in economy after the yield system installation, occupancy will increase, and there will be more sold-out nights. But what if there is no increase in demand compared to last year. As a result of the yield management system, it is anticipated that there will be a reduction in the number of turn downs multi-night stays. And the proper overbooking of rooms leads to a decrease in the amount of empty rooms on sold-out nights.

Thus, occupancy will increase through the better yield practice. The scientific measurement approach is the tool with which it can be precisely determined whether the occupancy increased because of the yield management practice or due to marketing programs or improved economic conditions. It begins by identifying periods where the system does not restrict the hotel or resort in accepting bookings. Scientific measurement isolates the impact of the marketing programs and economic factors from the impact of the yield management solution. It shows what room revenue increases can be attributed to the yield management solution.

True system measurement is required for hotel owners and executives, who need to justify the purchase of the system, precisely understand return on investment, and prove system impact for a rollout. In the hospitality industry, there have been many approaches and technologies offered to provide yield management benefits. Likewise, there have been many attempts to help hoteliers see and understand what their yield management systems are doing for them.

Revenue Management and Market Segmentation

Rather than forecast by market segment or rate product, the best practice in yield management goes further and forecasts by the value of each rate. For example, if a hotel has five retail rate products, each with single and double occupancy rates, a system should forecast the market's willingness to pay each of those rates.

All hotel revenue management systems optimize based on the relationship between forecasted demand and remaining capacity. Some other industries also incorporate competitive data in their calculations. These industries, such as airlines, have reliable access to competitive pricing data. Astute hotels in our industry traditionally "shop" competitors by making telephone inquiries in the guise of reservation requests. With the advent of web-based booking engines, it is possible to "shop" competitors electronically.

In some markets this works well. In other markets, web rates are not representative of rates available via other distribution channels. Nevertheless, whether done electronically or by telephone, hotels do shop one another. Revenue management solutions should provide a mechanism for adjusting rate availability in real time based on the findings of these shopping calls. Competitor pricing can have an effect on both your hotel's demand and on the market's perception of the value of your rates. If available competitive rates for a specific stay pattern are higher than yours, some portion of competitive demand will "spill" and appear as demand for your hotel. In addition, your rate of $219 may appear as a real bargain as prospective guests shop around and find no rates in comparable hotels for less than $299.

We use a concept called the Rate Threshold and provide for simple and direct user control. Full utilization of the Rate Threshold capability requires a synergistic capability in the hotel's reservation systems. Without this extension: if you raised your Rate Threshold to $269, all rates between $219 and $268 would be closed. With the extension you can specify that certain rates (e.g. Volume Accounts A) not be affected. The rationale behind this decision is based on the fact that the Volume Account A demand is needed by your hotel to sell out. You don't want to turn it away and encourage it to go elsewhere.

Indifference Rates

The indifference rate is a measure of the real financial or strategic value of a particular rate. Every rate product has an "indifference rate" schema that may vary in large or small amounts from the corresponding quoted rates. As an example, if your hotel sells a weekend rate of $159 that includes breakfast, the indifference rate might actually be $149 for single occupancy and $139 for double occupancy. These indifference rates reflect the estimated cost of the breakfast at $10 per person.

It is not uncommon for a hotel to intentionally give an indifference rate that is not based on financial calculations but has an underlying strategic justification. Suppose your hotel is located in a state capitol. The rate product associated with the government segment has a low rate that would often be closed during weekdays in peak demand seasons. Since the government segment exhibits significant demand during the lower-demand season, you decide to intentionally give the government rate product an inflated indifference rate.

You justify this in hopes that providing greater availability to your rooms during times of high demand will encourage loyalty that will keep government guests coming when demand is low. Indifference rates in a yield management system gives you the ability to customize the apparent value of particular rate products for yield management purposes. This is important both to accurately reflect the real financial value of rate products and to assign a strategic value when appropriate.

Yield Management System

Yield management systems should support three states of yieldability:

— Fully Yieldable: Rates are subject to rate hurdles, rate thresholds, and system generated stay controls.

— Non-Yieldable: Rates are not subject to either rate hurdles or TLP-generated stay controls. If there are available rooms, non-yieldable rates can be sold.

— Stay Pattern Yieldable: Rates are not subject to rate hurdles but are subject to system generated stay controls. If the top retail rate (usually called Rack) is open, then any rate designated as Stay Pattern Yieldable remains open-regardless of the prevailing rate hurdle.

The third of these three yieldability statuses allows the hotel to enter into "last room availability" contracts and still yield manage them from a stay pattern standpoint. In other words, when system optimization closes Tuesday one-day stays to allow Tuesday's remaining capacity to support longer stays, last room available rates would also be closed for a Tuesday one-day stay pattern.

Therefore, rate products that fall outside the control of other yield management systems can be controlled by stay patterns.In order to implement this yieldability feature, yield management systems should further refine the rate value forecast into separate forecasts for each rate value by yieldability status. In this way, the systems also optimizes the mix of fully yieldable and stay pattern yieldable demand.

A market segment approach to hotel yield management opens or closes entire segments or rate products at one time. The approach recommended there controls rate availability at the value level - a far more refined and precise approach. One future vision of hotel revenue management goes even further. It speaks to a day when each guest is a market segment of one and the availability of rates for a requested stay would depend on a guest's past history or forecasted future with the hotel or brand. One can imagine lower room rates being available to guests with a history of dining in the hotel when compared to those that dine out.

Similarly, requestors who demonstrate ongoing hotel or brand loyalty might have lower rate requirements than others without such a history. Forecasting and optimization at the market segment level runs counter to this vision of one-to-one revenue management - a strategy which many believe is the ultimate future of hotel yield management. OPUS 2 is working with the Fidelio OPERA development team as well as other PMS and CRS vendors to make this capability available to the industry.

Role of RM in Slow Economy

When profits are down, a hotel can do one of two things to increase RevPAR over last year: Cut Expenses or Increase Sales. Expenses can be cut rather simplistically- make a list of all unnecessary expenses and put the freeze on spending. Unfortunately the subject of sales will be more the challenge for most, as revenues have peaked in the last few years, making achieving those same levels of growth difficult to keep up with. Dissecting the two components that make up RevPAR, Rate and Occupancy, both at the surface seem unshakable in terms of increasing- after all, demand has "plateaued" in most markets already, and the rate growth which was a phenomenon for so long, has since slowed considerably. With rate protected from significant decrease, hotels may be able to salvage any unnecessary dramatic decrease in RevPAR.

If revenues are going to be down, than let's make sure your revenues are down just as much as your competitors. Keeping up with the Pace of growth of your competitor was important when RevPAR growth was in the double-digits. You were right to want to grow rate and RevPAR as aggressively as everyone else when times were good, so should you be now, when times are less than desirable: All negative growth is not the same! Let's say your competitor shows a – 2.8% RevPAR decrease over the same month last year. It would be wrong to assume you're doing "just as bad" if you show a – 8% decrease.

Rate Flexibility and Price-Cutting

If softening up on rates seems to be how your market of hotels is reacting to a slowing economy, be sure you identify the pricing strategy being employed by most. There's a fine line between lowering rates across the board and merely allocating additional inventory or rate types available that otherwise would not have been available during those same time periods. An example would be traditionally lower weekend rates being allocated through the midweek, or perhaps a discounted rate attached to a several-night stay. The Yield Management systems used by large hotel companies today make these combination possibilities materialize into camouflaged length-of-stay packages which on the surface might seem impossible to detect of your competitors without some deeper investigating.

5

Tourism and Economic Development

There are variety of challenges that face the tourism sector. How these challenges are met will certainly influence the sector in the long-term, and it is clear that positive initiatives by the industry will enable local and regional economic development, including that which has a poverty alleviation agenda, to take place in parallel with the needs of a viable economic business.

In fact, it was argued by some that these two components of tourism should not be separated. To achieve this aim there needs to be a co-ordinated approach across the sector and this includes the.financiers, developers, operators, hoteliers and Government. This task might best be achieved through adoption of a framework to guide those involved in the sector. The National Guidelines for Responsible Tourism developed in South Africa were published by the Department for Environmental Affairs and Tourism in 2002 and they were adopted as the national sector planning guidelines for tourism. The guidelines cover the economic, social and environmental agendas for responsible tourism.

The section on Guiding Principles for Economic Responsibility is a specific checklist of actions that people in the industry could take to increase the positive impact on local economic development. These guidelines were developed with and for the industry in South Africa. It is recommended that, using the South African example as a guiding principle, different guidelines could be developed for other destinations and that there is scope to develop guidelines for particular parts of the industry for example hoteliers, tour operators and guides.

Poverty Reduction and Local Economic Devolopment

Poverty is a multi-faceted concept which embraces not only insufficient levels of income but a lack of access to essential services such as education, water and sanitation, health care and housing. At the same time, the World Tourism Organization estimates that tourism accounts for up to 10% of global gross domestic product, making it the world's biggest industry. The potential for tourism to contribute significantly to poverty alleviation is considerable. The UN Millennium Development Goals include specific commitments to reduce by one-half the proportion of people living in extreme poverty by 2015.

Work since 1998 by the Pro-Poor Tourism Partnership has demonstrated that tourism can contribute to poverty reduction and that for many of the least developed countries, and in many rural areas, tourism is one of the few current viable strategies for economic development. The World Tourism Organization's report on Tourism and Poverty Alleviation published for the World Summit on Sustainable Development in Johannesburg in 2002 drew substantially on the work of the Pro-Poor Tourism Partnership www.propoortourism.org.uk and there are now a range of initiatives taking place on pro-poor tourism.

In each of tourism sectors the significance of Socially Responsible Investment has a differential impact depending upon the extent to which there is perceived commercial advantage. The following points illustrate the general consensus of the delegates; specific areas of concern and opportunity are addressed subsequent to this.

— There was general agreement about the importance of facilitating local community access to the tourism market (comprising tourists and the tourism industry locally) in order to maximise linkages and minimise leakages.

— Support for strategies which assist the development of local capacity to realise these opportunities.

— Developers and.financiers, hoteliers and tour operators can all act to create those opportunities to assist local communities to benefit from them.

— The importance of measuring and demonstrating impacts on local economic development and the reduction of poverty was emphasised, it is time to move beyond statements of general principles and to measure and report the impacts of initiatives in specific terms.

— It is time to move from pilot projects and experiments to programmes of action.

— Scalability is the current challenge. How do we take what we know about how to enhance the impact of tourism on local economic development and the reduction of poverty and implement it at the destination to make real change?

Role of Government

Role of government was not the focus a number of issues were raised:

— Establishing a 'whole government' agenda for tourism development is rarely achieved; this applies both between departments at national level and between national and local government.

— How can other departments of government be engaged in the issues of tourism development? Ministries of Tourism are often seen as junior players in government and it can be very difficult to engage ministries of.finance, trade and industry in cross government efforts to harness tourism for development.

— Tourism is often seen as an industry which benefits elites. When people look at the industry they see hoteliers and tour operators, they see wealth. How do we raise awareness in government, and amongst national decision makers in other sectors, about the contribution which tourism makes to local livelihoods and engage them in joint initiatives to increase the local economic development and poverty reduction impacts?

— If pro-poor growth and poverty reduction through tourism is to become part of national strategy then it is essential to engage other national government ministries. This requires that the positive impacts on the local and national economy and in particular success in achieving poverty reduction targets can be convincingly demonstrated, measured and reported.

— Tourism is mentioned in some national Poverty Reduction Strategy Papers (PRSPs) but there is little referencing between national tourism policy and the poverty reduction strategies.

Investors and Developers

Many leading commercial banks have adopted the Equator Principles which are intended to provide a common framework (benchmarked against World Bank group criteria) for commercial lenders. It is intended that the Equator Principles should become an important element of lender due diligence and borrower compliance and that the principles will become part of the project management process and extend over the lifecycle of a development.

The benefits for developers, seeking commercial.finance, of compliance with the Equator Principles may be expected to include more favourable repayment terms and less intrusive covenants in loan agreements as banks lend more selectively in order to minimise their risk. For investors and.financial institutions the issues of risk management are no less significant, the repayment of, and return on, their investments is dependent upon the licence to operate, successful risk management and market advantage of the borrower.

By adopting a proactive approach through the Equator Principles they can manage portfolio volatility and increase returns. Where developers and investors are proactive in minimising negative environmental, social and economic impacts and maximising the positive impacts they have a competitive advantage in securing planning permissions or licenses and in bidding for development contracts. Different considerations apply in the design and construction phases and in the operational phases of a project. Developers are likely to focus on securing construction and development contracts and. Financial institutions are often partners in this process. Their joint focus is on the development and construction phase, but as hoteliers point out, their capacity to adopt a CR approach in the operational phase is, to a significant degree, dependent upon decisions made in siting, design and construction.

Hotel and resort management companies often have little or no influence at that stage and subsequent retrofitting to comply with regulatory frameworks, insurance requirements and industry best practices, as they develop over the lifecycle of the development, is expensive. Risk needs to be managed over the project lifecycle as a whole. The licence to operate, risk management and commercial advantage are key considerations for developers and their funders. The International Finance Corporation has developed Tourism and Hospitality Development guidelines which apply to developments which it.finances. Whilst the agenda has been dominated by risk management there are commercial advantages for developers, construction companies and banks.

In winning licenses and construction contracts there is commercial advantage in being able to demonstrate not just low levels of negative environmental and socio-cultural impacts but enhanced positive economic and social impacts. This can be achieved through the creation of additional employment and SME opportunities for local communities by adopting strategies and development plans maximizing the local economic development and poverty impacts whilst minimizing negative livelihood impacts. The additional investment and partnering, mentoring and transaction costs associated with a broader approach to local economic development are likely to be small in comparison to the commercial advantage which comes from enhancing the economic impacts, particularly in countries with high levels of youth unemployment.

By engaging with local communities in tourism development projects and demonstrating both willingness and acumen in maximising the local economic benefits developers secure their licence to operate and create a better business environment for the hotel and resort management companies, with a richer product offer in the neighbourhood. Local sourcing and maintenance requires the development of a range of local enterprises which will benefit the development and the local economy by providing employment, local enterprise opportunities and supplies of goods and services which benefit the local community as well as the tourism development. The development of this strategy requires that both local sourcing and market access issues are addressed in the design and development phases.

If the approach is to be credible the local economic benefits need to be clearly specified, targets need to be set and the deliverables monitored. Processes like community labour agreements and established economic impact measurements including the measurement of local sourcing and job creation can be used for this purpose. Local communities can often, but not always, gain from the infrastructure that comes to their area as a result of tourism development. Companies will increasingly be challenged to report on these benefits - all of which contribute to risk management and ensuring the licence to operate.

Hotels and Resorts

Risk management and the licence to operate require that hotels and resorts maintain good relationships with their "neighbourhood" and return a profit to the owners. The hotel sector moved earlier than other travel and tourism industry sectors to adopt and implement environmental management principles and there are many examples of local initiatives around hotels and resorts that are designed to address issues of economic and social sustainability. The experiments and local initiatives need now to be scaled up and applied more widely.

Hotels and resorts are to a significant degree dependent upon the maintenance and development of the environment in which they operate. Hotels and reports have an obvious and real interest in their neighbourhood for risk management and product quality reasons - the hotel or resort is committed to the local area, it cannot just move on if the environment is ruined or the neighbourhood becomes unattractive. The managers of hotels and resorts have a long-term interest in the maintenance and enrichment of the locality, to "create better places for people to live in and for people to visit." If the destination value declines so, generally, does the value and profitability of the property; contributing to the development of the destination enables the hotel or resort to manage risk, increase product quality and secure commercial advantage.

There are direct commercial benefits in extending the season, increasing bed occupancy,.filling beds out of season through a festival and extending length of stay. Improving the destination can assist in achieving all of these commercial objectives. Hotels and resorts can achieve a considerable amount by acting separately, however, destinations are often composed by a variety of properties serving different market segments and with different management strategies and the sector is very vulnerable to those who whilst they benefit from initiatives do not contribute to them. At the destination level there are benefits from collaborative action by hotels and resorts working with local authorities and communities and with the wider local industry.

Local economic development and the reduction of poverty is achieved where hotels and resorts:

— maximise their employment of local labour and through management and training interventions, by investing in people and ensuring that increasingly senior posts go to local employees;

— work with local communities and micro enterprises to ensure supplies of food and beverages, soft furnishings, maintenance, arts and crafts and entertainment are locally sourced.

The development of local linkages of these sorts requires that the challenges of quality, quantity and continuity of supply at a fair market price are met.

Tour Operators

Tour operators have established relationships with local suppliers; particularly their inbound operator in the destination. Their ability to sell trips is very reliant upon the perceived, and actual quality, of the destination. Tour operators are reliant on the quality and safety of the destination, they also play a significant role in shaping the way the destination is perceived by the way that they market the location.

Many operators are responding to changing market trends in the UK by placing increasing emphasis on locally sourced services, food and drinks, richer excursion and activity programmes. Tour operators seek market advantage through the quality of the experiences which they offer and that often necessitates close engagement with local communities and micro enterprises. Increasing numbers of operators are seeking to secure repeat business by enhancing the quality of the holiday experience in these ways and securing both increased levels of repeat business and referrals. Where investors and developers, hotel and resort management companies and managers and tour operators can identify ways of working together to enhance the quality of the destination, they and the local community gain.

Benefits of CR Approach to Stimulating Local Economic Development

Minimising risk

Business has been using tools to manage environmental risk for some time. There is now increasing emphasis on the economic and social aspects of the triple bottom line of business. Brand image and value are key elements for an industry where the product is intangible at the point of purchase and where the experience is much more than the directly purchased transport, accommodation and guide services. Reputational risk is a significant issue in an industry that is highly competitive and differentiated; and where the product purchased by the consumer extends beyond what is owned and directly managed in the supply chain.

Licence to operate

Good relationships with local communities, positive recognition of demonstrable concern for the natural and cultural environment and the maximisation of the contribution which the industry makes to local livelihoods, economic development and the reduction of poverty are all important to the industry's licence to operate. Enterprises, particularly where they collaborate to achieve local economic development, can improve the general environment for business and enable them to stay ahead of legislation. Resentful communities can make it significantly more expensive for the industry to operate and reduce the quality of the experience.

Market advantage

Extending responsible business practices beyond the environmental agenda to address the economic and social aspects builds reputation, particularly for those companies that establish a leadership role. The market is changing to reflect socially, environmentally and culturally aware holidaymakers. These market trends require a richer experience, generally beyond the confines of the hotel or resor.t There is market advantage and repeat business to be secured by enabling clients to enrich their experience and this will increase the local economic benefit

Product quality and cost

In an increasingly differentiated and competitive market there is commercial advantage in operating in, and to, destinations which offer a rich mixture of experiences and activities. The traditional provision of resort activities increasingly needs to be supplemented with complementary products many of which will be locally owned and provided by SMEs. Businesses benefit where collectively their efforts create a larger range of opportunities for local sourcing and a larger pool of labour with appropriate skills from which they can recruit. Cooperation between businesses makes the strategy easier to achieve, reduces cost and avoids the freeloader problem.

Staff morale

Changing consumer attitudes towards what constitutes a good holiday experiences and the relevance of the CR agenda also applies to staff. Adopting a more responsible business agenda can assist with the recruitment, motivation and retention of quality staff and reduce costs.

6

Trends in Loadging Industries

Many owners who practice "green housekeeping" have found they can remain competitive and save a little "green" too, by reducing waste, energy consumption and water use throughout their businesses. The hospitality industry is very competitive, and as an owner or operator of a resort, loadge, inn, motel, or hotel, you probably look for ways to save money while maintaining quality services.

Laws of Recycling

The law places a high priority on reducing waste and reusing items even before recycling. Local ordinances and the state Waste Reduction and Recycling Law require all businesses and property owners to:

— Provide separate containers for the materials banned from landfills and incinerators

— Regularly educate the occupants and users about the recycling program at their facility

— Arrange for the collection and delivery of the recyclables to a recycling facility.

Process of Recycling

Step 1: Work with your hauler to get started

Get a list of what is accepted for recycling. Work closely

with your hauler to identify collection methods, frequency of collection, container needs, and costs for collecting recyclables and trash. Discuss potential recycling contamination problems and solutions. Consider all items that you might need to dispose of, including appliances, furniture, kitchen grease, fluorescent bulbs, etc. By recycling, you can reduce your overall solid waste disposal costs.

Step 2: Establish your recycling collection program

You may decide to put a container for recyclables in each guest room, and have another can for garbage. Label them clearly. In many cases, guests can mix recyclables like cans and bottles with each other in the recycling container with few problems since rooms are serviced daily. Remind guests that it takes no more time to put an item in a recycling bin than it takes to put it in a garbage can! Put recycling containers in these areas: the lobby or other common areas; vending areas; any food preparation areas; housekeeping closets; the pool or recreation area; conference rooms and offices; and in maintenance buildings and grounds. There are many attractive and functional containers on the market. DNR has several free publications that describe how to set up a recycling collection program in detail.

Step 3: Train your employees to practice good habits at work

Help your staff incorporate waste reduction and recycling habits into their daily responsibilities. Teach your employees the importance of keeping recyclables separate from garbage to minimize contamination of the recyclables. Incorporate this training into their general employee orientation. On-going education is the key to overcome contamination and insure employee cooperation. Form a committee made of staff from housekeeping, administration, maintenance, and other areas to develop and maintain your program. Solicit ideas from your employees for additional ways to recycle and reduce waste.

Step 4: Educate your guests

Give guests a flyer that describes your recycling and waste reduction programs when they check in. Put informational table tents that describe your recycling and waste reduction program in each guest room. Pre-printed table tents, like the one pictured, can be ordered for a small fee from the "Green" Hotels Association. Or, you can make your own and have them printed locally. Laminated tents will last longer. Recycling is one step you can take to make your business more "green," but if you really want to save resources and more of that other "green stuff," practice waste reduction.

Here are some tips that have worked in large and small resorts, loadges, motels, and hotels.

Waste Reduction Tips for Guest Rooms

Reduce solid waste

— Substitute refillable liquid soap dispensers for individually-wrapped bar soaps in bathrooms. Though the initial expense for these dispensers may seem high, you will realize a quick return on your investment. Refills and items purchased in bulk are usually less expensive and generate less waste than individual containers.

— If you continue to use bar soap, donate partiallyused bars to day care centres, senior centres, shelters, churches, etc., instead of throwing them away.

— Substitute washable drinking glasses for disposable glasses if you have dishwashing capabilities. It is cheaper to wash and reuse them than to purchase disposable ones and pay to have them hauled away as garbage.

— Take hangers left in guest rooms to dry cleaners or laundromats for reuse. Bring other reusable items left in rooms to resale stores when appropriate.

— When remodeling, give reusable furniture, bedding, carpet, fixtures, etc., to resale stores or donate items to community groups like day care centres, shelters, or churches. Get a receipt for tax deductions.

— Instead of putting a complimentary newspaper in each room, encourage guests to pick up a free copy in the lobby if they want one.

Reduce energy waste

— Replace standard light bulbs with energy efficient compact fluorescent bulbs. These bulbs cost more initially-about $15 each-but pay for themselves over time since they last much longer and use about one-quarter of the electricity of an incandescent. Using long-lasting bulbs also reduces labour costs since you don't have to change them as often.

— Compact fluorescent bulbs are found in most hardware stores. See "Resources for Loadging Operators" for other sources.

Reduce water waste

— Repair all water leaks immediately!

— Install a water-saving toilet dam in the toilet tank. Toilet dams, available at hardware stores, can save about one-third of the water commonly used per flush with no change in effectiveness.

— When remodelling bathrooms or replacing broken toilets, install standard low-flush toilets that use only 1.5 gallons per flush.

— Install low flow water aerators in shower heads and sink faucets. These inexpensive items, commonly found in hardware stores, incorporate air into the water flow. Each shower uses 25-50% less water, yet supplies the same amount of pressure in the spray. Aerators also save energy since less hot water is used.

— Encourage guests to leave sheets on the bed during their stay instead of having them changed every day. This reduces the amount of laundry you have to do, saving water, soap, energy, time and money!

— Encourage guests to take new towels only when they really need them. Remind them to leave dirty towels on the floor so housekeeping staff will replace only those towels. Here is a sample of a preprinted message that can be hung on the bathroom door. To order copies, see "Resources for Loadging Operators" in this flyer.

Reduce waste in other areas

— Use linen hand towels on a continuous roll instead of paper towels in the employee, dining and lobby restrooms.

— Cut up old linens and use them as cleaning rags. Or, donate slightly-worn linens and towels to community groups or shelters for reuse.

— Replace old appliances with newer, energy efficient appliances. Recycle the old one, of course!

— Buy products you use regularly in bulk whenever possible.

— Use rechargeable batteries in pagers, cell phones, etc. Recharging units and batteries are available in hardware and discount stores. Check with your suppliers for information on how to recycle the used batteries that eventually wear out.

— Put reusable dishes, mugs, and glassware at your continental breakfast table. Encourage employees to use reusable mugs and glasses for coffee breaks instead of disposable cups.

Less waste in the office

— Minimize paper use by copying on both sides of your paper, or use the blank back sides as scratch paper.

— Use refillable toner cartridges instead of disposable ones in your copier and computer printers. Your local office supply store can help you locate companies that service refillable cartridges.

— Buy recycled products whenever possible. Ask your suppliers or shop at discount stores for items like recycled toilet paper, fax, copier, notepaper and computer paper; garbage can liners, pillows, carpets and carpet pads made of recycled plastic soda bottles; landscape edging made of plastic food containers; picnic tables, benches, and parking stops made of plastic milk jugs; and construction materials like recycled ceiling tiles, insulation, and floor mats.

— Remove your name from unwanted mailing lists by calling the 800 phone numbers on catalogues. Or, send your name and your business' name to: Mail Preferences Services, Direct Mail Marketing Association, PO Box 9008, Farmingdale, NY, 11735.

— Choose suppliers who can provide reusable or recyclable packaging and packaging that has recycled content in it.

Live lightly with the environment

— Use water-based paints instead of oil-based paints. Water-based paints can be cleaned up with water. Donate unused paint to a community-service agency or a local paint exchange.

— Left-over oil-based paint is considered a hazardous waste and must be brought to a hazardous waste collection event for proper disposal. Call your DNR Hazardous Waste Specialist for more information.

— Use cleaners without oil-based solvents.

— If you're using lawn chemicals, take every precaution to keep them off of paved driveways, sidewalks, and streets so they don't run into storm drains when it rains. Follow directions exactly and only buy as much as you need.

State hazardous waste regulations prohibit businesses from disposing of waste lamps and light bulbs in landfills due to the mercury content that exceeds hazardous waste limits. These include fluorescent, mercury vapor, metal halide, high-and low-pressure sodium-vapor, and some incandescent lamps.

Trends in Loadging Industry

The loadging industry is heavily dependent on consumer confidence or how people feel about the current economic environment. Business travel, the largest segment in the industry, fluctuates directly to overall economic conditions. Leisure travel is usually avoided or postponed in times of economic uncertainty. The demand for loadging will not pick up until people are more confident about the state of the economy. The following are some of the major trends facing the loadging industry:

— *Consolidation:* The joining or merger of two firms is referred to as consolidation. There is a long-term trend toward consolidation in the loadging industry due to the benefits of size and market penetration. Marriot Loadging, for example, now operates 11 brands ranging from Fairfield Inns to Ritz Carlton hotels. Larger consolidated companies can offer economies of scale that provides effective cost controls, frequent traveller programs, reservation systems, sales and marketing programs. Acquisition activity has been slow in the last three years after significant activity in the late 1990's.

— *Third party reservation:* Companies like Travelocity, Expedia, Priceline.com and Hotels.com are used increasingly by travelers for reserving their hotel and motel rooms. By the year 2005, an estimated 1 in 5 hotel bookings will be made online, up from 1 in 12 bookings in 2002. According to Jupiter Research, online hotel reservations will grow from $5 billion in 2002 to $14.8 billion in 2007. According to Cendant Corporation, customers shopping for a room online want a friendly and efficient booking experience, great prices, and a well-known and trusted brand.

— *New technologies:* Technology is being used to attract potential customers and to keep operating costs lower at hotels and motels. High-speed internet, wireless internet access and teleconferencing capabilities are some examples of technologies that are attractive to business travelers. Some hotels are using automated guest check-in to keep their costs down.

— *Operations:* During times of declining occupancy and economic uncertainty, loadging operators are continuing to explore new and effective cost controls. The challenge is to maximize cash flow without hurting customer service. Outstanding customer service and guest rooms are critical factors in maintaining and improving market share.

— *Customer market segments:* Some companies are paying special attention to certain customer segments that may not be very sensitive to economic conditions. These can include seniors, fraternal and religious groups and wedding parties.

— *Development:* Extended stay hotels have emerged with a unique, apartment-style format (with kitchen, dining and work areas) for longer-term stays. The growth of condominium hotels represent an alternative to traditional lender financing and, at the same time, provides a "built in" customer base. Boutique hotels that offer a "home away from home" feeling are becoming more popular as these hotels offer unique personalities achieved through their designs and surroundings. In a bid for additional sources of profit, hotels are adding new services and amenities such as spas.

There is a slowdown in new hotel construction as lenders are more interested in deals such as refinancing, consolidation, renovation and repositioning of existing properties. Lenders are also becoming stricter about their terms. Local and regional banks, the biggest funding source for limited-service hotels, are requiring developers to have strong existing relationships with the banks and solid project characteristics like location, brand and management.

Successful existing properties are continuously renovating their properties. Furniture, fixtures, equipment and building materials need constant update regardless of economic conditions. Excess supply is a significant problem faced by the loadging industry. Occupancy levels have fallen in the last few years due to room supply increasing faster than room demand. Hotel companies are solving this problem by reassessing their capital plans so that they can decide whether to undertake certain projects.

Benefits and Costs for Tourism for Remote Communities

Remote Destinations

Remote destinations need to understand the basic principles governing tourism and tourism development so that they can plan appropriately and take anticipative action, thereby safeguarding the region as a great place to live for the regional community and as a worthwhile place to visit for tourists.The considerations shared here will help regional and other decision makers to balance the needs and aspirations of tourists and host communities with national interests and the need to safeguard natural resources and ecosystems for future generations.

Use of Resources

Tropical savanna destinations, like destinations across Australia's outback regions, offer an essentially nature-based tourist product. In addition to the magnificent scenery, offering drive-through and bushwalking experience, the extensive coastline, rivers and waterholes offer fishing opportunities and wetlands and billabongs harbour extensive birdlife. In the process of enjoying these resources, tourists also consume them. They take fish, generate rubbish and waste, cause congestion, and by their mere presence detract from the enjoyment of other visitors and local people.

Tourists also consume other types of resources in host regions, such as accommodation and catering, entertainment, infrastructure and services. They further consume intangible aspects of the tourist product such as the local culture and the feeling of place. The type and extent of resource use differs between destinations depending on visitor numbers, visitor nights, visitor types and resource availability.

All the resources that constitute a destination's tourist product are shared by members of the host community, tourists and other users. It is therefore essential to understand the cumulative impact and extent of resource use/extraction. The use of resources can then be assessed in the context of the contribution tourists make to a destination. There are two important steps towards an integrated analysis of tourism benefits and costs.

Firstly, it provides an estimation and assessment of tourist spending (financial contribution) as well as fish catch (resource extraction). Secondly, it shows the extent to which tourists require access to basic infrastructure and resources by converting visitor days into 'resident equivalents'. This reveals the extent to which the true demand for infrastructure and services is underestimated if based only on resident population. The experiences and challenges of most savanna and outback destinations are similar.

In relation to Coral Bay on the Western Australia Carnarvon-Ningaloo coast: "Many negative impacts of tourism can be attributed to incremental growth and the absence of appropriate plans and management actions. The future of tourism in the region depends on its sustainability and the maintenance of the natural environment, the very attribute that attracts visitors to spend their discretionary dollars in [this region] rather than competing destinations in Australia and abroad."

Tourism benefits

All tourism players such as tourists, businesses, tourism managers, host communities and society, need to derive benefits from tourism for tourism to be truly successful. However, the aspirations of these players are at least partially competing. Tourists seek to maximise 'consumer surplus', ie. get the best experience possible for the least cost, while businesses seek to maximise (shortterm) profits and host communities are interested in long-term income and employment as well as net benefits.

Tourism success is predominantly measured in tourist numbers. This measure is useful when assessing tourism at a national scale since economic activity generated can be assumed to be linear to tourist numbers. Thus, from a national - or even state perspective - it is useful to pursue an increase in tourist numbers, both international as well as inter- and intra-state. Equalling tourist numbers to tourist success is a dangerously floored concept for small host communities such as Normanton/Karumba and others right across the tropical savannas.

Here, benefit is not necessarily related to tourist numbers but to yield and net benefit. Yield is about the financial bottom-line of tourism and net benefits assess yield in the context of social, cultural and environmental impacts. As demonstrated the question of yield is not only linked to the types of visitors and their daily spending, but also to duration of stay. Therefore 'visitor days' is proposed as a superior measure to 'visitor number'. Tourists who spend more and extract/use fewer resources produce higher net benefit than those who spend little and use resources heavily.

To increase net benefits of host communities from tourism it is absolutely critical to have a fact-based understanding of tourism in the region, including tourist numbers, tourist market, visitor profiles and activities. Perceptions and anecdotal evidence (eg. about assumed tourist numbers and market segments) can be misleading for planning and management. Specifically the quest for more tourists without consideration of yield and net benefit is a hazardous concept.

The visitor market at any specific location across the savannas may differ from other locations. While it is important to understand the visitor market it is equally important to identify what types of visitors are missing. For example, there are only very few international tourists visiting Normanton/Karumba. On the basis of such understanding the host community can develop a vision for tourism for the destination and start to take pro-active and strategic steps to maximise community net benefits. When evaluating tourism benefits it is further important to consider the distribution of benefits and costs in the host community.

For the Karumba/Normanton region it has been demonstrated that indigenous people, despite representing a majority of population, have only a marginal involvement in tourism and therefore receive few benefits from tourism.

In addition, they are also the socio-economically weakest group and are affected most by local businesses increasing prices for goods to generate a tourist rent. Savanna regions are 'peripheral' destinations, as is the case for Carpentaria Shire. This brings specific challenges in terms of changing product, attracting different tourists to diversify the tourist market, adding secondary benefits from money re-spent locally and combating seasonality of visitation.

Future of Tourism

The tropical savannas are largely a domestic tourist destination. Increasingly, grey nomads are dominating the visitor market right across the north, from Cape York to the Kimberley. Given the demographic profile of the Australian population, the number of grey nomads is bound to increase significantly over the next decades as the baby boomer generation retires. The ABS estimates that the number of people older than 65 years will increase from 2.4 million (year 2001; 12.1% of population) to 2.94 million within a decade (an increase of 23%) and to 5.05 million by 2031.

Many people retire before the age of 65. Consequently, many more grey nomads will travel to and through northern Australia's outback regions, in the pursuit of adventure, solitude and pristine environments. More demand on outback roads will lead to increased maintenance costs and more roads will be sealed. Towns such as Burketown, which are currently 'protected' from the gravel-road adverse travellers, will become mainstream destinations. The fish stocks in adjacent rivers will be attracting the tourist anglers that are now becoming frustrated with declining catch in the waters accessible from Karumba.

Many visitors consider it their right not only to travel to remote regions, but also to camp and fish wherever they want to, and to do so free of charge. However, increasing visitation and resulting pressure on savanna ecosystems and communities requires a change of public attitude to the effect that it is a privilege to visit remote regions. This in turn means that with the right to visit comes an obligation to firstly minimise ones' impacts through careful resource use and secondly to pay for the services received.

An attitude change to the effect that 'free-riding is un-cool' requires a concerted and continued education effort at the national, state and regional levels. It is more difficult to foresee trends relating to international tourists to the region. International travel is subject to many uncertain factors such as exchange rates, price of aviation fuel, political conditions and security issues. However, some economic forecasters predict that tourism will become the largest exportearning sector in Australia in the near future. Increasing international visitor numbers to savanna regions would exacerbate the urgency of rethink of tourism in remote regions.

7

Appropriate Planning for Tourism in Destination Communities

Each culture has particular values, habits, and norms, and tourists need to recognise and respect local cultures, and codes of conduct or guidelines can be extremely useful as tools to minimise social and cultural impacts. Tourists often need and usually appreciate tips and information on how to behave. Much of the socio cultural damage caused by tourism is due to a lack of knowledge and understanding. The following points should be addressed in guidelines and codes of conduct for tourists:

— local customs and traditions;
— use of technological gadgetry;
— religious beliefs; bartering and bargaining;
— permission for photographs and videos;
— indigenous rights;
— language;
— treatment and status of local officials;
— invasion of privacy;
— off limit areas;
— responses to begging;
— alcoholic beverages;

- keeping promises;
- smoking; and
- tipping.

With pre-travel information, visitors can often prepare themselves for travel to places where the culture is known to be quite different from their own. Tourists are able to obtain information about the culture of the host community, especially unacceptable behaviour, and essential actions, such as correct greeting behaviour and tipping, from commercial guide books, travel agents and tour operators.

There is a need for governments and the tourism industry to create tourism awareness by initiating programmes to inform the public about tourism, and to obtain feedback from local people about their perceptions of burism. Tourism is particularly dependent on the use of community spaces and resources, and community receptiveness, as in the case of township tourism.

Socio-Cultural Sustainability

Social sustainability is the ability of a community to absorb visitors for either long or short periods of time without being influenced negatively by people different from themselves (in other words, without experiencing social disharmony) or attempting to alleviate any disharmony by adapting their functions or relationships. Although societies are able function harmoniously in the presence of tourism, the possibility nevertheless remains that relationships within that society and its lifestyle, customs and traditions may well change as a result of the introduction of visitors with different habits, styles, customs and means of exchange.

Even if a society survives under these circumstances, its culture can undergo irreversible alterations. Vital to sustainable tourism is responsible behaviour on the part of the visitor and the prevention of any form of distortion of the local culture. To sustain the hosts' desire for tourists to visit and the guests' desire to return, the negative impacts of cultural tourism must be kept to the minimum through skilled management, an area in which social scientists and anthropologists can offer assistance.

Non-Sustainable Dimension of Cultural Tourism

Continuous use of cultural sites

The overuse of sites such as cultural villages and townships can become a particular problem, as has happened with heritage tourism elsewhere in the world. This overuse can result in both damage to buildings and landscapes and an unsatisfactory experience for visitors. The problem can be caused by too many visitors in total, too high a proportion of consumers visiting at the same time, or the wrong kind of visitors whose behaviour is not appropriate. All of these are management problems, and often it may be beyond the skill or financial resources of those who own the cultural tourism resources in question to solve them.

Lack of local control

The mechanisms that are used to elicit the views of the community provide an opportunity for a minority of self-appointed community spokespeople, or people with strong views, to dominate the process; the views of the so-called `silent majority' may thus often go unheard. Moreover, professionals may undervalue or even ignore local views that run contrary to their own. This is particularly prevalent when `public participation exercises' are held to legitimise decisions that have, in all probability, already been taken.

Even if a community could speak with one voice, its ability to control local tourism development would be limited by a number of factors, as given below:

- — If a destination community tries to control tourism activities, the power of the tourism industry allows for tour operators simply to move on to another destination where they will notface similar constraints.
- — A community may wish to limit the growth of tourism in an area, but government policies may require the maximisation of the attraction of foreign tourists to the destination to help the balance of payments of the country.
- — Externally based organisations may already have a strong voice in the area because of their ownership of local businesses. An example of this would be hotels owned by national hotel chains or transnational companies.
- — The stimulus and funding for the development of cultural tourism in South Africa often comes from outside the local area due to lack of economic empowerment in both rural and urban communities.

In South Africa, amongst indigenous populations in particular, history has shown that in most cases, local people may have little say in the process, which is clearly at odds with the concept of sustainable tourism. It is perhaps especially a problem in the heritage field, where the story of a community is told to tourists by outside professionals rather than by local people. This is an extremely contentious issue in South Africa, particularly in the cultural tourism context, where there is a scarcity of site guides.

The lack of local control may often lead to developments that are inappropriate for their location because the outside agencies lack the necessary knowledge. Furthermore, it can lead to some or most of the benefits derived from the development being exported away from the local area. The challenge is, therefore, to find ways of making cultural tourism products such as township tourism and cultural villages more sustainable in themselves, and to be better able to contribute towards the development of sustainable tourism in general.

Trivialisation of authenticity

The needs of the tourism industry, and the tastes of tourists, can lead to the trivialising of culture and a loss of authenticity. Traditional dances, for instance, are shortened to accommodate the schedules of tour groups, and traditional cuisine is internationalised to make it acceptable to the palates of visitors.

Sustainable Development

The sustainable development approach implies that the resources for development are conserved for indefinite future as well as present use; sustainable development is considered to be "development that meets the needs of the present without compromising the ability of future generations to meet their own needs". This approach thus ensures that future generations everywhere will have sufficient resources to adequately sustain themselves and maintain a reasonable quality of life. The concept of sustainable development emerged in the mid nineteen-sixties. However, the term was first used in the Bmntland report, entitled Our Common Future, prepared by the World Commission on Development and Environment in 1987.

Sustainable development brings together the apparently contrasting concepts of economic development and environmental conservation. The vision put forward by the Bruntland report was one of economic development not concerned purely with attaining maximum economic growth but also with issues of fairness between the individuals and groups making up today's society as well as fairness between the present generation and those generations still to come.For people whose present quality of life is not of an acceptable standard, the resources, if sustained, will be available for them and their children potentially to achieve quality of life in the future.

Achieving sustainability is now the underlying principle for all types of development, including tourism. The achievement of sustainability is an objective that will require much time and effort, and careful planning and management of resources development are the key means to achieving it. Keyser argues that the use of phrases such as `beyond the rhetoric of sustainable development' and `operationalising sustainable development' clearly points to the need to stop talking about sustainable development and start acting to turn it into reality.

Sastainable Tourism

The former is seen as sensitive, soft, `intelligent' tourism that is complementary to the concept of sustainable tourism. However there are several aspects to cultural tourism that may well prevent it from being a sustainable activity in its own right, and may in fact make it incompatible with the principles of sustainable tourism. The concept of sustainable tourism, popularised following the release of the Bruntland report, represents a direct application of the sustainable development concept.

Sustainable tourism is tourism that meets the needs of present generations without compromising the ability of future generations to meet their own needs. Some commentators prefer the term `sustainable tourism development', since the term `sustainable tourism' could imply an emphasis on the well-being of the tourism sector itself, in the sense of `sustained tourism', rather than on the communities where tourism takes place.

The term `sustainable tourism', however, is more widely used, with some arguing that the concept of sustainable tourism should take into account the sustainability of tourism as well as that of the local community. This contention is based on the argument that the term is meaningless if there is no tourism sector to which the adjective `sustainable' can be attached. As with `sustainable development', the label `sustainable tourism' is susceptible to appropriation by those pursuing a particular political agenda. Sustainable tourism embraces a community- oriented approach, encouraging community involvement and participation. Definitions of sustainable tourism emphasise three fundamental features:

— *Quality* : Sustainable tourism involved providing quality experiences for visitors, while improving the quality of life of the host community.

— *Continuity* : Sustainable tourism ensures the continuity of the natural resources upon which it is based, and the continuity of the culture of the host communities.

— *Balance* : Sustainable tourism balances the needs of the tourism industry, supporters of the environment, and the local community.

Socio-cultural impacts usually occur slowly over time and tend to be invisible and intangible. Swarbrooke notes that the social impact of tourism is usually permanent, or all but impossible to reverse. Social dimension of sustainable tourism that offers a complete perspective on the socio - cultural aspects of sustainable tourism. All the Stakeholder in tourism are clearly interrelated, and indeed interdependent, each with both rights and responsibilities that need to be recognised.

The researcher believes that it is necessary to recognise that sustainable tourism may be an impossible dream, and the best we can hope for is to develop sustainable forms of tourism. This may be because tourism is inherently non-sustainable, or because unforeseen future political, economic, social and technological change may make current approaches to sustainable tourism management obsolete. We must recognise that sustainable tourism is an overtly political subject, in that it concerns the distribution of resources, both now and in the future. The fact that some people will gain and some people will lose as a result of sustainable tourism means that it is inherently political, and its political nature means that sustainable tourism is about who has the power - host communities, governments, the industry or the tourists - and how these role-players recognise that definitions of sustainable tourism and devising strategies to try to achieve it will normally reflect who has the power in any particular situation.

The idea of community involvement as a cornerstone of sustainable tourism is problematic. Communities are rarely homogeneous, and thus will rarely take a single homogeneous view on any issue. There is a need to develop mechanisms for arbitrating the conflicting views concerning tourism that will emerge in any community. Tourism management should not allow articulate minorities to dominate the process to the exclusion of other citizens; sustainable tourism is thus about stakeholders whose interests have to be balanced. Swarbrooke notes that in some instances the community may wish to pursue policies that run counter to sustainable tourism; it cannot thus be assumed that community involvement will automatically ensure more sustainable forms of tourism.

The sustainable development strategy needs to shift towards emphasis on implementation, since many sustainable tourism strategies have been devised, but there are as yet few examples of successful initiatives. This is quite evident in the White Paper on Tourism Development and Promotion of 1996. Sustainable Turism development needs to be interpreted in tenns of what destinations and the tourism industry can do to implement and operationalise sustainable tourism development.

Responsible Tourism Development

Responsible Tourism as a concept has gained much

momentum in the 1990's and is quite synonymous with the concept of sustainable tourism development, alternative tourism, ecotourism, green tourism, and soft tourism. The White Paper on the Development and Promotion of Tourism in South Africa identifies the concept of `Responsible Tourism' as the most appropriate concept and guiding principle for tourism development in South Africa. "Responsible tourism destinations conserve nature and increase the living standards of local communities, by supporting these destinations, and contributing to their success, you can help them achieve these aims.

Responsible tourism allows you to meet local people and experience their culture and way of life, which will make your visit more meaningful and enjoyable. As a responsible tourist, we encourage you to ask your hosts what they are doing to develop the local economy and protect the environment". Responsible tourism is seen as a positive approach by tourism industry partners to develop, market, and manage the tourism industry in a responsible manner, to create a competitive advantage. According to the Responsible Tourism Handbook (003) and the South African White Paper on Responsible Tourism of 1996, responsible tourism implies:

— Tourism industry responsibility to the environment, flhrough the promotion of balanced and sustainable tourism, and a focus on environmentally based tourism activities;

— Responsibility of government and business to involve the local communities that are in close proximity to tourism plant and attractions, through the development of meaningful economic linkages;

— Responsibility to respect, invest and develop local cultures, and protect them from over-commercialization and over-exploitations-,

— The responsibility of local communities to become actively involved in the tourism industry, to practice sustainable development, and to ensure the safety and security of visitors;

— The responsibility of both employers and employees in the tourism industry, both to each other and the customer (responsible trade union and employment practices); and

— Responsible government as well a responsibility on the part of tourists to observe the norms and practices of South Africa.

According to the Responsible Tourism Handbook and the South African White Paper on Responsible Tourism of 1996, the key elements of responsible tourism include:

— Avoidance of waste and over-consumption

— Using local resources in a sustainable manner

— Maintenance and encouragement of natural, social and cultural diversity

— Sensitivity to the host culture

— Local community involvement in planning and decision making

— A prerequisite assessment of the environmental, economic and social impacts prior to tourism development

— Ensuring that the host population is involved in and benefits from tourism

— The tourism that is marked should be responsible, respecting the local, natural and cultural environment

— The impacts of tourism must be monitored and open disclosure of information ensured.

"Responsible Tourism" is therefore a concept underpinned by sound environmental, social and economic principles, offering a way to minimise environmental and cultural impacts, by benefiting local communities and reducing poverty. Responsible tourism therefore involves participation by all stakeholders. This includes private sector, government, local communities, disadvantaged communities, minority groups, consumers, NGO's, the media, employees and others. By comparing the description and principles of responsible tourism defined in the White Paper with the principles of sustainable tourism development described previously, one will see that the principles and descriptions are essentially the same.

The sustainable tourism development concept embraces a community-oriented approach, encouraging community involvement and participation. As in Soweto, host communities throughout the world play an integral role in the tourism industry. What they typically lack, however, is the power to influence the nature and direction of tourism development. The level of choice exercised by host communities in becoming a destination is questionable in the case of tourism in general, and particularly so in developing countries. Thus, in worst-case scenarios, host communities are actively disadvantaged by having tourism occur in their own backyards, which is why the term `host' can be hotly contested.

For example, in many contexts in South Africa, indigenous peoples have been displaced from land so that national parks or wildlife areas can be created. In such cases the rewards. reaped from subsequent tourism development are typically pocketed by outside tourism operators and the government, while local people must deal with diminished livelihood options.

Indeed, the central role of the community in tourism planning has come to be recognised as one of the tenets of sustainable and socially responsible tourism. However, while community-based planning is an important driver in academic and bureaucratic approaches to tourism development, it is important to recognise that such an approach does not automatically lead to sustainable tourism development; a key point to remember is that the local should not be romanticised, as often seems to be the case in discussions of tourism planning.

Nevertheless, a community-based approach provides the possibility that the need for consultation regarding the use of shared resources and the needs of neighbours will open the way to the resolution of tourism conflicts. When examining the role of the community in tourism it is impossible to separate the social, economic and political processes operating within a community from the conflict which occurs between stakeholders. Conflict and disagreement between members of a community over the outputs and outcomes of tourism are, in fact, the norm. Tourism planners therefore typically have to achieve a compromise between various stakeholders and interests in tourism development in an attempt to arrive at outcomes acceptable to stakeholders within the wider community.

Indeed, much of the recent proliferation of tourism literature dealing with co-operation and collaboration in tourism destinations is a direct response to the need to find mechanisms to accommodate the various interests that exist in tourism development. One of the responsibilities of the host population is to recognise the desire of many tourists to meet and interact with local people and to be prepared to foster the host-guest relationship in tourism. The host population should have an active say in the kind of tourism appropriate to their own lifestyle, culture and natural resources, and to be free to reject tourism as an economic option if other options are available. Participation by host communities in tourism planning and development is fundamental to the process.

The United Nations Environment Programme advocated that tourism should be subject to environmental planning and management, taking into account the well-being of the local population, which too often has to accept a large influx of tourists without having had a voice in such development. The demands of the public that their concerns be incorporated into the decision-making process has resulted in the emergence of public participation programmes and requirements that environmental impact statements be prepared.

A thriving and healthy tourism industry depends upon an equally healthy and thriving local community. It is the local community that benefits from tourism but, at the same time, it is the local community that bears the costs of tourism and has to pick up the pieces once the tourists have gone. In other words, tourism is a resource industry, and local communities are as much a resource, or part of the tourism product, as are tourist facilities and attractions. Therefore, the basic requirement for the community approach to tourism development is that all members of communities in tourist destination areas, rather than just those directly involved in the tourism industry, should be involved in the management and planning of tourism.

Pearce et al. include the education of both local people and communities, community ownership of tourist facilities, the facilitation of local residents' way of life and the undertaking of constant monitoring and research as equally essential ingredients of communitytbased tourism development. The purpose of this approach is to ensure that the objectives of tourism development coincide with the community's wider social and economic goals, that the tourism industry gives back to the community while extracting a living from it, and that both the industry and its community base can benefit mutually from a Ion,-,term partnership.

Tourism is an economic activity that involves tourists who are willing to spend money in return for certain goods and services, and organisations and businesses that will provide those goods and services at a profit. Under such circumstances, balanced and harmonious tourist-host relationships will occur only when the tourism product is small scale, locally owned and controlled, and not the major source of income and employment for the local community. As soon as the hosts become dependent, either on tourists or on outside organisations, a form of exploitation results. The tourist host relationship becomes based upon conflict and the local community begins to suffer from the social and cultural impacts of tourism.

Clearly most destination communities currently do not dictate the terms or conditions on which tourism takes place in their home area, yet it is they who must live with the direct consequences of tourism. These consequences often include negative social and environmental impacts, even in situations where communities are benefiting economically from tourism. To ensure a strong likelihood of economic, political and social benefits of tourism accruing to host communities, there needs to be full participation.

Full participation is said to occur where communities supply the majority of goods and services to tourists, have considerable input into planning decisions, and collectively manage common resources. The latter point is particularly relevant in situations where tourism is based on natural and cultural features. When tourism ventures are largely dependent on local cultural resources, and are locally managed, this allows communities to participate with equity in the tourism process. Thus access to information pertaining to the pros and cons of tourism and how it may impact on their lives is important for host communities, particularly for those in less developed countries where infor mation flows are often poor.

Empowerment should be a precursor to community involvement in tourism, as it is a means to determine and achieve socio-economic objectives The local community needs to be empowered to decide what forms of tourism they want to be developed in their respective communities, and how the tourism costs and benefits are to be shared among different stakeholders. A framework that specifies four dimensions of empowerment (economic, social, psychological and political) helps explain what empowerment can mean for host communities involved in tourism, as well as how disempowerment may manifest itself. It demonstrates multiple ways in which communities need to be empowered if they are to have at least some management control over tourism and secure maximum benefits from engaging in tourism initiatives.

Economic empowerment : Economic gains from involvement in both formal and informal sector activities can lead to empowerment for host communities, but what is more important than the total amount of these economic benefits is the spread of the benefits. For a community to be economically empowered it will need secure access to productive resources in a tourism area. This is particularly important in the case of common property resources and in situations where protected areas have been established.

Social empowerment: Social empowerment refers to a situation in which a community's sense of cohesion and integrity has been confirmed or strengthened through its involvement in tourism. Social empowerment perhaps most clearly results from tourism when profits are used to fund social development projects identified by the community, such as water supply systems or clinics in the local area. Social disempowerment may occur if tourism results in crime, begging, perceptions of crowding, displacement from traditional lands, loss of authenticity or restitution and inequities in the distribution of the benefits of tourism.

Psychological empowerment: Psychological empowerment should ideally mean that a community's confidence in its ability to participate equitably and effectively in tourism planning, development and management is maximised. This may involve capacity-building and reinforcement of the self-worth of community members so that they can play an active role in decisiorrmaking or power-sharing processes with external stakeholders.

A host community that is optimistic about the future, has faith in the abilities of its residents. A community that is relatively self-reliant, and demonstrates pride in its traditions and culture, can be said to be psychologically powerful. Tourism that is sensitive to cultural norms and builds respect for local traditions can, therefore, be empowering for local people. Preservation of tradition is extremely important in terms of maintaining a group's sense of self-esteem and wellbeing.

Political empowerment: Once community members are politically empowered by involvement in tourism, their voices and concerns guide the development of any tourism initiative from the feasibility stage through to its implementation. A community is usually diverse in terms of class, gender, caste, age and ethnicity, so it is important that democratic structures that encourage the involvement of a range of interest groups are in place. Forming organisations, or working through traditional organisations structures, can certainly help communities gain greater control over tourist development in their areas and give them political strength to deal with outsiders, including the private sector and government officials.

Nature of Tourism Development

Another issue critical to understanding the management of host community tourism is scale. Studies reveal that small-scale initiatives have gained much support in discussions of community involvement in tourism because these initiatives are more likely to be owned and managed locally, and thus provide greater local benefits than tourism enterprises controlled by outsiders. Essentially, when local people can meet many of the needs of tourists themselves, they are more likely to retain some control over tourism. Controlling one's own enterprise is a positive step in the direction of self-determination for people otherwise dependent on the tourism industry for menial jobs or handouts, and is more likely to lead to self-fulfilment.

If tourism moves `up scale' in an area, local people can lose important economic advantages as well as control over tourism enterprises. While community enterprises certainly offer opportunities for residents to manage tourism on their own terms, other configurations, such as joint ventures with private-sector partners, also enable host communities to play a management role. Whether destination communities always see small-scale or alternative forms of tourism as preferable to mass or luxury tourism should also be questioned. While small-scale tourism is perceived to fit in well with the philosophy of alternative tourism, in practice mass tourism may be the preferred option if it brings in more money to local communities.

Some communities may prefer mass tourism that involves, for example, one bus load of tourists arriving per day at a set time for a cultural performance and to buy crafts and then returning to their hotels, rather than tourism where outsiders come to stay in their village, as the latter is more culturally invasive. Communities may in fact be concerned that small-scale enterprises simply cannot compete with larger tourism ventures. Therefore, while some host communities will wish to pursue small-scale, alternative forms of tourism, others will prefer mass tourism. It is in the latter cases, however, that concerns are more likely to arise about the lack of community control over tourism.

8

Hospitality Operations in Global Age

The hospitality industry is one of the world's largest employers and arguably one of the largest traders of foreign currency. It is often also a focal point for local society, and is clearly at the center of the transfer of ideas and the cross fertilization of cultures. At its heart, the hospitality industry plays an important part physically in bringing people together in a global community. And those countries suffering from trade imbalances due to high imports frequently look to tourism and hospitality to close the gap. Hospitality is thus not only an industry, it is a concept — and a major force in the rapidly evolving global marketplace.

Globalisation is typified by the rapid movement of people, information and capital across national borders worldwide in ways that would have been difficult to envision not too many years ago. In many countries, where tourism has become a major export industry, the hospitality sector is the focal point for concepts of Globalisation to take root. Indeed, tourism has become the world's largest export industry, involving as it does enormous cross-border flows of people and capital.

The hospitality industry is thus at the very core of the Globalisation of international business. Hospitality companies therefore need to consider the implications of the global context in which they operate and must be prepared to address the questions that arise from this changing environment. The Globalisation of business and lifestyles is characterized by communicating over vast distances in foreign languages, frequent travel to overseas countries, dealing in many currencies, and coping with a variety of political and social systems, regulatory environments, cultures and customs. While these aspects of Globalisation are easy to identify, understanding the underlying current and future trends can be problematic. Analysis, however, reveals that a number of issues are reshaping the global hospitality industry. These are:

— International expansion with common product and brand position;

— Sales and marketing programs that fully capture global economies of scale;

— Organizational structures that allow global delivery of services with local operational control;

— Cross-border employee training to support operations; and

— Use of the world capital markets as sources of funding.

Those hospitality companies that believe that they can grow and retain a niche position without acknowledging the imperatives of Globalisation need to take another look. Put another way, most hospitality businesses will need to think "globally" if they are to survive. That goes for organizations competing in the mature European and U. S. markets, which are now seeing stiff competition from other parts of the world, especially Asia. The sheer size of the vast U. S. market, in particular, can promote an insular point of view, but hotel companies that concern themselves only with the dynamics of this domestic arena also need to hear the "wake up" call.

Globalisation will ultimately touch virtually all aspects of the hospitality industry. Increasingly, customers, management processes, employees, products, and sources of capital will be competed for and will move across national boundaries. Companies which are unprepared for this will be left behind. Local or regional entities may believe that Globalisation is not their concern.

Impacts of Hospitality Industry

Globalisation is a natural outgrowth of trends that have evolved during the past 50 years. International hotel chains were invented after World War II; they grew in the 1960s, and expanded greatly in the following two decades. Industry and economic trends in this decade have further propelled the growth of internationally-oriented hotel companies for a variety of reasons.

Severe overbuilding of hotel markets, particularly in the United States during the 1980s, halted new development almost entirely, while scarcity of growth and development opportunities in markets around the world has further supported the trend toward industry consolidation. Many companies committed to growth have found that opportunities in their back yards have been limited because of overbuilding, and they have been forced to look beyond mature domestic markets to offshore opportunities.

The pressures to expand beyond national boundaries have largely arisen from the need for growing hotel companies to reach 'critical mass'— the point at which a network of properties is sufficiently large to satisfy the travel needs of the hotel company's most valued customers. For different companies with varying products and locations, critical mass will vary in scope. A hotel organization, for example, may reach a point in which there is no other viable option than to expand across national boundaries if it wishes to grow, achieve critical mass and benefit from the economies of scale that accompany it.

If this is the case, leadership will need to recognize the imperative of organizing as a global company. As an example, consider an international hotel company that is well established in North America and Europe. In today's world market, company leadership may cast attention on the potential for moving into burgeoning Asia/Pacific markets to compete with established regional companies. Companies considering such strategic options can succeed against strong local and regional competitors only if they capitalize on the advantages derived from being a global company.

While the large international chains continue to expand on a global basis, there are in the United States a number of brand names that have yet to reach the critical mass required for marketing success. The need for hotel companies to achieve critical mass and the attendant economies of scale suggests that we will see a diminishing number of larger companies in the future as the imperatives of global expansion persist. Economies of scale are real, not imagined, and marketing on a global basis creates a significant competitive edge. It is certain that brands and products will be increasingly marketed on a truly global basis. Growth and development functions will thus become even more critical for those organizations that have not yet achieved critical mass.

For those companies pursuing a global strategy and accustomed to hotel management contracts, franchising relationships and non-recourse financing, significant adjustments will need to be made to the growth and development model. In a number of markets around the world, the bifurcation of ownership from management and management from marketing is a concept yet to achieve real maturity. The process that promotes these concepts is a slow one and global-minded companies will need to respond accordingly.

The differences in financing, owning, operating and marketing hotel properties will thus eventually narrow in a more global environment. The challenge for companies growing into markets where local partnerships and alliances are required for success will be to convince their foreign counterparts of the benefits of structures that have been successful in their home countries. A company going offshore with a business concept, however, cannot assume that it will be wholly accepted. Differences will gradually break down, but for the time being it may be necessary to adjust to local realities.

Hospitality customers increasingly seek predictable services that support their ability to move quickly and easily around the world. Indeed, the businesses and lifestyles of these multi-cultural travellers have themselves been shaped by Globalisation. The concept of projecting single brands globally is thus alluring, as well as being fully within the grasp of many hospitality companies. Nevertheless, there continues to be uncertainty about the benefits of establishing a single-brand presence in a global marketplace, in contrast to responding to the unique conditions at the local level. That challenge was addressed by an executive in another industry in the Economist Intelligence Unit study co-sponsored by Arthur Andersen — The Successful Corporation of the Year 2000. "We like to say we speak English with a Swedish accent, " says Goran Carstedt, president and CEO of IKEA North America. "I think global companies that understand how to organize and distribute their global competence to local needs will be the winners in the future. "

A number of international hotel companies have sought the economies of scale attendant to developing single brands and products, and providing them in a uniform fashion to as many markets around the globe as possible. A countervailing trend is that many people — both tourists and business travellers — seek the unique qualities and customs of an individual locale. In response, some international hotel companies have tried to reflect local culture in the way their hotels are designed and operated.

This is clearly an arena in which there is no one right answer, but rather a balance of complex factors required.

For example, there is a general consensus that "global travellers, " who travel frequently whether for business or recreation, usually prefer a uniform product, because they want the convenience and comfort of predictability, and they demand a high level of service. Those who travel less frequently, but have a fairly high level of sophistication may avoid such dominant global brand and product concepts. A third group is looking for what they are accustomed to, and are attracted by brands they are familiar with; in essence, they prefer to stay in environments that reflect their home-based experience.

Customer expectations are related to the level of the product, and hotel products at the lower end of the spectrum tend to be easier to standardize globally, in part because these properties are more clearly defined by physical attributes, which can be duplicated. At the upper end of the product quality spectrum, customers seek subtle differences in services and quality, which are not easily replicated.

Strategic Concept of Globalization

For the larger well-established international hotel companies that have circled the world in the quest for new opportunity, Globalisation has been a strategic concept for a number of years. International hotel companies have had to confront virtually all of the issues facing global enterprises — and in many cases more. Unlike a manufacturer with an overseas plant, for example, a hotel company must export its entire operating business to function in diverse cultural and geographic settings. Hotel companies must have the capability of establishing an entire business concept in dramatically different local environments.

As the new century approaches, formulating organizational structures that can integrate individual businesses in one seamless global structure will remain an on-going challenge. Information technology clearly is one major factor shaping the opportunities for how global hotel companies organize themselves, offering the ability to communicate with customers electronically and linking far-flung operations. It is also clear that global organizations also benefit by becoming flatter, in contrast to pyramid-shaped structures with strong central authority. Such decentralized organizations can narrow the distance between employers and employees, at the same time putting management and staff closer to the customer.

Organizational structures that are based on hierarchical systems with authority centralized at a headquarters location, as a result, may be increasingly obsolete because they distance management from the customer, while at the same time failing to empower line management and staff responsible for delivering services. Fortunately, "flatter" and more decentralized organizations are greatly facilitated by the increasing sophistication of technology and communications.

In addition, hotel company employees represent a melting pot of cultures, customs and languages, requiring new visioning and management skills to manage effectively, as well as a commitment to education and training that is unprecedented in its breadth. Today's hotel schools will need to increase their focus on issues that have to do with a global environment — communications, international marketing and law, history, social studies, geography and language. Company-wide training in a global organization to assure consistent leadership, operational skills and service delivery also represents a considerable challenge.

All of these factors suggest that companies expanding globally can benefit greatly by forming strategic alliances. A number of companies are moving towards such alliances with regional partners as a key strategy to provide entry to new and relatively unfamiliar markets and assure a higher level of local knowledge. Going it alone is increasingly expensive and frequently more risky. Substantial sums of money can be spent trying to conquer a region, and there may be considerable wisdom in forging alliances with local and regional partners. Foreign hotel groups have long found it difficult to establish a U. S. presence and distribution system, for example, and will probably need to enter into alliances, rather than establishing a new product from the ground up in an extremely competitive market.

At their best, alliances capitalize on the strengths of large, multinational corporations while drawing on the benefits that tend to accrue to smaller, more differentiated companies. Creating an integrated organization from such alliances presents a challenge, however. The overriding issue operationally is how best to maintain a firm, fixed center while encouraging flexibility and proactive approaches to local conditions. Also at issue is the choice of partner. Here, a shared operational philosophy and product/customer orientation are mandatory if the combined whole is to become bigger and more successful than the sum of the parts.

Operational Paradox

A recurrent issue for hotel companies in a global context is the need to develop global brands and image, while at the same time empowering management and staff closest to the customer in day-to-day operations. On the one hand, decentralized structures allow a hotel company to give authority to employees at the property level. Once the customer walks in the door, the service is controlled and delivered at the local level — with virtually no headquarters interface, even if those services have been centrally designed. But a key — and potentially controversial — question arises.

Customers want to be served locally in the hotels they patronize. But they want to make reservations and communicate electronically on the Internet — pointing to a bifurcation of the economies of scale possible in a global organization between marketing and operations. While operational issues must be dealt with locally, marketing is very much a corporate, chain-wide function that lends itself to realizing the benefits of global structures. As a result, it is possible that the economies of scale that can be achieved by a global organization may have less to do with operations — the running of a hotel — and much more to do with marketing.

Companies need to resolve this seeming paradox. They will need to secure a balanced position between these two objectives, which are potentially conflicting — decentralization for operational needs while taking advantage of global structures in the marketing arena. One might conclude that it will be marketing-driven organizations, especially franchisors with strong brand names, that are better able to capitalize on Globalisation and its communications benefits than those companies that persist in operating from a centralized base. For forward-looking companies, headquarters must be viewed not as a physical place but a dynamic function that exists either electronically or in person wherever it is needed. The "marketplace" has become the "marketspace".

Global Economy

As hospitality companies grow into the global economy, they will need to look to global capital markets for support. Investment capital, however, continues to be in short supply and this situation will continue for some time. Companies that wish to attract investors will need to demonstrate that they can offer better returns and performance than in the past. And, at least in the eyes of the world's financial markets, they will need to demonstrate their viability as companies in a global marketplace.

For the first time real estate is now being traded as a commodity in securities markets, and we can therefore expect hospitality products in the future to be viewed in the same manner. The securitization of real estate in the United States represents a significant trend, and it behooves savvy futurists to track these trends as they develop elsewhere in the world. Indeed, the world's financial markets are at the cutting edge of Globalisation, driven by the revolution in communications. With investment portfolios passed between the Americas, Europe and Asia/Pacific in a time continuum without interruption, 24-hour financial markets are here and are destined to impact significantly the way their customers use them.

Hospitality companies that seek capital from the public marketplace (a trend which is clearly going to continue and expand) will need to function as global enterprises. If the public markets on a global basis are going to serve corporations and produce optimum results, those public companies that feed into any or all of the three major financial centers of the world need to view themselves and to be viewed as global enterprises in order to benefit fully from what these markets have to offer.

Hospitality companies that want to trade in the financial markets will need a business concept that is relatively easy to communicate and comprehend. Those companies that provide homogeneity in products and market orientations will be the most attractive to global capital markets. Companies with simple and well-defined products such as Coca Cola have become recognized by customers and investors around the world. Hospitality companies that want to trade in the financial markets will need a business concept that is relatively easy to communicate and comprehend.

A truly global enterprise will have the ability to react quickly to market opportunities, no matter where they present themselves by applying business concepts that have been proven in the context of a global undertaking. Hotel companies expanding globally will also need to confront varying traditions, structures and attitudes to property investment and valuation in different countries. It is possible that there will be a more common set of standards in the future but we are still far from that level of standardization.

Capitalizing Hotel Organization

No hotel company operating today can be unaware of the swift pace of global change and its impact on every facet of the hospitality industry. With just five years left in this century, we can expect change to be the only constant. New business practices are evolving virtually as fast as our technologies, while resistance to change has become one of the primary causes of business failure. The specter of constant change raises fundamental questions as to the creation of shareholder wealth in a capital-constrained, highly competitive environment.

The future success of hotel organizations will be driven in large part by the ability to foresee — and capitalize — on change. Beyond this truism, however, there is an urgent need to identify what will be required in the competitive environment of the future with its intense focus on serving customer needs. The hospitality industry — as is the case with business generally — is subject to deep currents of change set in motion as economic and social systems shaped in the industrial era evolve to a knowledge-based era driven by technology advances.

Customers will have the strongest influence on the corporation in the year 2000. The customer will be "king" in the new century. A strategic planning focus is not only essential, but must embody a concept of planning for the future that anticipates change, rather than being based exclusively on historical models. In structuring organizations for the future, companies must build management capabilities to deal with one of the most critical challenges — diversity in the marketplace. Employing information technology to drive business success in this information-driven era is not only the path of least resistance, but vital to virtually every aspect of operations.

Customer Focus

Recognizing that the hotel industry has a somewhat split personality reflecting the inherent conflicts between its real estate and operational aspects, it is important to understand the industry's real estate origins and how they are shaping the challenges ahead. The origins of the industry's real estate persona are embodied in the classic theory of location - "if we build it, they will come. " As a result of this "building" complex, the industry has tended to have a real estate and asset orientation, rather than a customer focus. From the hotel company perspective — especially that of the brand-oriented "chain" — the varied interests of a diffused property ownership group can be quite different than the singular interest of the chain that operates and markets the properties.

Even when the ownership of geographically dispersed hotel properties is controlled by a single hotel organization, the financial structuring tends to be property-specific. Corporate financial strategies are frequently subjugated to the needs of the last property deal brought into the company's fold. Each property in a so-called "chain, " is frequently the subject of a unique and distinctive ownership and financial structure. This phenomenon — quite common in the real estate sector, but unusual for business enterprises generally — makes for elusive economies of scale in the structuring and financing of property-driven expansion.

Collectively, these factors have produced low comparative returns in real estate, although criticism levelled at commercial real estate returns is somewhat less germane to the hotel industry, where management and franchise fees can produce high returns for those companies where property ownership is held by third parties. Nevertheless, average returns in the real estate industry in the United States, for example, are just over 10 percent, compared to small company stock returns at almost 20 percent and large company stocks at an average of about 15 percent.

While hotel chains have adopted traditional corporate frameworks, there are a number of predominantly real estate-driven, family-owned businesses in the hotel sector that continue to operate as relatively unstructured organizations. In meeting the future, these businesses will need plans, people and processes in order to establish viable corporate forms that can compete in tomorrow's marketplace and capitalize upon its opportunities. In today's changed environment, the hotel organization must deal with a number of new realities.

Investors in our industry are no longer satisfied with long-term capital appreciation and psychic income that heretofore were often the justification for otherwise seemingly uneconomic investments in hotel property or, indeed, hotel chains. The first reality is that there is a very specific and identifiable relationship between bottom line performance and value. Improvements in business operations raises values. It is not surprising, therefore, that the new owners attracted to this industry in recent years have new sets of demands. This transformation from an old-guard group of investors and owners to income and return-driven newcomers has meant that the once "quiet enjoyment" of operators in their management of hotels for third parties is being disturbed, interrupted and overturned.

These challenges all take place in an environment where capital has become extremely selective in markets that have little stability. A global shortage of capital will not remain a short-term problem, and future hotel organizations must have a stronger alignment to capital providers — a critical "customer" group. Hotel companies will need to compete by offering better returns and performance than in the past. Hotel chains have found their development timetables quashed in recent years, making it difficult to achieve goals of critical mass often required to improve performance. These factors are driving consolidation in the brand "sweepstakes. " Capital markets, therefore, continue to favour well-established companies, a reality that must drive entrepreneurial organizations to meet the future now by planning for an evolving corporate context in which to operate.

Look Forward Factors

Hotel developers, owners and management companies will all need to develop new strategies, skills and processes that look forward to the competitive demands of the future. These ultimately must address issues related to vision and planning, as well as organizational skill sets and processes to attract and retain customers. To stake a claim in the future, current business practices should be examined in light of what can be expected to be the key success factors in the year 2000.

Embrace a global change orientation: As the information age produces greater worldwide integration of business activities, a global knowledge base will become invaluable. Success in local and regional hotel markets will be shaped decisively by a global business environment that defines capital movement, customer expectations and applications of new technologies.

Focus on the Customer: If the customer is "king" in the 21st century, hotel organizations will be best served by focusing less on their hotel assets as measures of success, and more on their customers.

This involves a fundamental shift in viewing the real estate asset as the wealth creator — to the customer as the key to building shareholder wealth. A customer focus must imbue business decisions at all levels of developing and operating a hotel organization. Pursuing such a course will inevitably impact shareholder wealth. To accomplish this, however, customers need to participate in the product development process. Fully realizing a customer focus in the industry poses a significant challenge. The hotel industry must confront problems due to conflicts between operational needs and real estate goals.

Quite simply, an operator must remain customer-focused, but the short-term strategies to meet these needs may be inconsistent with the long-term objectives of property owners. Balancing those goals will be essential. A customer focus implies a significant shift in what drives hotel development — placing primary emphasis on the customer with the locations to follow. Nevertheless, a hotel organization with its large investment in fixed assets — the real estate — can never be as nimble as a consumer products company in adjusting products and services to match rapid shifts in the marketplace.

The Japanese taught us that the concept of "zero defects" in products and services can yield tremendous benefits. But today an even more rigorous standard dominates — quality that surprises. In practical terms, the hotel industry finds it extremely difficult to meet the standard of zero defects in service. Hotel services are based primarily on people, not computers or other equipment. Quality that surprises takes the concept of zero defects a step further. Yesterday's surprising product or service is today's status quo. Twenty years ago, a business executive did not expect a consistent and predictable level of service wherever he or she travelled in the world. Today that is a standard — not the exception — as is the expectation for sophisticated technology in hotel rooms to support business needs. With customer discrimination so acute, it is not surprising that brand loyalty is a diminishing "commodity" in the hotel industry.

Find the ingredients for visionary leadership. Today's hotel organizations need to recognize the need for visionary leadership. The ability to forecast the future — to anticipate change rather than react to it — will be one of the single greatest determinants of market dominance in the years ahead. The old "command and control" model of leadership is giving way to a focus on leadership in ideas, information, inspiration, vision and teamwork. Warren Bennis, an authority on leadership in the U. S., puts it this way — "For the most part, failing organizations tend to be over-managed and under-led. The leader sets the tone for the moral character, the vision, the corporate culture and the fiber of the institution. "

While visionary leadership is essential, it must be linked to business operations and foster a risk bias, rather than a procedural bias. This will allow the organization to stretch and, in turn, change. And it must be shared by empowered professionals and staff throughout the organization, including those who meet the customer. Overcoming the resistance to change can be a daunting task, particularly in large hotel organizations in which diversions from the status quo may threaten established management lines. It suggests that a culture based on conformance may need to be replaced by an emphasis on flexibility, learning and cooperation. Management competencies will need to be aligned in order to achieve the desired result. For many organizations, this may mean a shift from traditional hierarchies typical of companies in an industrial era to a flatter organization with a more transparent interface between leadership, organizational functions and employees.

Create a defensible position through corporate strategy: For many of the industry's leaders, vision is driven by the strategic planning process, a function which has become critical for success.

Strategic planning, however, has at times been a step-child in the hotel industry, and it is often the first to be cut when organizations are down sized. It is clearly in transition. There also has been a tendency to decentralize and simplify this function — both actions of potential benefit. Strategic planning must be led by the top people in the organization — the CEO and COO. On the other hand, it should be close enough to the customer to ensure that planners can "listen" to and be influenced by customer needs.

Empower Management: Beyond the ability to envision the future, core management capabilities will make the difference — they are essential. A clear vision without the management skills to support it cannot be a recipe for success. First and foremost, hotel management must have strategic development skills and the ability to integrate complex factors affecting success. Market volatility has become the norm, in part caused by the rapidly changing tastes of customers. Customers are increasingly approaching the hotel industry with widely different social, economic and political backgrounds, to say nothing of employees. Being able to deal with these diversities in a positive and constructive fashion that capitalizes on the differences, rather than working to find ways to mitigate them, is the clear path for successful management in the future.

The organization will also need to be imbued with a sense of entrepreneurship that reacts proactively to the market's diversity. Traditional organizations that follow well-documented rules must give way to leaders who can balance a sense of discipline with that of flexibility. Talent and resources must be marshaled and leveraged. In an industry with high fixed costs and labour intensity, the concept of leverage in the hotel business is an all-important one. Improving labour productivity through technology must be a goal for today's forward-looking hotel organization. Management must also be able to narrow the gap between the employer and the employee, forcing a flatter organization in the process. This will put management closer to the customer and speed the two-way communication process up and down the organization.

Be in the information fast lane: The traditional role of information technology (IT) as a back office support for accounting and bookkeeping has clearly moved front and center stage. IT today influences all aspects of business from corporate strategies to organizational structure — and from the very business processes it is designed to support to performance measurement. In a world where the customer is "king, " IT must also deliver in two critical areas: sales and marketing and customer service.

Technology was once viewed as a way to reduce costs by replacing people. That attitude has been firmly supplanted by one that seeks IT support for the creative work that all organizations must pursue. IT must allow organizations to react more speedily to market needs and, of course, produce the fulfillment of customer demands both quickly and accurately. To do this IT must operate on a decentralized basis. IT delivers, but it has to be the right information to the right people, and it needs to be done on a timely basis.

Hospitality in Next Millennium

The hospitality industry will find itself in a competitive landscape that is greatly altered by new technologies, business practices and consumer demands. Indeed, this decade stands as a bridge between the socioeconomic forces that shaped the Industrial Age and the emerging capabilities and markets of the Information Age. There is thus a pressing need for executives leading the hospitality industry into the next century to define how their companies can marshal change in support of competitive advantage.

Customer

The Hospitality 2000 study sends a clear signal that the industry will need to shift its primary focus in the future from the physical assets (the hotels it owns and manages) to the industry's virtual assets (its customers). And this view is by no means supported by just a slim majority - it is held by industry executives around the world by a margin of five to one.

If this shift in focus from assets to customers does in fact take place, it will clearly drive great change in our industry, with broad implications for every aspect of the hospitality business. The traditional "marketplace" (our destinations, neighbourhoods and hotel buildings) will be greatly expanded to incorporate virtual, customer-focused activities to be known as the "marketspace" a completely reconfigured market context and environment that will allow for the delivery of an array of products and services, some traditional, others less so. For those responsible for marketing success in the future, this shift has two important implications.

From Revpar to Revpac: Currently, revenue per available room (known to industry insiders as REVPAR) is a widely accepted metric for hotel success, reflecting the yield from physical assets (the occupancy and pricing of the guest room). As the customer more clearly becomes the strategic focus, the industry will find that REVPAC (revenue per available customer) will become a key measure of performance.

From Central Reservations to Customer Information: CRS Becomes CIS -Understanding emerging customer needs will be pivotal to the success of hotel organizations. Industry executives indicate that usage and access to global distribution systems (GDS) will be an important strategy in the future. But there will also be a need to integrate data generated at the property level with reservations systems and corporate information in a total system solution that provides for data warehouses and networked communications. Technology thus supports the shift from a primary focus on reserving the physical room, to better understanding and serving a broad array of customer wants and needs.

In this period of global transition, it behooves hotel organizations to examine the key factors that will not only define success, but the ability to survive in coming years. The Successful Corporation of the Year 2000 surveyed more than 600 senior executives around the world. Its mission was to identify the characteristics needed to lead successful businesses in the next century. These executives offer a number of compelling messages regarding the key success factors of the future.

Market

As the hospitality industry considers its future beyond the year 2000, we can be assured of continuing change in the marketplace, although executives surveyed globally varied widely in their views. The study highlights differences among respondents based in the Americas, Asia/Pacific and EMEIA (Europe, the Middle East, India and Africa).

Demographic and Lifestyle Factors: Not surprisingly, lifestyle and demographic changes are likely to have dramatic impact on the market trends of the future, but regional differences revealed in the Hospitality 2000 study abound. The Globalisation of world business and lifestyles -and the growing number of international travellers - will be major forces in marketing hospitality products in the year 2000 and beyond. Indeed, executives surveyed in Hospitality 2000 cite international travellers as the most important lifestyle change for the hospitality industry. But the focus on international travellers is most important in Asia/Pacific, according to respondents.

Leisure and Business Travel: Most executives surveyed, regardless of geographic location, believe leisure travel will significantly outperform the business travel segment in the future. However, the study reveals major global differences in perceptions of growth. Asia/Pacific respondents by a margin of 10 to one forecast that leisure travel, rather than business travel, will show the greatest increase in the future. While leisure and business travel are expected to achieve growth, the meetings market - including associations, corporate, and social groups - is not forecast to grow and may even experience a slight decline in demand. Planners of convention centers and convention hotels, therefore, need to carefully consider the implications of these findings.

Customer Purchase Decisions: Reflecting the conventional "locational "bias in the real estate industry, virtually all respondents indicate that location will continue to be the most important influence on the customer's purchase decision, followed by service quality. While less than two-thirds of the respondents indicate that brand affiliation is a strong influence on the purchase decision, 83 percent acknowledge that business travellers will prefer branded products in the future and only two-thirds believe the same about leisure travellers an ambivalence that will undoubtedly be brought into greater focus and reconciled as Globalisation continues and branding becomes more prevalent in all types of business.

As to frequent traveler programs - the bane of some companies' marketing existence - only 60 percent of our respondents put much stock in such programs as significant influencers of the buying decision. This is driven quite probably by the fad that these programs are more valuable to the limited number of chains and their customers where there are extensive property networks and customer-tracking systems in place.

Future Marketing Strategies: Essential to marketing strategies is information about guest wants and needs. And yet an overwhelming number of respondents, 93 percent, indicate that they rely on the traditional in-room guest comment card approach to tracking guest satisfaction, a system fraught with weakness principally associated with lack of control and poor response rates from those customers who actually have something important to say. It is encouraging to note that the industry's leadership expects to rely more heavily on third-party market research and focus groups as a means of assessing guest needs and satisfaction in the future. Three key marketing approaches: increased use of global distribution systems, linking hotel reservation systems to airline and travel agency networks; enhanced yield management techniques; and service improvements designed to increase guest satisfaction.

Growth Strategies: Of the growth strategies ranked by executives, strategic alliances topped the list, followed by mergers and acquisitions. Joint ventures, franchising, and management contracts followed in importance. Not surprisingly, new development the most capital-intensive and time-consuming of the growth strategies - is at the bottom of the list in the Americas.

Product

Decisions about hotel products must be seen through the lens of changing customer demands - current and future - with an understanding that they are the primary assets of a hotel organization. The adage -"build it and they will come" no longer applies. Consistent with this philosophy are key findings related to forces driving the building of brand equity. The two major forces cited are:

— The need to increase market share by those companies seeking critical mass; and

— The importance of adapting products to meet the evolving needs of the market due to changing lifestyles and demographics.

As a result of rising customer expectations and the increasing needs of business travellers who wish to take their offices with them when they travel we can expect new product innovations within the guest room, particularly in the area of technology. Eighty percent of industry executives recognize that increased capital will need to be spent on technology upgrades in the hotel room. Anecdotally, however, there seems to be some ambivalence as to whether business travellers want their office setups in the room or downstairs in the more sociable atmosphere of the business center.

Food for Thought: Historically, food and beverage operations have contributed significantly to the industry's revenues, and yet they have also been viewed with mixed feelings by the hoteliers responsible for delivering the profits. The conventional wisdom has frequently been that "the real money is in the rooms. " Supporting this view is the strong preference expressed by our respondents for leasing food and beverage facilities to third-party operators in the future. Themed restaurants are also popular among respondents, reflecting the continuing convergence of the entertainment and hospitality industries. This is a trend of great significance and one that truly responds to the customers' focus on collecting experiences as much as material goods.

Global Chains Dominate: Given the importance of branding, it is not surprising that the Hospitality 2000 findings suggest that franchising will play a significant role in the future of this industry. Both consumer and investor preference for branded hospitality companies will continue to drive the growth of franchising. And, two-thirds of those polled furthermore believe that the franchising side of our industry will become dominated by a few multi-branded conglomerates relying on international growth. But for management companies, there was tough news. Ninety percent of our respondents foresee management fees driven by profits as opposed to revenues, and a future in which the term of management agreements will tend to be shorter.

Organization

In the future, a customer focus (both internal and external) will imbue business decisions at all levels of the hospitality organization. Global hotel chains as growing the fastest in the future. While change is occurring at an unprecedented rate, the Hospitality 2000 survey results indicate that visioning for the future is not always on the minds of many of the industry's executives. Close to one in four respondents reveal that they do not have a long-range plan in hand. Of those that do, there is quite a wide range in how far ahead our industry's leadership is prepared to forecast and plan.

As the hospitality industry changes, recruitment of skilled management will be critical. Eight out of ten industry executives agree that the ability to recruit experienced management personnel will be an important human resource challenge. Industry executives are also concerned with the availability of skilled employees and the adequacy of a hospitality education.

The hospitality industry moves into the knowledge-based era of the next millennium, hierarchical and matrix-like structures will need to give way to flat, flexible learning organizations that look to the market for guidance, take risks and balance analysis with creativity. Those organizations that pursue such courses will clearly be better able to compete in a customer-focused marketspace.

Capital

If current trends are anything to go by, the competition for capital is likely to increase steadily in the future. In response, hospitality companies will need to focus on enhancing shareholder wealth and producing satisfactory returns. As hospitality companies expand into the global economy, they will need to seek investment capital outside of the local or traditional framework. The majority of responding executives will be looking to public markets and institutional investors to provide the capital for the industry's future growth. Other prominent sources are expected to be foreign investors and the pension fund community - long sought after as a result of its huge capital base. Whether the pension funds can overcome their traditional ambivalence about real estate generally and their sharp views about the complexity of the hotel 'business" remains to be seen. But on the public markets front, the actual evidence is clear. Securitization of the hotel industry is well underway, at least in the United States, and is likely to continue to expand in the future.

Influences of Technology

The 21st century will bring the era of the fully-automated hotel, connecting the customer to a universe of diverse products and services offered by an array of providers. Technology will provide the opportunity to improve the delivery of products and services. However, many people state that technology cannot replace the human element in delivering quality service. Clearly, technology is widely viewed as a means to enhance and facilitate service, but not as an alternative to providing quality service.

While there has been speculation that technological innovation may reduce business travel. Our respondents are clearly split on the question of whether technological innovation such as video conferencing and the Internet will contribute to a decline in business travel. While over one-half explicitly disagree with such a view, close to one-quarter do not take a position one way or the other. The remaining respondents agree that technology will cause some decline in business-related travel.

Opportunities in Lodging Industry

Fast paced change in the lodging industry requires a

constant look to the future to identify new business opportunities. Big profits have been made in recent years by those with the foresight to anticipate and capitalize on trends in their early stages of development. Here explain a variety of current and future industry trends, focusing on those that may trigger new ideas for innovation in the lodging industry.

Trends to Watch in the Lodging Industry

— Aging Baby Boomers

— Institutionalization of Hotel Ownership

— Globalisation of Businesses

— New Developments in Telecommunications and Technology

— Shifting Economic Cycle

The following factor will have tremendous influence on the lodging industry in the near term and may be the foundation for innovation and future business opportunities.

Aging "Baby Boomers"

The baby boom generation represents approximately 78 million individuals who, sometime within the next decade, will move into the "over 50" age category. Just about every major U. S. industry, has focused on this trend. For example, the housing and health care industries have developed real estate products, such as retirement lifestyle communities vacation home communities, empty-nester communities and assisted care facilities targeting both active and non-active seniors. While some hotel chains have geared marketing campaigns toward the aging baby boomers, the lodging industry has yet to create a brand segment to this group.

Institutionalization of Hotel Ownership

The buying binge that has been occurring recently in the lodging industry has left large concentrations of hotel assets in the hands of relatively few major portfolio investors. Several new industry giants have emerged with portfolios valued well in excess of $1 billion. This new breed of owners consists of large, well capitalized hotel companies, REITs, pension funds, and investment funds. These entities are developing sophisticated asset management capabilities and expertise in capital markets and financial management. They are also expanding uses of technology and bringing "real estate" business savvy to investment decision - making.

The "bigger is better" philosophy has taken hold as a result of the desires to diversify risk rap economies of scale, and achieve overall lower costs of capital. Further consolidation will continue, and innovative service providers and deal makers can reap significant benefits by meeting the capital and service needs of these of these new giants.

Globalization of Business

Globalisation of businesses and economies is a trend that has taken hold in the 1990s and will continue for many years to come. With this trend comes increased international travel and corporate desires to expand globally and create worldwide brand identities. Many countries now embrace the concepts of democracy and free enterprise and welcome foreign investment. These conditions bode well for increased cross-border investments and global expansion in the lodging industry. Concentrating on hugely underdeveloped consumer and travel markets, such as Latin America, Southeast Asia, and China could mean big opportunities for hotel investors and hotel chains seeking opportunities for brand expansion.

New Developments in Telecommunications and Technology

The age of "the net" is upon us. Sweeping changes are occurring in telecommunication technology and regulation. Mainline businesses and consumers are logging on enmasse to the internet. These developments have significant implications for the lodging industry, both positive and negative. On the negative side, desktop video conferencing is becoming a realty which, in theory, could reduce the need for out-of-town business meetings. On the positive side, hotel companies can use the Internet to reach consumers more directly - effectively by-passing travel trade intermediaries. This could deepen the "brand lock" hotel companies now have on consumers. Use of the Internet - and technology in general - is a must for hotel companies wanting to stay ahead of the competition and realize big profit gains.

Shifting Economic Cycle

Hotel occupancies and room rates throughout the U. S. are reaching all time highs. Property values within most lodging segments are coming closer in sync with property replacement costs. Institutional portfolio investors are buying properties competitively, using cheap sources of capital. Economists cannot agree on whether inflation or recession is lurking around the corner. After experiencing four solid years of recovery, the growth cycle in the lodging industry is likely to flatten over the next two years, or even dip a bit beyond that - depending on what happens with new construction and interest rates. The story of big gains through property turnaround may be over for the near term, and high-yield investors will likely get out of hotel investments. Investors looking for more stable and predictable returns, particularly large institutional investors, will continue to buy hotels. Tax reform could also affect the current cycle, depending on what happens with capital gains rates and the 'flat tax' proposal.

Customer Loyalty Systems

The global hospitality industry in the new economy of the 21st century indicate that customer ownership will be the key to securing and maintaining competitive advantage. These megatrends, including consolidation, convergence, the cyclical nature of the industry, the efficient use of real estate, distribution systems, knowledge, outsourcing of non-core competencies, technology, and branding will have a profound influence on the day-to-day operations and long-term strategic direction in the hospitality and leisure industry in the coming decades.

Worldwide Partner in Charge, Hospitality and Leisure Services, Arthur Andersen, "Globalisation is rapidly eliminating boundaries and borders; the rapid proliferation of technology is redefining the meaning of time and space as we know it. The result is the customer is empowered like never before. If the industry does not stay ahead of the curve and remain close to its customers, it faces the prospect of disintermediation as their service becomes increasingly commoditized through the proliferation of electronic commerce. "

Relationship management is the key to securing a stable customer base, but this is only possible through a deep understanding of customer needs and preferences. Hospitality and leisure companies should invest in three key strategy areas.

Customer Relationship Management: The business realities emerging with the New Economy drive the need for greater awareness in several aspects of customer ownership. To be successful and dynamic, leading edge hospitality companies will not give away markdowns unnecessarily, identify the most valuable customers, optimize promotions/advertising effectiveness via stealth one-to-one communication, ensure retention of valuable customers through targeted campaigns, and gain share-of-wallet by better understanding their customers.

Knowledge Management: Consistent with the drive to secure a greater share of the customer, the industry must actively seek ways to harness relevant knowledge from its guests, suppliers, employees and competitors. For the majority of hotels, ERP platforms currently in place are out of date and not integrated into customer data and guest satisfaction databases. There is also a need for the industry to begin to benchmark its performance in order to advance and evolve a universally recognized best practices operating standard.

Outsourcing Non-core Competencies: Increasingly, this is a key trend that extends beyond laundry and valet parking. A more significant area of operations is draining revenue from the bottom line – the finance and accounting function. Arthur Andersen research reveals that finance and accounting processes at the average hotel are running at more than two percent of revenue. This is more than double the best practice standards in a number of other industries. Less emphasis on non-critical functions will give hoteliers more time to focus on brand-building activities and satisfying their customers.

Global Importance of Tourism

Travel & Tourism takes many different forms - from a trip only a few hours away from home to long distance travel overseas. A common belief is that most Travel & Tourism involves large numbers of visitors from developed countries travelling by air to destinations in emerging countries. In fact, in most countries, the domestic tourism market is larger than the inbound market. Of course, the social and cultural impact of inbound visitors is often greater than that of domestic tourists.

Travel & Tourism has a number of advantages over other industry sectors:

— it creates jobs and wealth whilst;

— at the same time, it can contribute to sustainable development;

— it tends to have low start-up costs;

— is a viable option in a wide range of areas and regions;

— is likely to continue to grow for the foreseeable future; and

— the industry is, in a large part, aware of the need to protect the resource on which it is based - local culture and built and natural environment - and it is committed to these resources' preservation and enhancement.

Whether tourism is domestic or international, it involves visiting a destination away from the area in which one lives and using the services available in that destination. Therefore, tourists' requirements are for travel services to reach their destinations and once there, for services such as shelter, water, food, sanitation and entertainment. What makes tourism special is that, many of these different products and services are often supplied by different operators: usually small or medium sized businesses in local ownership. This makes tourism a highly fragmented and diverse industry and so co-ordinated, industry-wide action is difficult to achieve.

The influence of Travel & Tourism's demand also extends far beyond traditional tourism companies, into upstream suppliers like aircraft manufacturers or food producers and into the downstream service providers for travellers, like retail shops. Despite the difficulties caused by fragmentation and lengthy supply chains, there has been a steady growth in environmental good practice across the industry in recent years. There are examples of - airlines and airports reducing pollution and noise impacts; cruise liners practising marine conservation; hotels implementing energy consumption and waste disposal programs; car rental companies investing in increasingly fuel efficient fleets and railways sound proofing to dampen noise. The result is that there are a number of excellent initiatives in place designed to improve the environmental management of Travel & Tourism businesses. Of course, more needs to be done.

Solutions

Providing Leadership: WTTC with 105 members is the global business leaders' forum for the Travel & Tourism industry. The WTTC have set in place an extensive strategy to promote a culture of sustainable development and have put in place a three-tiered structure for its achievement. This involves:

Policy: In 1996 the WTTC, the World Tourism Organization and the Earth Council, joined together to launch an action plan entitled "Agenda 21 for the Travel & Tourism Industry:

Environmentally Sustainable Development" - a sectional sustainable development program based on the results of the Rio Earth Summit in 1992. Since the launch of the document, the three organisations have begun a series of regional seminars to increase awareness of the conclusions, and to adapt the program for local implementation. The program has held regional seminars in London and Jakarta in 1997 and Victoria Falls and Dominica in 1998.

WTTC has recently introduced a major addition to the program – the "Alliance for Sustainable Tourism", which invites public and private sector Travel & Tourism organisations to record their Agenda 21 based activities on a central web site and commit to co-operation with all other partners. In order to develop the program from global principles to community based action, WTTC is also discussing with the International Council for Local Environment Initiatives (ICLEI) on how the principles of "Agenda 21 for Travel & Tourism" can be built into Local Agenda 21 programs. Furthermore, WTTC is considering pilot projects in 5 cities around the world to serve as models for other destinations.

Practice: In 1994, WTTC initiated the "GREEN GLOBE", an Agenda 21 based industry improvement program, which provides guidance material and a certification process linked to both ISO standards and Agenda 21 principles. There are now 500 "GREEN GLOBE " members in 100 countries dedicated to improving environmental practice. The first certification has commenced with hotels groups in Jamaica and Manchester (UK). "GREEN GLOBE" has also developed a specific Destination Program, which provides a methodology for Travel & Tourism destinations to implement sustainable development.

The ultimate aim is that "GREEN GLOBE" will become the primary global standard of environmental commitment by the global Travel & Tourism industry and will be recognised by the public as such. Currently, "GREEN GLOBE" has the support of over 20 international industry organisations representing thousands of businesses world-wide and the support of the World Tourism Organization, the United Nations Environment Program and the Earth Council.

Information: WTTC have also developed "ECoNETT", a web-site containing advice and data on good practice and sources of help and advice. "ECoNETT" is increasingly recognised as a focal point for environmental information, good practice, new techniques and technologies.

International Hotel & Restaurant Association (IH&RA)

The International Hotel & Restaurant Association (IH&RA), based in Paris, represents over 700,000 establishments in more than 150 countries. Its membership comprises some 50 national and international hotel and restaurant chains, over 110 national hotel and restaurant associations, independent hotel operators and restaurateurs, industry suppliers and 130 hotel schools. The IH&RA has offices in

Asia-Pacific and Latin America. It is also the voice of the world's hotels and restaurants and plays a global role in representing, protecting, promoting and informing the industry to enable its members to achieve their business objectives.

The IH&RA has:

— raised environmental awareness and developed programs through joint workshops withnational hotel associations and regularly encourages them to develop their own environmental awareness programs;

— established an annual Environmental Award sponsored by American Express and judged by the United Nations Environment Program (UNEP) that recognises efforts by independent and chain hotels to "green" the industry;

— published advice including practical publications such as the "Environmental Action Pack for Hotels" with the International Hotel Environment Initiative and UNEP and "Environmental Good Practice in Hotels" with UNEP;

— supported regional initiatives such as the Caribbean Action for Sustainable Tourism; and · joined forces with UNEP and the International Hotel School Directors' Association to develop an "Environmental Teaching Resource Package for Hospitality Educational Institutes".

Corporate Initiatives: The International Hotel Environment Initiative (IHEI), based in London, England, is a program of The Prince of Wales Business Leaders Forum. Founded in 1992 by a consortium of chief executives from 10 multinational hotel groups, IHEI is an educational charity designed to encourage continuous improvement in the environmental performance of the global hotel industry. It does this through:

— raising environmental awareness in the hotel industry by promoting good practice internationally;

— developing hotel-specific guidance, enabling hotels of all sizes to implement environmental programs; and
— multiplying the reach and impact of IHEI by working with partners, including hotel associations, governments, NGOs, tourism bodies and businesses.

IHEI is a catalyst and conduit for hotels to pool their resources and to share experience via a noncompetitive platform. In 5 years it has evolved into an organisation with global impact. IHEI has worked in 111 countries, stimulating and assisting with the establishment of local initiatives such as New Zealand's "Environmental Hotels of Auckland, the Asia Pacific Hotel Environment Initiative" and the Caribbean Action for Sustainable Tourism. Member hotels now represent over 1 million guest rooms and more than 8,000 hotels on 5 continents.

The Co-operative Research Centre for Sustainable Tourism, based in Australia, was established in 1997 to enhance the strategic knowledge available to the Travel & Tourism industry through:

— long-term high-quality scientific and technological research which contributes to the development of an internationally competitive tourism industry;
— strengthening the links between research and its commercial and other applications;
— promoting co-operative research; and
— stimulating education and training, particularly in graduate programs, through active involvement of researchers from outside the higher education system in educational activities, and of graduate students in major research programs.

In addition to individual projects implemented at each of the 26 hotels, the goals set for the chain as a whole were ambitious: (I) to reduce the amount of waste sent to landfill by 50% across the chain, by launching an extensive recycling program; (ii) to redesign purchasing policies to ensure that waste is reduced at source, and supplies used in the hotels are nature friendly.

The Caribbean Action For Sustainable Tourism (CAST) is an alliance for sustainable growth developed by the Caribbean Hoteliers Association with the support of the WTTC, the IHEI and the Caribbean Tourism Organisation. CAST has developed workshops, training courses and guidance material for its members on a wide range of environmental issues, including:

— setting up environmental management systems;

— energy efficiency;

— renewable energy; and

— waste water management.

Agents and Partnerships for Change

The public sectors, particularly national and local government, have an important role to play by setting the agenda and providing the framework in which action should take place. The regulatory environment also plays an important role in creating the conditions suitable for sustainable tourism. Self-regulation involving the agreement and co-operation of industry is always likely to be the most effective solution. Therefore, the role of trade associations and industry organisations in distributing information among their members and encouraging participation is essential.

The major partnerships to be formed are between:

— industry and the public sector - to ensure consistency with the framework;

— industry and the voluntary sector - to tap into the enormous resources of expertise and good will that this sector is able to generate; and

— industry and the public - both travellers themselves and the people who live in the places they visit to develop more sustainable forms of tourism.

Areas for further action

The industry is already doing much to improve its performance in terms of sustainable development. The challenge for the new millennium is to move from the existing ad hoc approach to a more systematic one. To do this will involve a partnership between industry and national governments to deliver the following:

1) Governments:

— Integration of travel and tourism policy into broader government policies, especially the environment;

— Incentives for the Travel & Tourism industry, backed up where necessary by effective regulation.

2) Public/Private partnership:

— Infrastructure planned and developed with a long-term view and within a reference framework;

— Indicators and environmental impact assessment tools to enable effective local management and appropriate development.

3) International bodies:

— Co-ordination at an international level of environmental action undertaken by all sectors of the Travel & Tourism industry;

— Review of existing voluntary initiatives to improve the quality of reporting, their transparency and credibility, and the assessment of their contribution to sustainability.

4) Companies:

— Commitment to place sustainable development issues at the core of the management structure;

— Innovation of process and application through new technology;

— Commitment to education and environmental training of staff.

Influencing Consumer Behaviour to Promote Sustainable Tourism

At the 1998 World Travel Market, WTTC hosted, as a part of its Environmental Awareness Day, a seminar entitled "Does the Consumer Care?" At this event, MORI presented the latest findings from their Business and the Environment survey - an annual UK survey devoted to public attitudes to theenvironment. The survey is now in its tenth year and illustrates the challenge facing the Travel & Tourism industry in influencing consumer behaviour to promote sustainable tourism.

Here, Travel & Tourism is now more associated with environmental damage than it has been in the past. Despite this decline in perception, the industry's economic success is not dependent on its green record - public sensitivity to environmental problems on holiday/business trips has not increased and is no more of a deterrent to repeat travel than it was previously.

There is a downward trend in the public's willingness to pay extra for environmental protection and environmentally friendly products, including "green" Travel & Tourism. Awareness of companies making environmental commitments is only marginally up. Therefore, the challenge is to persuade the consumer that it is in their interests to adopt and promote a sustainable approach in their activities and purchasing decisions. Education programs and the development and widespread acceptance of codes of conduct are useful tools in achieving this step. Once this message has been conveyed, it is then important to back this up with the necessary information to enable consumers to make informed choices. It is here that "ecolabels" and award programs have value.

Solutions

Education programs: The Foundation for Environmental Education in Europe (FEEE) seeks to promote environmental education by carrying out campaigns and improving awareness of the importance of environmental education. It is composed of a network of international organisations. The FEEE (headquarters in Denmark) runs three major campaigns in Europe for providing safe and clean beaches and marinas.

The award itself is given annually to beaches and marinas that satisfy a number of essential criteria in three separate areas: water quality; beach management and safety; and environmental information and education.

GREEN GLOBE s Dodo Campaign, is based on a cartoon character, who features in 65 Travel & Tourism videos. Dodo explains and promotes the actions that visitors can take to reduce the impacts of their travels. The videos are aimed at children and are designed to be fun, whilst conveying important messages about sustainable Travel & Tourism. The aim is to have these videos shown on inflight and in-room television channels to raise awareness and influence consumer behaviour.

Codes of conduct: Codes of conduct are also used to try and influence consumer behaviour. For example,"Guidelines for Responsible Environmental Tourism" are prepared and distributed by the American Society of Travel Agents to all customers who book holidays through their members' branches. The Guidelines aim to "encourage the growth of peaceful tourism and environmentally responsible travel" and include 10 recommendations to encourage tourists to act responsibly and show respect for their hosts and the environment of their destination(s).

The Pacific Asia Tourism Association (PATA) : is an industrial association, which promotes the Pacific Asia area's Travel & Tourism destinations, products and services.

PATA also serves as a central resource of information and research, travel industry education and training, as well as quality product development with sensitivity for culture, heritage and environment. In 1992, PATA introduced its "Code for Environmentally Responsible Tourism" to strengthen the principles of preservation in the region. Businesses, organisations and individuals wishing to affirm their support for the PATA Code are encouraged to participate in the PATA Green Leaf program.

The Africa Travel Association has produced "Responsible Traveller Guidelines"; the Japanese Association of Travel Agents has produced the "Declaration of Earth Friendly Travellers" and there are many more examples of industry codes aimed at educating and influencing their customers.

Eco labelling: There are numerous examples of industry sponsored labelling schemes, whose aim is to recognise good industry practice and influence consumer behaviour into purchasing the labelled products. For example, the "Green Key, Denmark" certificate operated by the Hotel, Restaurant and Leisure Industry Association (HORESTA) has 56 criteria that includes environmental information, water & energy consumption and waste management. Special features also include ecological food products, outdoor areas, non-smoking rooms, and adaptations for access by disabled persons.

Awards: There are a number of industries that runs and sponsors award programs to highlight and promote examples of good practice. For example, British Airways has run the "Tourism for Tomorrow" awards since 1992 to encourage action to protect the environment. The awards are directed at tour operators, hotels, national parks and heritage sites, and other activities associated with tourism. By selecting projects showing best practice in their field as role models, others are encouraged to follow suit and consider the environment in the everyday running of their tourism business. The awards are run annually, with a winner selected from each of five regions and an overall winner. In addition, two special awards are made for mass tourism destinations.

The awards are run in association with the British Tourist Authority, the Association of British Travel Agents, the Pacific Asia Travel Association and the American Society of Travel Agents. Entries to the awards have been increases every year. American Express also sponsors a variety of environmental awards for international tourism organisations.

Agents and Partnerships for Change

A broad based approach is called for which requires Travel & Tourism to work with:

— national governments to raise the profile of environmental and social issues within the education system;

— NGOs to raise awareness of tourism issues in their work and activities and provide feedback to the Travel & Tourism industry;

— development organisations to communicate with host communities to understand their needs and requirements;

— local authorities to engage local people through the inclusion of tourism issues in Local Agenda 21 plans;

— national and international trade associations, labour representative organisations and training providers to increase awareness and training of staff in environmental and social issues;

— Travel & Tourism publications (such as travel guides);

— Travel & Tourism journalists to raise the profile of reporting environmental and social impacts of tourism among consumers and tourism businesses; and

— the Internet as a source of information for potential travellers.

Areas for further Action: The WTTC/MORI data shows the scale of the task still remaining. The industry has developed a number of initiatives to influence consumer behaviour. However, if consumers do not understand or are not aware of the issues involved and do not demand more sustainable products then, in the long term, it will not be in the industry's interests to move in that direction. The priority for future action, therefore, should be to raise awareness among travellers of the issues associated with tourism and the impact their activities can have on local destinations and cultures.

Promoting Broad-based Sustainable Development through Tourism while Safeguarding the Integrity of Local Cultures and Protecting the Environment.

The Travel & Tourism industry has a vested interest in protecting the natural and cultural resources that are the core of its business. Travel & Tourism has less impacts on natural resources and the environment than other sectors and it has already done much (see Section B) to address the issues arising from its activities.

There are examples, however, from around the world where the impact of Travel & Tourism has been damaging to the local environment and people. Some of the factors which contributes to the harmful impact of tourism are:

— a lack of awareness on the part of those making decisions about tourism development of the social, economic and environmental balance to be pursued in achieving sustainable development;

— a lack of commitment by tourism operators and travellers to contribute to the maintenance of the local environment and culture of the host destination;

— a weak institutional framework with inadequate controls can lead to tourism development which is both inappropriate and intrusive;

— unfairly traded tourism, whereby local communities are unable to share in its benefits;

— large flows of visitors in remote or sensitive locations can place considerable strains on local resources (particularly water) and supply systems. Travellers' expectations of the goods and services, which should be available, can lead to these items or services, being imported from outside or local supply chains, being distorted to meet demands; and

— tourism can change a destination's cultural make-up and, if poorly developed, can increase crime, prostitution and other social problems.

Solutions

In order for tourism to realise its potential to achieve broad-based sustainable development, an effective partnership between Government and all sectors of the industry will be required. The following illustrates what is being done:

International Co-operation : IH&RA and the United Nations Organisation for Education, Science and Culture (UNESCO) have signed a co-operation agreement to encourage world-wide hotel chains to sponsor UNESCO cultural heritage sites and attract tourism to them via their marketing campaigns.

National Governments: In India, the government is pump priming local "eco-tourism" activities, which are primarily driven by local women. In Mexico, the government is kick starting village development for "eco-tourism" lodges in the Chiapas region involving the whole community. In England, the government has recently held a national consultation on sustainable tourism and, as a result, is developing a new strategy for tourism, which incorporates the principles of sustainable development as a core component. The Caribbean Tourism Organisation has developed a comprehensive strategy to develop "eco-tourism" in the Caribbean region. This strategy is closely integrated with the goals of the Association for Caribbean States (ACE) for a green Caribbean.

Destinations: "GREEN GLOBE" has developed a specific "Destinations" program to recognise those tourist destinations where there is a concerted effort by all those involved in the local tourism industry to improve the quality of the environment. The Destinations process provides a framework to guide tourist locations towards achieving sustainable development based on the principles of Agenda 21. The Destinations programs are tailor made to reflect local circumstances, such as the level of environmental awareness, action taken to date and available resources. Each program is based on achieving progressive environmental improvements. Targets are set within a realistic timetable and are developed by a steering group made up of key partners. The island of Jersey has become the first "GREEN GLOBE" Destination. Vilamoura in Portugal, Dominica in the Caribbean and 3 destinations in the Philippines have also entered the Destination program.

For example, in 1996 Lusotour SA, a tourism development company, enacted a management plan for Vilamoura whereby employees are given responsibility for individual environmental tasks. The company has invested money into rehabilitating the surrounding natural environment, which includes pine forests and a lake that has significance to local wetland areas. Guests are provided with a copy of the environmental policy and are encouraged to participate in the scheme through specialised brochures.

The campaign includes recycling; treating diseased pine areas; regular cleaning of the beaches and marinas; development of a sewage treatment plant and new buildings in the resort are designed to minimise visual and environmental impacts. For its work in Vilamoura, Lusotour SA is also a winner of the British Airways Tourism for Tomorrow Awards. The "Afrikatourism" brand has been developed by the Open Africa Foundation to encourage products, which embraces sustainable ecological, economic and social development based on Africa's unique cultural, natural and wildlife heritage. "Open Africa" is also developing a continuous network of "Afrikatourism" routes from the Cape to Cairo, known as the "African Dream". The Dream helps to create awareness of the many rural and environmental projects, which exist throughout Africa. "Team Africa", a transcontinental alliance of governments, corporations, institutions, professionals and individuals, provides leadership and motivation in the development of the "African Dream".

Host Communities

"Whale Watch Kaikoura" is an initiative of local Maori people from a small town on the East Coast of New Zealand's South Island. Within a kilometre of the Kaikoura shore is an area ideal for whales, where visitors are guaranteed to see them all year round. The Whale Watch began 11 years ago and is now a booming tourist destination, run by indigenous people with a strong sense of heritage and a view of the future based on strong principles of sustainability.

Jordan Tourism Investments, has revitalised the traditional village of Taybeh, in Jordan, into a cultural tourist resort, with the help and agreement of villagers. With many of the younger generation moving to the cities, the village was losing its character. By restoring its 19th century buildings and reviving old crafts, the village is now thriving again. The village lies 9km south east of the historic city of Petra. Opened in July 1994, the village now accommodates around 60,000 guests each year.

Uluru and Kakadu National Parks are both owned by indigenous Australians, the local Aboriginal communities, and jointly run with the National Parks and Wildlife Service. They are both major tourism destinations and involve indigenous participation in planning, management, and ownership of tourism infrastructure, as well as interpretation for visitors. They bring significant economic, social and cultural benefits to the local indigenous communities. The Conservation Corporation in Africa has established a series of high quality game parks in which local communities are major stakeholders and beneficiaries of tourism. This initiative is also helping to re-invigorate local crafts.

Agents and Partnerships for Change and Areas for further Action

The challenge facing the tourism industry in moving towards a more sustainable future is set out in "Agenda 21 for the Travel & Tourism Industry". To achieve the goals set out in this document will require a partnership between government departments, national tourism authorities, international and national trade organisations and Travel & Tourism companies. Working together in close co-operation such partnerships should aim to deliver the following:

— Close co-operation between the public and private sectors to deliver a regulatory regime, which encourages voluntary action but supplement, where necessary, with regulation in areas such as land-use and waste management.

— Agreed common standards and tools to enable the measurement of progress towards achieving sustainable development.

— Certification criteria developed and more widely applied to industry initiatives.

— A commitment to the controlled expansion, where appropriate, of infrastructure.

— Environmental taxes, where applied, should be fair and non-discriminatory. They should be carefully thought out to minimise their impact on economic development, and revenues should be allocated to Travel & Tourism associated environment improvement programs.

— International, national and local funding bodies should include sustainable development as a part of their criteria, so that in time, all funding would be dependent on sound environmental practice.

— Contemporary research into sustainable tourism needs to be funded and developed. Issues requiring attention include design, carrying capacity, tour operator activities, environmental reporting, auditing and environmental impact assessments.

— Environmental education and training should be increased, particularly in schools, for future hotel and tourism staff.

— Greater investment and commitment to the use of new technology.

Coastal Impact of Tourism

Tourism provides an essential lifeline for many coastal communities. Faced with the prospect of increasing financial hardship, more and more coastal communities have turned to tourism as a means of generating income and survival. Tourism's impact on the coastal zone has, therefore, been largely positive. Of course, as in any area, if Tourism is not properly managed and developed, it can be harmful.

Impacts arise from the construction of infrastructure (hotels, marinas, transport, waste treatment facilities, groynes etc.) and from recreation (golf courses, water sports, theme parks etc). Coastal communities are now faced with tourism on a considerable scale, and the host to guest ratio can be very high in such areas. At the same time, coastal communities must try to maintain the resort's attraction as tourist demands change, sometimes quite rapidly.

With coastal regions being primary tourist destinations, sensitive marine and coastal environments can suffer dramatically. For example, as a result of large-scale sea-front tourist development, considerable beach and dune erosion can occur. Tourism also impacts on environmental quality in the following ways:

— ribbon development, infrastructure requirements, particularly transport links;

— the treatment and disposal of solid and/or liquid wastes, particularly during peak tourist seasons, may be inadequate or at worst non-existent; and

— water is often consumed excessively, not only for drinking but for showers, laundry, swimming pools, maintenance of golf courses etc. This can affect the quantity and quality of fresh water available to indigenous coastal populations.

Recreational activities can also have a significant impact on the coastal zone:

— golf course's impact can be considerable, with those situated directly on coastal habitats (especially sand dunes) in particular;

— erosion of reefs and coral from divers and swimmers;

— pollution from boats and jets skis; and

— noise from motor boats and jet skis, cars and buses, nightlife and other activities.

Solutions

The development of a sustainable tourism industry in the coastal zone offers numerous opportunities. Opportunities includes, those for nature conservation – which, given the increasing interest in high quality natural and cultural experiences, can help to reverse the decline in market share of many coastal destinations. Tourism also provides important opportunities for strengthening local industries. Where industries are in decline, tourism ventures can help supplement declining income.

The following examples illustrate what can be done to make the most of the opportunities offered by tourism in the coastal zone: Calvia is a Municipality on the Mediterranean coast that has undertaken an Agenda 21 project to assist the sustainable development of its tourism sector, in order to counter the negative impact of short-term tourism development since the 1960s. The local council has now implemented a transferable policy aimed at modernising, improving and diversifying the local tourist industry, involving all stakeholders, including the local population. A Project Plan was enacted, and achievements so far include:

— indigenous development, based on the sustainable use of available resources;

— high quality services and an appropriate bed night capacity;

— a ban on new development on 1,700 acres;

— active participation of the residents in community life; and

— environmental management of municipality buildings, waste recycling, reduction in spending on electricity, and use of environmentally friendly materials for office use.

Quicksilver Tours, Queensland, Australia, is owned by one of the largest tourism operators to the Great Barrier Reef. Quicksilver have five large catamarans, which take about 1,000 tourists a day to dive on the reef. They have their own reef site with fixed diving platforms. They employ a team of biologists, both for environmental management and assessment as well as widespread environmental interpretation. Recent assessment of the reef, in the vicinity of the operation, shows that it is being maintained in pristine condition.

Kingfisher Bay Resort is found at Fraser Island, Queensland. It is a large five star "ecotourism" resort built in a beautiful, but fragile environment off the Queensland coast. Its concept, design, construction and management were conceived using the latest ecologically sustainable principles. It is a state-of-the-art "ecotourism" resort, which has won Australia's top tourism awards, and its economic and environmental success has influenced new coastal tourism developments.

Maho Bay's camps and studios in the US Virgin Islands have based their product on a commitment to minimise impact on the environment, conserve natural resources, engage in active and passive environmental education of their guests, and contribute to the local economy. Specific initiatives introduced at Maho Bay include the following: use of new technology; purchasing policies; waste management; environmental education; energy and water conservation; and support for local communities and culture.

These initiatives show an appreciation of the need for alternative solutions to issues such as packaging and waste disposal through landfill. These are issues, which as the industry grows, will be increasingly important for the Travel & Tourism industry as a whole to address.

Agents and Partnerships for Change and Areas for Further Action

The agents, partnerships for change and areas for further action in relation to tourism in the coastal zone are similar to the development of broad based sustainable tourism in general as set out in Section A number of issues do, of course, have particular importance for the coastal zone.

Above all, the key to success is better participation at destination level among all the stakeholders concerned (such as at Calvia). In the case of the coastal zone, there are a number of additional organisations with an interest in coastal policy, marine conservation, shipping etc., which needs to be identified and included in partnerships for the coastal zone.

Successful planning for tourism is very important for the future of the industry in coastal regions, because a significant percentage of tourism occurs within the geographical parameters of the definition of a coastal zone. Concerted support from all countries involved (and the industries within them) is vital to protect the shared natural resources that coastal zones represent. Historically, the influence most hoteliers have on the environmental impact of their business is limited to working within existing buildings, or after a new site has been completed. In April 1998, the

IHEI convened a group of hoteliers, tour operators, architectural firms and sustainable development specialists with the goal of creating a partnership to be called the "Siting and Design Programme". The new initiative's mission will be to define responsible planning and design specifications that will cause minimal environmental damage at new sites. Particular attention will be paid to sites located within ecologically sensitive areas and upon waterfronts. The "Siting and Design Programme" will strive toreach hotel owners, investors and developers to bring these issues to the attention of the entire industry.

9

Sustainable Tourism Management

The study of ecotourism offers many opportunities to reflect on the importance of sustainability, and the possibilities of implementing approaches which move us in a new direction. Ecotourism must do more than create a series of activities to attract visitors, offering them an opportunity to interact with nature in such a way as to make it possible to preserve or enhance the special qualities of the site and its flora and fauna, while allowing local inhabitants and future visitors to continue to enjoy these qualities. The study of ecotourism also suggests that there are significant obstacles.

Overcoming these obstacles requires more than well-intentioned policies; it requires a new correlation of social forces, a move towards broad-based democratic participation in all aspects of life, within each country and in the concert of nations. Strategies to face these challenges must respond to the dual challenges of insulating these communities from further encroachment and assuring their viability.

The obstacles are an integral part of the world system, a system of increasing duality, polarized between the rich and poor —nations, regions, communities, and individuals. A small number of nations dominate the global power structure, guiding production and determining welfare levels. The remaining nations compete among themselves to offer lucrative conditions that will entice the corporate and financial powers to locate within their boundaries. Similarly, regions and communities within nations engage in self-destructive forms of bargaining —compromising the welfare of their workers and the building of their own infrastructure— in an attempt to outbid each other for the fruits of global growth.

The regions unable to attract investment suffer the ignoble fate of losers in a permanent economic olympics, condemned to oblivion on the world stage, their populations doomed to marginality and permanent poverty. Sustainability is not possible as long as the expansion of capital enlarges the ranks of the poor and impedes their access to the resources needed for mere survival. Capitalism no longer needs growing armies of unemployed to ensure low wages, nor need it control vast areas to secure regular access to the raw materials and primary products for its productive machine; these inputs are now assured by new institutional arrangements that modified social and productive structures to fit the needs of capital.

At present, however, great excesses are generated, excesses that impoverish people and ravage their regions. Profound changes are required to facilitate a strategy of sustainable development: Ecotourist development strategies may contribute to promoting a new form of dualism: a dual structure that allows people to rebuild their rural societies, produce goods and services in a sustainable fashion while expanding the environmental stewardship services they have always provided.

When given the chance and access to resources, the poor are more likely than other groups to engage in direct actions to protect and improve the environment. From this perspective, an alternative development model requires new ways to encourage the direct participation of peasant and indigenous communities in a program of job creation in rural areas to increase incomes and improve living standards. By proposing policies that encourage and safeguard rural producers in their efforts to become once again a vibrant and viable social and productive force, here proposes to contribute to an awareness of the deliberate steps needed to promote sustainability.

Ecotourism is widely believed to be the perfect economic activity to promote both sustainability and development. Here describes the relationship between these two goals and end up with some reflections on the organization of specific projects.

Sustainability

Sustainable development has become a powerful and controversial theme, creating seemingly impossible goals for policy makers and development practitioners. Prevailing trickle-down approaches to economic development enrich a few and stimulate growth in "modern" economies and sectors within traditional societies, but they do not address most people's needs; moreover, they contribute to depleting the world's store of natural wealth and to a deterioration in the quality of our natural environment. A new discourse of sustainability is emerging, one that troubles thoughtful people, who are realizing the difficulty of implementing such an approach. When fully understood, people realize that present levels of per capita resource consumption in the richer countries cannot possibly be maintained much less generalized to people living in the rest of the world.

In present conditions, the very accumulation of wealth creates poverty. While the poor often survive in scandalous conditions and are forced to contribute to further degradation, they do so because they know no alternatives. Even in the poorest of countries, social chasms not only prevent resources from being used to ameliorate their situation, but actually compound the damage by forcing people from their communities and denying them the opportunities to devise their own solutions. For this reason, the search for sustainability involves a dual strategy.

On the one hand, it must involve an unleashing of the bonds that restrain people from strengthening their own organizations, or creating new ones, to use their relatively meager resources to search for an alternative and autonomous resolution to their problems. On the other hand, a sustainable development strategy must contribute to the forging of a new social pact, cemented in the recognition that the eradication of poverty and the democratic incorporation of the disenfranchised into a more diverse productive structure are essential.

Sustainability, then, is about the struggle for diversity in all its dimensions. International campaigns to conserve germplasm, to protect endangered species, and to create reserves of the biosphere are multiplying in reaction to the mounting offensive, while communities and their hard pressed members struggle against powerful external forces to defend their individuality, their rights and ability to survive while trying to provide for their brethren. The concern for biodiversity, in its broadest sense, encompasses not only threatened flora and fauna, but also the survivability of these human communities, as stewards of the natural environment and as producers.

Internationalization has stymied this movement towards diversity. The powerful economic groups that shape the world economy (transnational corporations and financial institutions, and influential local powers, among others) are striving to break down these individual or regional traits, molding us into more homogenous and tractable social groups. They would position us to support the existing structure of inequality and to engage in productive employment; and, for those lucky enough to enjoy high enough incomes, to become customers.

Self-sufficiency

A crucial issue in developing a strategy of sustainability is that of self-sufficiency. The existing process of integration into the global trading system promotes specialization based on monocropping systems. Although sustainability does not lead to autarchy, it is conducive to a much lower degree of specialization in all areas of production and social organization. Historically, food self-sufficiency emerged as a necessity in many societies because of the precariousness of international trading systems; specific culinary traditions developed on the basis of highly localized knowledge of fruits and vegetables, herbs and spices. Although the introduction of green revolution technologies raised the productive potential of food producers tremendously, we soon found out how hard it was to reach this potential and the high social and environmental costs that such a program might entail.

Food self-sufficiency is a controversial objective that cogently raises the question of autonomy. Although development practitioners are virtually unanimous in rejecting calls for extreme specialization, there is general agreement on two contradictory factors in the debate:

— local production of basic commodities that can be produced equally well but more efficiently elsewhere is a luxury few societies can afford, if and only if the resources not dedicated to the production of these traded goods can find productive employment elsewhere; and

— there are probably few exceptions to the observation that greater local production of such commodities contributes to higher nutritional standards and better health indices. In the context of today's societies, in which inequality is the rule and the forces discriminating against the rural poor legion, a greater degree of autonomy in the provision of the material basis for an adequate standard of living is likely to be an important part of any program of regional sustainability. It will contribute to creating more productive jobs and an interest in better stewardship over natural resources.

There are many parts of the world in which such a strategy would be a wasteful luxury. It would divert resources from other uses that could better contribute to improving well-being. But even when the importation of basic needs is advisable, people concerned with sustainable development raise questions about modifying local diets so that they are more attuned to the productive possibilities of their regions; in the current scene, the tendency to substitute imported products for traditional foods is having terrible consequences for human welfare in many societies.

Food self-sufficiency, however, is only part of a broader strategy of productive diversification whose tenets are very much a part of the sustainability movement. Historically, rural denizens never have been 'just' farmers, or anything else, for that matter. Rather, rural communities were characterized by the diversity of the productive activities in which they engaged to assure their subsistence. It was only the aberration of transferring models of large-scale commercial agriculture to development thinking in the Third World that misled many into ignoring the multifaceted nature of traditional rural productive systems. Sustainable development strategies directly face this problem, attempting to reintroduce this diversity, as they grapple with problems of appropriate scales of operation and product mix.

Democratic Participation for Rural Diversification

Sustainable development is an approach to productive reorganization that encompasses the combined experiences of local groups throughout the world. The techniques for implementation vary greatly among regions and ecosystems. A single common denominator pervades this work: the need for effective democratic participation in the design and implementation of projects. Without the mutual reinforcement that the international grouping of NGOs provides, the individual units would not be as effective in obtaining funds for their projects, in obtaining technical assistance for their implementation, and political support against intransigent or incredulous local and national politicians and institutions.

Sustainable development, however, is not an approach that will be accepted, simply because "its time has come." In the final analysis, it involves a political struggle for control over the productive apparatus. It requires a redefinition of not only what and how we produce but also of who will be allowed produce and for what ends. For organizations involved in projects of sustainable development in rural areas, the conflict will center around control of mechanisms of local political and economic power, and the use of resources. The struggle to assure a greater voice in the process for peasants, indigenous populations, women, and other underprivileged minorities, will not assure that their decisions will lead to sustainable development. But broad-based democratic participation is the best way create the basis for a more equitable distribution of wealth, one of the first prerequisites for forging a strategy of sustainable development.

Dualistic Development

Global integration is creating opportunities for some, nightmares for many. In this juxtaposition of winners and losers, a new strategy for rural development is required: a strategy that revalues the contribution of traditional production strategies. In the present world economy, the vast majority of rural producers in the third world cannot compete on world markets. Unless insulated in some way, their traditional products only have ready markets within the narrow confines of poor communities suffering a similar fate.

But these marginal rural producers offer an important promise: they can support themselves and make important contributions to the rest of society. Present policies are driving peasants from their traditional activities and communities. Peasants and indigenous communities must receive support to continue living and producing in their own regions. Even by the strictest criteria of neoclassical economics, this approach should not be dismissed as inefficient protectionism, since most of the resources involved in this process would have little or no opportunity cost for society as a whole.

In effect, we are proposing the formalization of a dual economy. By recognizing the permanence of a sharply stratified society, the country will be in a better position to design policies that recognize and take advantage of these differences to improve the welfare of people in both sectors. A strategy that offers succor to rural communities, a means to make productive diversification possible, will make the management of growth easier in those areas developing links with the international economy. But more importantly, such a strategy will offer an opportunity for the society to actively confront the challenges of environmental management and conservation in a meaningful way, with a group of people uniquely qualified for such activities.

The dual economy is not new. Unlike the present version that permeates all our societies, confronting rich and poor, the proposal calls for creating structures so that one segment of society that chooses to live in rural areas finds support from the rest of the nation to implement an alternative regional development program. The new variant starts from the inherited base of rural production, improving productivity by using the techniques of agroecology. It also involves incorporating new activities that build on the cultural and resource base of the community and the region for further development. It requires very specific responses to a general problem and therefore depends heavily on local involvement in design and implementation. While the broad outlines are widely discussed, the specifics require investment programs for direct producers and their partners.

What is new is the introduction of an explicit strategy to strengthen the social and economic base for a dual structure. By recognizing and encouraging the marginal groups to create an alternative that would offer marginal groups better prospects for their own development, the dual economy proposal might be mistaken to be the simple formalization of the "war on poverty" or "solidarity" approach to the alleviation of the worst effects of marginality. This would be erroneous. Rather than a simple transfer of resources to compensate groups for their poverty, we require an integrated set of productive projects that offer rural communities the opportunity to generate goods and services that will contribute to raising their living standards while also improving the environment in which they live.

Limitations of Ecotourism

As a result of ecotourism, many of the people living in the tourist region have come to resent the intruder; its annual visits have brought increasing government regulation of their lives, effective appropriation of their lands, intense social conflict and heightened immiserization. There are serious social and economic problems in the protected area. Many of these problems are simply local manifestations of the larger crisis of society, making it difficult for poor rural producers to survive by continuing their traditional activities. In this protected area, people have been particularly affected by specific conservation measures that intensified the adjustment process.

The declaration of certain important areas to be part of the nuclear and buffer zones of the reserve, led to a prohibition or severe restriction on traditional forestry activities, without offering the communities or their members compensation for the reclassification of their lands or alternative productive opportunities with which they might earn a livelihood elsewhere in the region. The region's problems and those of the communities did not begin in 1986 and cannot be attributed solely to the butterflies. Local systems of control by economic elites and political bosses were an important part of the local scene long before the visitors acquired their new found fame.

Industrial demand for sources of pulp, and local mechanisms to concentrate the wealth and opportunities were already creating pressures on the forests and dividing individual communities as well as pitting one against another. The opportunities created by the unbridled expansion of tourism and the arbitrary distribution of the spoils among a very small group of people compounded the problems. In this environment, a new approach to regional development is required. While there is a general recognition that ecotourism can offer more opportunities to the people, it is also clear that without other, complementary productive activities that create jobs and income, the people in the region will continue their environmentally destructive activities that also threaten the viability of the fir forests in which the Monarch nests.

A local network of NGOs and confederations of communities and productive groups has begun to play an important role in creating these opportunities. There appears to be an understanding of the great cost that was incurred as a result of the internecine warfare that the strategies of bureaucratic imposition created. The principal limitation is the lack of a mechanism for the various groups to implement realistic productive strategies; they need information about resources and markets, as well as mechanism to channel available resources more effectively. The organizations require a process of local cooperation, constructed on a firm basis of broad based effective local participation. This is the route to creating a "dual society" in which ecotourism would contribute to an overall strategy of sustainable development.

Sustainable Cultural Tourism

Cultural tourism began to be recognized as a distinct product category in the late 1970s when tourism marketers that some people traveled specifically to gain a deeper understanding of the culture or heritage of a destination. By its very nature, the art of traveling removes tourists from their home culture and places them temporarily in a different cultural milieu, whether in an adjacent city or in a village halfway around the world. But cultural tourism is seen as offering something more or different both to the tourist and the community that hosts the tourist.

Initially, it was regarded as a specialized, niche activity that was thought to be pursued by a small number of better educated, more affluent tourists who were looking for something other than the standard sand, sun, and sea holiday. It is only since the fragmentation of the mass market in the 1990s that cultural tourism has been recognized for what it is: a high-profile, mass-market activity.

Depending on the source and the destination, between 35 and 70 percent of international travelers are now considered cultural tourists. Based on these figures, as many as 240 million international journeys annually involve some element of cultural tourism. Today, arguably, cultural tourism has superseded ecotourism as the trendy tourism buzzword. It is not surprising, then, that destinations are clamoring to get on the proverbial cultural tourism band-wagon by promoting their cultural or heritage assets for tourist consumption, often without due consideration of the impact that tourism may have on them.

Cultural tourism did not go unnoticed by the cultural heritage management sector either. In fact, the growth of cultural tourism coincided with the emergence of a broader societywide appreciation of the need to protect and conserve our dwindling cultural and heritage assets. However, cultural tourism was seen as a double-edged sword by the cultural heritage management community. On the one hand, increased demand by tourists provided a powerful political and economic justification to expand conservation activities. On the other hand, increased visitation, overuse, inappropriate use, and the commodification of the same assets without regard for their cultural values posed a real threat to the integrity-and in extreme cases, to the very survival-of these assets.

At about the same time, then, cultural heritage management advocates began to promulgate policies to protect cultural values from inappropriate tourism uses. Thus began the parallel yet largely independent evolution of cultural tourism as both a product and cultural heritage management issue. To a large extent, both sectors still operate in parallel, with little real evidence being shown of true partnerships forming between them. But cultural tourism can, could, and should achieve both cultural heritage management and tourism management objectives. In theory, this aim is supported widely by both sectors. In practice, though, the achievement of this dual objective has proven elusive, as the pursuit of one objective has often been regarded as being inimical with the attainment of the other.

Instead, in many instances one element has been sacrificed or traded off. Tourism values are compromised to ensure that the cultural integrity of assets is maintained or that cultural values are not compromised for tourism gain. The resulting cultural tourism sector operates at a suboptimal level, failing to achieve either its tourism or cultural heritage management potential fully. Sustainability can occur only when the practice of trading off one set of values for another ceases and, instead, tourism and cultural heritage management interests work toward the achievement of com-mon goals. This task is complicated by the historic lack of understanding of the role each plays and is reflected in the sentiment that both sectors work toward different and mutually incompatible goals. Other than sharing the same assets, they often feel they have little else in common.

Each sector has a different disciplinary focus and mandate, serves a different role in society, has different political overlords, and is accountable to different stakeholder groups. The end product is ignorance, often leading to suspicion of the other's motives. This book seeks to dispel some of that ignorance and foster greater understanding of the mutual interests that tourism and cultural heritage management have in cultural tourism.

Cultural tourism as a name means many things to many people and herein lies its strength and its weakness. Politically oriented definitions of cultural tourism tend to be as inclusive as possible to show the level of consumer interest and thus provide further justification for investment in cultural heritage management activities. Likewise, the undercurrent of many marketing-oriented definitions is to strive for greater allocation of marketing resources to the sector. On the other hand, definitions that tend to focus on one or a narrow set of activities seek to position those activities as the core elements of cultural tourism and, by extension, position others as being peripheral to true cultural tourism.

Derived Definitions: Tourism definitions place cultural tourism within a broader framework of tourism and tourism management theory. Cultural tourism, for example, is recognized as a form of special interest tourism, where culture forms the basis of either attracting tourists or motivating people to travel. Others place it in a tourism systems context, recognizing that it involves interrelationships between people, places, and cultural heritage, or define it in the context of the temporary movement of people. Cultural tourism has also been conceptualized from a business perspective as involving the development and marketing of various sites or attractions for foreign as well as domestic tourists.

Motivational Definitions: A number of authors and nongovernmental organizations (NGOs) feel that cultural tourists are motivated to travel for different reasons than other tourists and, therefore, feel that motivation must be considered an important element when defining cultural tourism. The World Tourism Organization (WTO) defines cultural tourism as "movements of persons essentially for cultural motivations such as study tours, performing arts and cultural tours, travel to festivals and other events, visit to sites and monuments, travel to study nature, folklore or art, and pilgrimages". Likewise, the province of Ontario in Canada uses the definition of "visits by persons from outside the host community motivated wholly or in part by interest in the historical, artistic, scientific, or lifestyle/ heritage offerings of the community, region, group, or institution".

Experiential or Aspirational Definitions: Motivation alone, though, does not seem to encapsulate the full magnitude of cultural tourism. Cultural tourism is also an experiential activity, with many people feeling it also includes an aspirational element. As a minimum, cultural tourism involves experiencing or having contact of differing intensity with the unique social fabric, heritage, and special character of places. It is also hoped that by experiencing culture the tourist will become educated as well as entertained, will have a chance to learn about the community, or will have an opportunity to learn something about the significance of a place and its associations with the local community, its heritage, and a cultural or natural landscape. Some people even liken cultural tourism to a quest or search for greater understanding. These people suggest that by leading the observer into the cultural past, cultural tourism can help them see the present from a different viewpoint.

Operational Definitions: An operational definition is the most common definitional approach used. Most of the tourism derived, motivational, and experiential definitions also include an operational component, often to illustrate the point being made. Cultural tourism is defined by participation in any one of an almost limitless array of activities or experiences. Indeed, it is common to avoid defining cultural tourism, instead stating that "cultural tourism includes visits to. . . " By inference, if someone visits one of these attractions, that person must be a cultural tourist; thus the activity must be a cultural tourism activity. Motivation, purpose, or depth of experience count less than participation.

The tourism literature identifies the range of cultural tourism activities as including the use of such cultural heritage assets as archaeological sites, museums, castles, palaces, historical buildings, famous buildings, ruins, art, sculpture, crafts, galleries, festivals, events, music and dance, folk arts, theatre, "primitive cultures [sic], " subcultures, ethnic communities, churches, cathedrals and other things that represents people and their cultures. Likewise, the array of cultural tourism products can include existing structures, modified facilities, and purpose-built attractions. The scale can vary from one building, to a cluster of buildings, a streetscape, a precinct within a community, an entire city or town, a region, or arguably to entire countries.

The operational definition highlights the potential scope of this activity, while at the same time illustrating the very real problems that exist in setting meaningful parameters about what is and what is not cultural tourism.

By its very nature, cultural tourism has fuzzy boundaries, for it is almost impossible to ascribe absolute parameters either to the resources used or to the tourist using them. In fact, cultural tourism has become an umbrella term for a wide range of related activities, including historical tourism, ethnic tourism, arts tourism, museum tourism, and others. They all share common sets of resources, management issues, and desired aspirational outcomes.

Cultural tourism involves four elements:

— Tourism

— Use of cultural heritage assets

— Consumption of experiences and products

— The tourist

Tourism

To state that cultural tourism is a form of tourism may seem selfevident and rather tautological. It is important to appreciate that "tourism" is a noun and "cultural" is an adjective used to modify it. Cultural tourism is a form of tourism. It is not a form of cultural heritage management. As a form of tourism, the decision to embark on cultural tourism must be based on sound, commercial tourism reasons first and cultural heritage management reasons second. This point is sometimes not appreciated by some members of the cultural heritage management community who may see tourism as a means of achieving other agendas or who fail to appreciate just what is needed to make an asset work as a tourism attraction. As a tourism activity, it will attract nonlocal visitors (or tourists) who are traveling primarily for pleasure on limited time budgets and who may know little about the significance of the assets being visited. Successful cultural tourism products must be shaped with this type of visitor in mind.

Use of Cultural Heritage Assets

Cultural tourism's principal building blocks are a community or a nation's cultural heritage assets. The International Council on Monuments and Sites (ICOMOS), defines heritage as a broad concept that includes tangible assets, such as natural and cultural environments, encompassing landscapes, historic places, sites, and built environments, as well as intangible assets, such as collections, past and continuing cultural practices, knowledge, and living experiences. These assets are identified and conserved for their intrinsic values or significance to a community rather than for their extrinsic values as tourism attractions. In fact, the tourism potential of assets is rarely considered when they are first identified.

At this time, most documentation of an asset's significance concentrates on its aesthetic, architectural, historical, social, spiritual, or educational values, with tourism sitting hazily within the educational or social values sections. One of the paradoxes of cultural tourism is that although the decision to enter this sector must be driven by tourism considerations, assets are managed by the principles of cultural heritage management. In addition, cultural or heritage assets may serve a multitude of user groups, including tourists, but also including local schoolchildren, "traditional owners", and other local residents. These groups may value the asset for different reasons and seek different benefits from its use, making the task of presenting the asset appropriately more difficult. These competing approaches can be a source of friction between tourism and cultural heritage management interests.

Consumption of Experiences and Products

All tourism involves the consumption of experiences and products, and cultural tourism is no different. Cultural tourists want to consume a variety of cultural experiences.

To facilitate this consumption, cultural heritage assets must be transformed into cultural tourism products. The transformation process actualizes the potential of the asset by converting it into something that the tourist can utilize. This transformation process, though abhorrent to some, is integral to the successful development and sustainable management of the cultural tourism product. A distinction is made between a cultural or heritage asset and a cultural tourism product. A cultural or heritage asset represents the uncommodified or raw asset that is identified for its intrinsic values. Acultural tourism product, on the other hand, represents an asset that has been transformed or commodified specifically for tourism consumption.

Tourist

Finally, cultural tourism must consider the tourist. A number of the definitions suggest or imply strongly that all cultural tourists are motivated to travel for deep learning, experiential, or self-exploration reasons. Others recognize that the motivations for cultural tourism participation fall along a continuum, from those who travel exclusively or primarily for cultural tourism reasons to those for whom cultural tourism participation is an accidental element of the trip. The typology is based on the importance of cultural tourism in the decision to visit a destination and the depth of the experience for the tourist. In addition, the type, quality, and veracity of information tourists consume prior to arrival will shape their expectations of the asset and their expected behavior while visiting. Ideally, the asset managers can communicate directly to the tourist and accurately impart the desired information in a desirable manner.

Tourism and Cultural Heritage Management

The challenge facing the cultural tourism sector is to find a balance between tourism and cultural heritage management-between the consumption of extrinsic values by tourists and conservation of the intrinsic values by cultural heritage managers. This challenge was noted first by the cultural heritage community as long as twenty-five years ago and is only recently being recognized as an important issue by the tourism community. The advent of tourism as an interested and legitimate user group has made the heritage resource management process even more demanding. At times, conflicts have emerged between the two sectors as they vie to use the same resource base.

Greater urgency than ever exists as demand increases and as pressure is being placed on many assets to perform in a more businesslike manner in order to secure funding. The main stumbling blocks seem to be the continued operations of tourism and cultural heritage management in parallel rather than in partnership, combined with ignorance of the other's needs and suspicion of the other's motives. Integration and partnerships can be achieved only if each side develops a stronger understanding of how the other views the assets, values them, and seeks to use them.

The conservation sector seems to appreciate that use, be it by local residents or tourists, is an important element in creating public awareness of and support for conservation of tangible and intangible assets that will translate into greater political and finding support for further conservation activities. Many others in the conservation sector-sometimes begrudgingly, sometimes with open arms-accept that a partnership between heritage management and tourism is both necessary and beneficial. As a general rule, the tourism industry, historically, has been much slower to recognize the need for partnership.

10

The Impacts of Tourism

Different groups are often concerned about different tourism impacts. To generalize, where one group embraces the economic impacts of tourism, another group experiences social and cultural impacts , while another is affected by tourism's environmental impacts. In theory, the interests of each group could be completely separate. Ideally, all groups could be positively affected and would support the community's tourism efforts. However, when group interests are divergent, differing perspectives can make consensus on tourism development difficult.

In most cases, groups with interests in one area of tourism will also have interests or concerns about other tourism impacts. In these situations, there are common areas of interest and a greater likelihood that each group will show more appreciation for the concerns of the other groups. Finding commonality provides a starting point for resolving tourism issues.

Role of Planning

Specific plans and actions can increase tourism's benefits or decrease the gravity of a negative impact. It is important for communities to understand the wide scope of impacts and endeavor to agree on what positive impacts to emphasize. It is wise to acknowledge and identify possible negative impacts so actions can be taken to minimize or prevent them. A clear statement of the community's vision of tourism should be an integral part of a community's comprehensive plan. Active planning directs tourism toward the goals of the community, clarifying tourism's role and uniting multiple interests.

Planning is not enough. Active implementation and management of plans and prompt attention to emerging tourism issues will maximize positive and minimize negative impacts. Monitoring and addressing community attitudes should be an ongoing part of the management effort. Good monitoring efforts can identify trouble areas and give leaders an opportunity to defuse community reactions and make timely changes before a crisis occurs. Unfortunately, few communities are so proactive.

Elaboration of Tourism Impact

A goal of developing the tourism industry in a community is maximizing selected positive impacts while minimizing potential negative impacts. First, it is essential to identify the possible impacts. Tourism researchers have identified a large number of impacts. Grouping the impacts into categories shows the types of impacts that could result from developing tourism in a community. A community will not experience every impact. Some are dependent on particular natural resource features (mountains, coral reefs) or development and spatial patterns (special "tourist zones"). Others relate to the social condition of the community, particularly the ability to culturally or socially connect with tourists. Still others relate to types and intensity of tourism developments, i. e. , approval or hostility toward tourist activities.

Understanding that tourism development may result in many and complex impacts suggests that local elected officials, the tourism industry, and community residents need to work cooperatively and carefully to plan for its growth and development. Planning can help create an industry that enhances a community with minimal costs and disruptions in other aspects of community life. Having broad community involvement and embracing different perspectives during planning helps identify and resolve concerns that would otherwise create problems later.

The impacts of tourism can be sorted into seven general categories:

— Economic

— Environmental

— Social and cultural

— Crowding and congestion

— Services

— Taxes

— Community attitude

Economic impacts

Tourism increases employment opportunities. Additional jobs, ranging from low-wage entry-level to high-paying professional positions in management and technical fields, generate income and raise standards of living. Particularly in rural areas, the diversification created by tourism helps communities that are possibly dependent on only one industry. As tourism grows, additional opportunities are created for investment, development, and infrastructure spending. Tourism often induces improvements in public utilities such as water, sewer, sidewalks, lighting, parking, public restrooms, litter control, and landscaping. Such improvements benefit tourists and residents alike.

Likewise, tourism encourages improvements in transport infrastructure resulting in upgraded roads, airports, public transportation, and non-traditional transportation. Tourism encourages new elements to join the retail mix, increasing opportunities for shopping and adding healthy competitiveness. It often increases a community's tax revenues. Lodging and sales taxes most notably increase but additional tax revenues include air travel and other transportation taxes, business taxes, and fuel taxes. New jobs generate more income tax revenues. When considering the economic impacts of tourism, it is essential to understand that tourism businesses often include a significant number of low-paying jobs, often at minimum wage or less.

These jobs are often seasonal, causing under-employment or unemployment during off-seasons. Labor may be imported, rather than hired locally, especially if particular skills or expertise is required, or if local labor is unavailable. Some tourism-related businesses are volatile and high-risk ventures that are unsustainable. Greater demand for goods, services, land, and housing may increase prices that in turn will increase the cost of living. Tourism businesses may claim land that could have higher- value or other uses.

Additionally, non-local owners and corporations may export profits out of the community. The community may have to generate funds (possibly through increased taxes) to maintain roads and transportation systems that have become more heavily used. Similarly, if additional infrastructure (water, sewer, power, fuel, medical, etc.) is required, additional taxes may also be needed to pay for them.

Environmental impacts

Areas with high-value natural resources, like oceans, lakes, waterfalls, mountains, unique flora and fauna, and great scenic beauty attract tourists and new residents (in-migrants) who seek emotional and spiritual connections with nature. Because these people value nature, selected natural environments are preserved, protected, and kept from further ecological decline. Lands that could be developed can generate income by accommodating the recreational activities of visitors. Tourist income often makes it possible to preserve and restore historic buildings and monuments. Improvements in the area's appearance through cleanup or repairs and the addition of public art such as murals, water fountains, and monuments (part of making a community ready for tourism) benefit visitors and residents alike.

Tourism is generally considered a "clean" industry, one that is based on hotels, restaurants, shops and attractions, instead of factories. Tourism can also degrade an environment. Visitors generate waste and pollution (air, water, solid waste, noise, and visual). Natural resource attractions can be jeopardized through improper uses or overuse. Providing tourist services can alter the landscape's appearance. For instance, visual pollution may occur from billboard proliferation. As tourism develops, demand for land increases, especially for prime locations like beachfronts, special views, and mountains. Without forethought, natural landscape and open space can be lost.

The destruction of flora and fauna can happen when desirable plants and animals are collected for sale or the land is trampled. Tourists or the businesses that cater to them often remove plants, animals, rocks, fossils, coral, and cultural or historical artifacts from an area. Uncontrolled visitation or overuse by visitors can degrade landscapes, historic sites, and monuments. Where water is scarce, tourists can overwhelm the available supply. Travelers can also inadvertently introduce nonindigenous species, as can increases in the trade of animals and plants. A constant stream of visitors and domestic pets may disrupt wildlife by disturbing their breeding cycles and altering natural behaviors.

Social and cultural impacts

The social and cultural ramifications of tourism warrant careful consideration, as impacts can either become assets or detriments to communities. Influxes of tourists bring diverse values to the community and influence behaviors and family life. Individuals and the collective community might try to please tourists or adopt tourist behaviors. Interactions between residents and tourists can impact creative expression by providing new opportunities (positive) or by stifling individuality with new restrictions (negative). Increased tourism can push a community to adopt a different moral conduct such as improved understanding between sexes (positive) or increased illicit drug use (negative).

Safety and health facilities and staffing tend to increase at the same time safety problems such as crime and accidents increase. Traditional ceremonies may be renewed and revived by tourist interest or lost in alternative activities. Community organizations can be invigorated by facing the opportunities of tourism or overwhelmed by its associated problems. Calamities such as natural disasters, energy shortages, terrorism, political upheaval, disease outbreak, a chemical spill, or even widespread negative publicity could shut down tourism abruptly but sometimes can attract curious visitors. Tourism can improve the quality of life in an area by increasing the number of attractions, recreational opportunities, and services.

Tourism offers residents opportunities to meet interesting people, make friendships, learn about the world, and expose themselves to new perspectives. Experiencing different cultural practices enriches experiences, broadens horizons, and increases insight and appreciation for different approaches to living. Often, dwindling interest in host cultures is revived by reawakening cultural heritage as part of tourism development, which increases demand for historical and cultural exhibits. This interest by tourists in local culture and history provides opportunities to support preservation of historical artifacts and architecture. By learning more about others, their differences become less threatening and more interesting.

At the same time, tourism often promotes higher levels of psychological satisfaction from opportunities created by tourism development and through interactions with travelers. Tourism can come to a community with a dark social and cultural side, too. Illegal activities tend to increase in the relaxed atmosphere of tourist areas. Increased underage drinking can become a problem especially in beach communities, areas with festivals involving alcohol, and ski villages. It is easier to be anonymous where strangers are taken for granted; bustling tourist traffic can increase the presence of smugglers and buyers of smuggled products. Lifestyle changes such as alterations in local travel patterns to avoid tourist congestion and the avoidance of downtown shopping can damage a community socially and culturally.

Hotels, restaurants, and shops can push tourism development into residential areas, forcing changes in the physical structure of a community. Development of tourist facilities in prime locations may cause locals to be or feel excluded from those resources. As local ethnic culture alters to fit the needs of tourism, language and cultural practices may change. In places where longer- term visitors tend to congregate, social cliques, such as condo tourists or RVers, may be at odds with local interests and work to influence local issues. The "demonstration effect" of tourists and the addition of tourist facilities may alter customs, such as dating habits, especially those of a more structured or traditional culture. The potential of meeting and marrying non-local mates may create family stress.

Crowding and congestion impacts

Tourism often develops around specific locations and

concentrates there, providing growth yet avoiding sprawl. Historic buildings and grounds, which might otherwise slowly deteriorate, have great appeal for tourism development and can often be renovated to suit the industry. People congregate in attractive places. As people congregate, congestion and crowding produces stress, annoyance, anger, and other negative attitudes.

Hordes of visitors may impede local businesses, prevent residents from accomplishing normal activities, and compete for space. Tourism construction, especially hotels, may be inappropriate in scale and style with respect to other structures and the landscape. In some areas, recreational second homes and condominium developments create major crowding and congestion problems.

Services

Tourist expectations can upgrade service by local shops, restaurants, and other commerce operators. Tourism creates opportunities to develop new amenities and recreation facilities that would not otherwise be viable in a community. Tourist traffic in a community creates an opportunity for upgraded fire, police, and medical protection that also benefits residents. Traditional services may be forced out or relocated due to competition with tourist interests. Supply shortages may occur, temporarily, seasonally, or chronically. Water, power, fuel, and other shortages may be experienced with increased pressure on the infrastructure.

Taxes

Increased retail activity from restaurants and tourist shopping will add state and local sales tax revenue. Lodging tax revenue to the city (or state) should increase since travelers account for virtually all lodging tax receipts. Increased tax burdens to expand infrastructure and public services will be passed on to property owners through increased property taxes.

Community Attitude

Seeing visitor interest makes local residents more appreciative of local resources that are often taken for granted. Visitor interest and satisfaction in the community is a source of local pride. As tourism develops, local residents will enjoy more facilities and a greater range of choices. Tourism activities and events tend to make living in a place more interesting and exciting.

Heightened tension and community divisiveness can occur over tourism development, pitting tourism supporters against non-supporters. Also, tension between residents and tourists can occur. People will often feel stressed over the new, increasingly hectic community and personal pace of life. They may claim the result is no better than before or perhaps even worse. Where culture is part of the tourist attractions, over-amplification of cultural traits and creation of "new" cultural traits to satisfy tourist tastes may create a phony culture.

Residents may experience a sense of exclusion and alienation over planning and development concerns. They may feel a loss of control over the community's future as "outsiders" take over establishments and new development. Over-dependence on non-local developers and an influx of outside businesses creates a sense that the community is being manipulated and exploited by outsiders for the sole benefit of those developers or business people. Hotels built in monolithic cubes or restaurants with standardized franchise designs might clash with local standards and disrupt the aesthetic appearance of the community, damage unique community character, and spread "sameness."

Factors of Impact

Researchers generally divide impact sources into two groups: tourist factors and destination factors. Tourist factors are those which tourists bring to the destination and include such elements as demographic characteristics, social differences, and numbers of visitors. Destination factors are those that are part of the destination itself, such as travel linkage and circulation, local acceptance of tourism, and local vitality and leadership.

Tourist Factors

Number and type of visitors

— *Numbers* : small numbers of tourists are often relatively unobtrusive and may be a curiosity or an interesting diversion for community residents. As visitor numbers increase and they become commonplace, locals may ignore them. When the number of visitors reaches a point that residents feel a sense of displacement, obstruction, loss of community, or safety threat, resentment and resistance may result.

— *Demographics* : family status, age, education, profession, etc. , influence the actions and activities of tourists and their local visibility.

— *Transportation* : private vehicle or rental car, bus, train, air, or passenger ship dictates tourists' movements, influences whether choices are pre-selected, and affects the ease of reaching attractions and services.

Length of stay

— Day trips have less economic impact.

— Short (2-5 day) stays in a community maximize per-day economic impact for regional driving destinations, i. e. , tourist spending is maximized, but the pace can be hectic. Tourists who stay longer have wider range of needs and may spread the direct economic impact more broadly in the community. Seasonal visitors (1-6 months) may take more interest in non-tourism community matters.

— Annual events can create a large economic impact in a short period.

Mass arrivals and departures

— How and when people arrive (passenger ship, opening of festival) and depart influences traffic congestion and the availability of attractions and services to tourists.

— Smaller lodgings and restaurants can't accommodate large groups. Transportation options and availability may limit the choice of attractions and services.

Links to community residents

— Reduced economic impact when staying with friends or relatives.

— Better understanding of community values.

— High potential for repeat visitation.

Ethnic/racial characteristics: When the tourist population differs greatly in ethnic or racial origin or economic status from the local population, more consideration of resident concerns is needed to reduce the potential for resentment, social conflict, and crime. Careful planning and ongoing education can reduce points of conflict.

Economic characteristics

— Influences spending choices.

— Higher incomes may give tourists greater access to environment and have higher negative impact on the environment.

Activities selected

— Educational, cultural, and historical tourism often has lower social and environmental impact.

— Recreational activities may have a greater impact on the environment.

— Entertainment activities may conflict with the social values of local residents.

Ability to speak local language/accents: Perceived as making more meaningful connections with local people and culture.

"Demonstration effect" of tourists: Local residents copying behaviors of tourists can add new dimensions to local culture but sometimes the behavior is not appropriate to local values. Locals copying negative behavior of vacationers (excessive drinking, inappropriate dress, casual sex, etc.) create social problems.

Destination Factors

Local economic state: Troubled economies may benefit from tourism. However, government officials should plan so that new tourism developments are sustainable. Towns with strong economies can look for tourism that complements other community goals such as preservation of historic buildings, creation of recreational amenities, and expansion of food/lodging options.

Diversification of the economy: Economic diversity helps reduce the influence of negative impacts to the host community. If tourism has a poor year, other economic activities may offset the impact and vice versa.

Degree of local involvement in tourism and attitudes of tourism leaders: Local involvement helps align tourism with the attitudes of the rest of the community. Local ownership and management of tourism businesses keep profits from leaving the community. In most cases, if tourism businesses are cooperative in responding to residents' concerns, the industry will have strong local support.

Characteristics of tourism development

- Separation of active tourist areas from residential areas reduces conflict.
- Shared commercial areas. A mix of resident-oriented and tourist-oriented businesses adds to the vibrancy of

the retail area. Domination of tourist-oriented businesses pushes locals elsewhere and may create resentment.

— Shared cultural or recreational amenities (parks, museum s , plazas, beaches, gardens) can be more successful with tourism .

— Tourist strips can clog streets and may restrict resident access to public resources, especially beaches and shorelines. Gated or exclusionary tourist developments can create a class structure and local resentment.

Viability of the host culture

— A strong and active local culture combats tourism's tendency to change a community.

— Active programs to educate tourists in local cultural practices (especially public taboos) help reduce conflicts.

— Pride in culture influences tourists to honor local customs and adhere to cultural restrictions.

History of stability in the community

— Strong local economies give leaders more options in influencing tourism development to fit the community.

— Strong community leaders and active planning can place tourism more appropriately within the community's geography and can support suitable tourism projects while resisting inappropriate ones.

Pace of tourism development: Slower development provides time for residents and leaders to reassess tourism growth and make changes that better serve the community. Rapid development can strain a community's infrastructure and lead to serious resident dissatisfaction. Negative environmental impacts are also more likely.

Fragility of the environment used by tourists: Many of the most sought-after environments for tourism are also the most fragile. Extra effort to plan appropriate access and use of fragile environments helps insure their long-term viability and continued attractiveness for tourism.

Public transportation options

— Availability of local public transportation (bus, trolley, cab, shuttle, train) and alternative transportation corridors (bicycle, pedestrian) can reduce auto congestion.

— Poor access can make facilities inaccessible for motor coach or public transit.

Tourism is just one element of a community. While creative strategic development of tourism amenities and services can enhance the community or correct local deficiencies, tourism, like all business development, must assure that its products (attractions and services) attract customers. Overbearing rules and restrictions, and overburdening taxes can make tourism businesses less attractive or competitive.

11

New Age Technologies in Tourism and Hotel Management

The tourism and recreation industry is increasingly recognized as an important economic, environmental and social force which can bring both benefit and adversity. The business community and governments also know that the industry has had spectacular successes and colossal failures. A key element of a successful tourism industry is the ability to recognize and deal with change across a wide range of behavioral and technological factors and the way they interact.

In the 21st century, the tourism industry is undergoing major shifts in the leisure and tourism environment reflecting changing consumer values, political forces, and the explosive growth of information and other technologies. No aspect of the industry will remain untouched. These shifts will fall in ten principal areas. These changing realities make up the strategic context within which long term tourism industry commitments and investments should be made. They should guide the industry's decision processes and resource allocation. Only by understanding and acting upon reliable forecasts will the tourism industry be able to avoid the most common cause of bad decisions: incorrect assumptions about the external demographic, economic, political, and technology environment.

Table 1. Principle areas of shifts in tourism and leisure environment

Means Turning Away From	:	*And Turning Towards:*
1. Old Travel Patterns	→	New Travel Patterns
2. Established Destinations	→	Emerging Destinations
3. Old Products	→	New Products
4. Fragmented Tourism Industry	→	Economic Development Tool
5. Developer Control	→	Community Control
6. Financial Illusion	→	Financial Reality
7. Passive Customers	→	Involved Participants
8. Observing Technology	→	Orchestrating Technology
9. Mass Markets	→	Specialty markets
10.Mass Marketing	→	Direct Customer Communication

New technology has driven many of the tourism and resort developments we see today. It is appropriate to look at probable future technologies and how they will affect tourism - and how they can be incorporated into the planning for new tourism products and marketing. Science and technology are often the wild cards in tourism and resort planning—they seem to appear unexpectedly, creating entirely new markets or products, or causing segmentation of existing ones.

Tourism leaders must be able to imagine, perceive, and gauge the effects of oncoming Science and Technology upon demand, supply, and distribution. The most pervasive technological changes that will be applied to the tourism and recreation industry are both predictable and manageable. They will include advances in: communication and information technology, transportation, medicine, recreation equipment, the natural sciences, built environments and automation.

Communication and Information Technology (IT)

Breakthroughs in IT and video technology will have countervailing effects on tourism demand and the need to supply natural environments for tourism activities. Advances that will allow individuals to enjoy simulated environments in or near their own homes may also stimulate a stronger desire to visit the actual environments. However, the direction of change is not clear. Videophones, teleconferencing and virtual reality will reduce the need for routine business travel. Interactive television/PC's, Internet, and a variety of on-line services will support a paradigm shift toward direct consumer marketing. Voice activated language translators will enhance communication and visitor experiences, particularly in Asia.

Some major contributions of IT are :

— *Image Libraries* : That can call up travel information, scenes, and adventures from a variety of electronic media. Advances in Flat Screen technology will allow images to be portrayed on nearly any surface

— *Realistic Simulation* : of high risk recreational experiences such as sky diving, river rafting, etc.

— *Virtual Reality* : for entertainment, virtual reality provides interactive fantasy trips, experiences and competitive games in 3-D life size images and sensory response

— *Simultaneous Voice-Activated Language Translation* : for ease of visitor communication and employee training

— *Unlimited Worldwide Database Access* : for travel information, reservations and confirmed booking

— Miniature, multipurpose communication devices accessible worldwide

— *Smart Cards* : to speed up the processing of travelers as well as monitor activity and spending habits

— *Interactive Learning Devices and Distance Learning* : to expand education and training programs for employees and managers

— *Fiber Optics/ISDN* : to enable these advances to reach individual homes and businesses

— *Individually programmed experiences/Virtual sex* : a world in which your lawyers and lovers are both computer simulations and morality systems are in turmoil

— *Large-Scale Holography* : to create realistic walk through images and environments

— *Elimination of Long-Distance Phone Charges* : to encourage relocation of business activities to resort environments (The Internet already provides this for document and image transmission, and low cost voice transmission programs are now being released)

— *Practical Videophones* : for individual use and high quality teleconferencing. Time, not money will be the currency of the 21st Century. Businesses and individuals will have to learn how to make time with technology. Desktop video communications will be a key tool in this new environment-and it will have a major impact on routine forms of business travel

— *Virtual Communities* : where relationships exist solely through electronic communication and physical transportation is discretionary. The Internet chat rooms are but the first stage in this evolution.

Transportation Infrastructure

Future tourism transportation for the most part will be faster, easier, and more comfortable. Video mapping and location sensors for automobiles will become standard equipment in rental cars and an important distribution channel for tourism industry marketing. However, local transportation infrastructure will be under increasing strain. The rapid rise in the number of personal automobiles in developing countries will have a major impact on society and particularly the logistics of tourism. As airline and airspace capacity become increasingly limited, high speed, high capacity passenger vessels will play an increasingly important role in tourist travel.

Some of the major innovations in transportation infrastructure include:

— *Video Mapping and Location Sensors for Automobiles :* no more getting lost. Geographic Positioning Systems (GPS) combined with digital maps are already providing this service in Japan and a few locations in the US. They will become standard equipment in rental cars and an important point-of-sale distribution channel for tourism industry marketing

— *Advanced air traffic control (FANS) :* to increase airspace capacity

— *Rise in Number of Personal Automobiles in Developing Countries :* a major impact on society, the environment, and the logistics of tourism

— *Large-Capacity Air Transport :* up to 1,000 passengers capacity. These limits to aircraft size are caused partly by engineering issues but mainly by infrastructure limits at existing airports (runway layout, taxiways, gate spacing, etc.) It reminds me of the time when ships were built not to exceed the size of the Panama Canal. These Panamax vessels were the effective limit to ship size for over thirty years-until the quantum leap to the giant supertankers and bulk vessels that we see today. We can expect a similar pattern for passenger travel-but it will be a shift from air travel, and back to the sea.

— *High-Speed/Large-Capacity water transport systems :* VFB's (Very Fast Boats) transport 5,000 people at a time on wave skimmers capable of speeds of 200 mph. (Yokohama to Sydney in two days). Japan is already building prototypes of these "bulletboats" to move cargo between large coastal cities

— *High speed trains:* as an alternative for short haul air transport
— *Supersonic air transport* : faster and faster still
— *Transportation transformers (land/air/sea)* : for flexibility of access and routing/ decentralization of coastal populations
— *Hypersonic air travel/space plane* : anywhere to anywhere in under two hours

Recreation Equipment

As with information technology, advances in recreational equipment will cause both increases and decreases in tourism demand and supply. However, the net effect will be that more people spend more time, day and night, in natural environments. Some advanced recreational equipment are:

— *Geographic positioning systems (GPS)* : so you know where you are (for navigation, wilderness adventures, travel and photo diaries, and golf club selection)
— *All-weather lightweight clothing* for travel flexibility
— *Personal submarines* for unrestricted underwater observation
— *Self-correcting sports equipment* to guarantee success the "non-slicing" golf ball allows tourism industry golf tournaments to be completed in less than eight hours
— *Night vision glasses and other electronic sense enhancers* for nocturnal eco-experiences and extended use of daytime facilities
— *Simulation trainers* create a better prepared and more fit recreationist
— *Ability to breathe underwater* man returns to the sea

Built Environments

Science and technology improvements in built environments will increase the demand for recreation and leisure, but not necessarily tourism. Artificial environment resorts and theme parks will enable developers to bring resorts to within two hours of the resident market rather than depend on uncertain far distant markets. In-home leisure lifestyle centers will encourage electronic tourism and recreation.

Some innovative built environments which are developed with the help of science and technology are:

— *Artificial environment resorts and theme parks* : create warm weather attractions in cold climates

— *Simulated experiences* : will provide realistic competition to natural attractions

— *Telework Centers* : new communications technologies will enable more and more people to live and work anywhere they choose. This will be both a boon and a threat to resorts and sensitive natural environments.

— *Underwater habitats* : create new tourism experiences

— *Earth shelters and underground habitats* : protect natural views in resort areas

— *In home leisure lifestyle centers* : will encourage electronic tourism and recreation

— *Space tourism* : is on the drawing boards with plans to have a space hotel by 2025.

Automation

The revolution in robotics will be somewhat longer term in the field of tourism than in other industries. Some revolutionary inventions in the field are given below:

— *Free Ranging On Grid (FROG) driverless vehicles* : automatically move goods, clean up, and maintain amusement parks and golf courses

— Routine hotel and attraction maintenance provided by robots

— *Artificial intelligence systems* : manage fragile environments

— *Individual "personal assistants"* : reside in your computer and know your special preferences. They make routine travel arrangements (on voice command) and scan the Internet for travel and recreation opportunities that meet your individual preferences. This assistant is searching out products that tourism providers have on offer.

— *Audioanimatronic pets and "wild" animals* : perhaps the greatest benefit to the travel industry. When you leave the house to go on a trip, you don't need a pet sitter, just turn off the dog.

— Universal Cashless Transactions

— *Personal security and privacy protection devices* : battle against the invasion of smart cards and databases

The tourism industry needs to use technology to improve productivity in reaching a broad and diverse customer base. To do this, it must be flexible and responsive to rapid change as well as be stable and responsible to its existing customer base and suppliers. The tourism industry needs to incorporate new technologies, decentralize decision making, and incorporate new and more youthful ideas.

Possible responses from the tourism industry include:

— Identify changes in technology that will affect the growth, quality, and marketing of tourism

— Examine the extent to which new telework and video communication technologies could affect routine forms of business and personal travel

— Provide quality and timely information that encourages the successful deployment and application of new technology throughout the industry. Work to increase the productivity and competitive advantage that will accrue to those in the industry that use new information technology to improve their plans, decisions, and processes

— Maintain a technology clearing house that keeps members posted on the latest developments
— Consider areas where the tourism industry can be proactive and orchestrate technology to its benefit rather than adapt to technology that has been placed upon it.
— Cooperate in developing and managing a branded electronic information system through established networks such as the Internet
— Develop education programs, seminars, and conferences that address tourism and technology issues
— Develop a working relationship with key technology providers and developers so they become knowledgeable about the needs and opportunities within the tourism industry.

Hotel Telecom Services

The early 1980s marked the beginning of an era of profitable hotel telephone departments. The advent of call accounting systems nabled hoteliers to easily mark up calls to a profitable level. Guests had little choice back then but to use the guestroom phone and grumble about the cost. This era has come to an end. With few exceptions, most hotels have seen between a 15 percent and 25 percent drop in telephone revenues over the last five years. The main reason for this decrease is guest choice. The guest now has a variety of choices for communicating including fax over the Internet, e-mail, cell phones, calling cards and now even Internet-based phones.

All these alternatives offer a less expensive means of communicating than using the traditional hotel guestroom phone and other services such as fax. A fax machine in the guestroom was considered a premium amenity for many years. With the Internet explosion, however, the machines have seen less use. While some hotels continue to enjoy a reasonable revenue stream, others have reported declines in revenue. E-mail and Internet faxing have contributed to the drop in usage. Calling cards have led the shift from 0+ to 1-800 dialing. This shift not only has depleted revenue from commissions but also ties up much needed trunk lines. Modem calls are also another source of PBX congestion, but contrary to popular belief, not as much as calling cards.

Cellular phones have become so widely used that some cell phone providers have had trouble keeping up with the demand. AT&T's one-rate plan was so successful that for a time subscribers were unable to complete calls in certain areas. These problems have now been addressed for the most part. What is of concern to hoteliers attempting to eke out a profit in telecom is the proliferation of nationwide cell phone plans that include no roaming or long-distance charges and nights and weekends free.

A guest on such a plan has an average cost of about 5 cents per minute for long distance, depending on the mix of anytime vs. night and weekend. Assuming that the wireless reception quality is acceptable, it is very difficult for the hotel to compete on a cost basis. High-speed Internet access (HSIA) is fast becoming an expected amenity. With more guests carrying laptops than ever before and Internet business activity rapidly increasing, the guest must have the best connection available. HSIA also relieves the congestion on the PBX caused by modem calls. While some revenue-sharing business models have proven unsuccessful, there are realistic approaches to installing and providing HSIA on at least a break-even basis, if not generating a small profit.

Self-Contained Guest

Typically, this guest carries a notebook computer, a small printer, a cell phone and perhaps a pager. The guest has spare batteries for the phone, an antenna booster that enhances reception and the ability to connect to the Internet wirelessly. The guest sends and receives faxes over the Internet or with a direct dial wireless connection. The phone receives voicemail messages when in use or turned off during charging. Theoretically, the self-contained guest needs no hotel telecommunications services.

Guests to Use the Hotel's Telecommunication Services

Hotels are unable to compete on price with devices that the guest has brought with him. What the hotel can do is offer a better experience at a reasonable price to entice guests to use the hotel's telecom infrastructure. No matter what cell phone the guest may carry or what service provider is used, no wireless connection is as good as a land-line connection. Given a choice, most guests would prefer to use the hotel phone if they can afford to.

Wireless Internet connections, while improving, offer an experience that is, at best, the speed of a dial-up connection. Generation 3 cell phones promise better connections, but that is some time in the future. Therefore, it is not possible for the guest to attain anywhere near the quality wirelessly that a high-speed Internet connection furnished by the hotel can provide. Some hoteliers have recognized this advantage in quality by offering package plans. One small hotel chain is offering unlimited local calls and high-speed Internet access for $9.95 a day. The take rate on this package has been as high as 25 percent.

Other chains are tying such packages to their loyalty programs. The guest must first enroll in the program to be eligible for the packages. This approach has led to an increase in enrollment. Such packages can require a two-way interface with the call accounting system. This two-way interface allows the call accounting system to recognize package plans vs. normal call accounting billing for other guests. Other properties are looking at the feasibility of offering fixed-rate long distance, such as 12 cents per minute.

This is a variation from traditional hotel long-distance pricing, but is more attractive to the guest. No matter what strategy a property takes in the telecommunications department, one thing is for certain, it needs to be a different one from the past. Given the hotel's advantage in quality over the guest's portable devices, the proper packaging of services will lure even the most avid self-contained guest back to using the hotel's telecom services.

Hotel Information Systems : Total Enterprise Management Solutions

Hotel Information Systems (HIS) uses leading enterprise technology to provide multi-property management and centralize all key areas of operations. We have combined our years of hospitality experience with Internet technology expertise to develop an enterprise-class system that brings our clients a foundation for sustainable competitive advantages.

Driving Forces

Products : HIS epitome Enterprise Solutions deliver the transactional framework and a set of convenient tools to centrally analyze critical operational data, and manage rates, inventory and the many new buy-side channels. HIS offers products include:

- Property management tools
- Corporate management tools
- Call center management tools

— Strategic analysis and planning tools
— Reservation portal solutions

Services : Our products are deployable on multiple platforms, integrated by utilizing intelligent transport and messaging technology. HIS offers services such as:

— Systems design and integration
— Infrastructure and data analysis
— Project management
— Implementation
— Training
— Support services
— Specialized engineering

Technology : We have built products from the ground up using proven Internet technology making them completely platform neutral, globally deployable and highly scalable. Our solutions provide the ability to:

— Leverage existing IT investments
— Lay the foundation for future computing
— Add functionality at your own pace
— Integrate your corporate systems
— Integrate your business processes with your partners, suppliers and customers
— Use one comprehensive solution for any operation, from a single property to the largest chain

HIS epitome Enterprise Solutions provide global hotel organizations with tools to:

— Increase operational efficiency
— Improve guest loyalty
— Centralize processes
— Maximize yields

— Provide timely operational knowledge
— Manage the many new buy-side channels
— Leverage current IT investments
— Transform transactional data into strategic intelligence
— Provide the foundation for future business agility
— Increase profitability

Hospitality eDistribution in the New Economy: Restructuring the Concept of Value Chain

The logical consequence of eDistribution is inescapable: the traditional value chain collapses in what can be described as a "frictionless environment," as suppliers interact directly with consumers through networked technologies. In a frictionless environment, when interaction costs at the margin are close to zero, the cost structure and strategic implications of distribution clearly change very significantly. To grow and succeed, management at hospitality and travel companies of any size must juggle multiple distribution channels, customer segments and intermediaries in their distribution of goods and services.

All entities have zeroed in on a business-to-consumer strategy with the intent to influence purchase decisions and own consumer loyalty. Classic economic models place the producer of goods at one end of the chain and the consumer on the other end, with packaging, shipping, storing and retail middlemen often connecting the two. The Internet, however, has redefined the traditional model and all of the relationships within this value chain. Regardless of whether the good is a product, a service or a combination of the two, the entire consumer purchasing process is undergoing re-evaluation with new business models poised to change or destroy the traditional methods of distribution.

In the so-called "old economy," distribution intermediaries existed to compensate for the lack of knowledge on products and pricing, as well as bringing buyer and seller together over a physical distance. As the Internet becomes the ultimate connectivity tool, however, products and services no longer require a physical distribution presence. Intermediaries can continue to contribute to the product or service. But as technology forces out physical inefficiencies in distribution, there are fewer places where middlemen can find safe haven from disintermediation.

The implications of a collapse of the traditional value chain are immense. Because much of the hospitality travel product is experienced-based, the role of distribution can be seen at its simplest as the ability to initiate an experience. Distribution, therefore, becomes part of the product itself. A redefined value chain has both positive and negative implications for each player in the chain.

Generally speaking, suppliers benefit from lower distribution costs, better product image control, enhanced brand value and a better relationship with the customer. Intermediaries are likely to experience the greatest short-term turbulence, as each scrambles to assess the value they create and how to sustain it in the value chain. The consumer is most likely to gain, given the opportunity for better service, lower prices, tailored marketing and more options.

Traditional suppliers

Regardless of distribution method, the products themselves, such as physical guest rooms, airline seats and rental cars, remain largely unchanged in the new economy, although customer information can be used to customize products and services. What is markedly different, however, is an extraordinary increase in competitive pressure to "own" the customer. Since connectivity to the customer is no longer a technology hurdle, each player in the value chain is attempting to develop customer loyalty.

Owning or, at a minimum, significantly influencing the channel is an important component of managing customer loyalty. Numerous supplier limitations have allowed nimble start-ups to take an early lead in the race to influence the consumer purchase decision. Most legacy information technology (IT) systems have not been engineered to handle the volume, content and query capabilities required of an online presence in the distribution channel. Customer relationship management (CRM) systems, for example, remain largely in an infancy stage - only the top few percent of frequent hotel guests for example, receive consistent customized service. Indeed, the vast majority of Web site screens do not mimic how consumers buy hospitality and travel products and services.

To secure a hotel booking online, for example, the customer typically enters an arrival date and length of stay. In reality these variables often are influenced by price, but this symbiotic relationship is not well represented at Web sites. Web sites will clearly need to provide more information and suggestions for customized and packaged travel if they are truly to serve the interests of travelers. Major issues for each of the key suppliers:

Airlines : The airlines have continued to be leaders in a shortening value chain by eliminating activities that do not add value, while developing such items as electronic ticketing and last-minute fares at low prices. Recently, five major airlines have announced they plan to create a megasite for eDistribution, a plan that responds to the threat of online travel agencies as they attempt to reintermediate themselves with customers. Whereas the airlines previously did not distribute their products directly to consumers, the new economy is requiring them to collaborate with their historical competitors with strategies to own the customer.

Hotel Companies : Channel conflict continues to be a significant issue among hotel companies. The price of a physical hotel room often varies widely depending on the source of booking (e.g., call center, Internet travel site, retail travel agency, corporate agent or direct contact with the property). Even though "single-image" inventory is widely favored in the industry, displaying the same image to all potential buyers remains challenging and is largely unfulfilled. Legacy reservation systems were not designed for true single image inventory. With available technology moving the industry toward price transparency, companies will feel intense pressure to compete on brand and differentiation, rather than price alone.

Hotels must also manage additional customer touch points, an activity that is not always successful in the physical world. Guest recognition and tailored service are hallmarks of excellent properties. Customer relationship management is powered by good data, however, which remains a rarity within the hotel community. Extending recognition and consistency of service to the Internet and new sales channels compounds the problem of effectively managing the entire guest experience.

Traditional Intermediaries

Changes brought by eDistribution have had the most profound effect on players that are positioned between suppliers and consumers in the distribution chain. These intermediaries are going through a period of transformation in how they do business:

Travel Agents: The new role for this group is that of knowledge manager. The retail travel agent is the best-known intermediary in the hospitality industry. A portion of a retailer's activities today remains value-added, while other roles are "old economy" in nature and becoming obsolete. The act of printing and issuing paper airline tickets is rooted in history when only Global Distribution System (GDS) terminals provided inventory access, and airlines required paper tickets for accounting. An area where travel agents do continue to add tremendous value is in advising travelers of destinations, tailoring travel to individual preferences, and saving time and money for the traveler before and during the trip.

Tour Operators: These intermediaries are also at significant risk from the collapse of the hospitality and travel value chain, as the Internet introduces new forms of competition. Tour operators aggregate travel products and repackage those products under a brand name. Tour operators in Europe own a much larger portion of the leisure travel market than in North America, with several large players dominating approximately half of the market. In the United States and Canada, the tour business is extremely fragmented, with few well-known brands and thin profit margins.

Suppliers connected with consumer groups have the potential to mimic and exceed the purchasing power of individual tour operators. Furthermore, customer loyalty is often stronger with the travel agent that sells packages in North America. Immense business and technology issues also exist for tour operators seeking to function in the new economy. Call centers create an artificial demand regulator, limiting the amount of product available on a free-sale basis by the number of agents answering calls.

If the same model and IT systems are opened to Web traffic, a virtually unlimited amount of demand could overwhelm free-sale and price-yielding techniques that are designed for a different business model. To compete, tour operators will need to use networking tools and offer complete excursions that are priced in real-time and tailored to their customers.

Global Distribution System (GDS) Providers

GDS and Switches GDS providers offer some of the most reliably engineered IT transaction systems in existence. In a frictionless environment, however, Internet connectivity could ultimately eliminate the need for the GDS. GDS providers are now powering many of the virtual travel agent and online supplier bookings, and are demonstrating that intermediaries can still play an effective role by delivering reservation capabilities faster and cheaper than individual suppliers on their own. The fact that the GDS and switching organizations such as THISCO and Wizcom are still used to book online travel indicates that new entrants have eliminated only a part of the traditional hospitality and travel value chain. Some friction in distribution still exists when these intermediaries are used to gain access to supplier inventory.

New dot.com intermediaries

Virtual travel agents represent a new form of intermediary, with some estimates placing the number of Web sites with travel booking capabilities at close to 1,000. Virtual travel agents charge a commission from suppliers (about 5 percent for hotels), but typically offer a lower flat fee for airlines. Many of these companies will clearly have to revisit their Internet strategies and business models over the next several years, as hotels, airlines and other suppliers become more aggressive in offering consumers direct access to inventory.

Many of these new dot.com companies have yet to be profitable and are running out of time and money to gain significant market share to offset high costs in technology and payroll. New intermediaries such as Priceline.com have used the Internet to create a demand collection system. Worldres.com has amassed a central inventory of more than 11,000 properties, of which many are bed and breakfasts and vacation rentals that could not conform to the GDS listing requirements. A large number of additional entrants are expected in this arena in the next twelve months, particularly in the business-to-business arena, allowing corporations of all sizes to more effectively buy travel products.

With the restructuring of the value chain, consumers stand to gain the most. Whether consumers choose to book online, or use the Internet for research and a physical travel agent to book, the level of knowledge, choices and convenience is unprecedented. The purchase experience will only improve as broadband access and multimedia content are married with product availability and one-to-one marketing activities. Distribution costs are eliminated when a value chain is shortened, and many of these savings are passed on to consumers in the form of bonus miles, last-minute fares and Web-direct-only pricing.

Vast amounts of information and the intensity of advertising "noise" can clearly be overwhelming to many consumers. But as the ease of use and customized offerings improve under the banner of powerful brands, the superiority of eBusiness applications for the hospitality and leisure industry will eventually become the norm. At that point, the new economy will no longer be "new," and the value chain will reflect the power of the Internet and its global networking capabilities.

Devolopment of Next-Generation Technology for the Hotel Industry

A new approach is needed in order to facilitate the development of next-generation, customer-centric systems that will better meet the needs of the global hotel community.Hotel Technology—Next Generation (HTNG) initiative, which aims to define a new approach to providing systems and technology services at the property, brand, management company, and ownership levels, worldwide. Comment and discussion are invited.

Hotels struggle daily to manage this complexity. They are handicapped by a complex decision-making process for capital spending, and also by a relative lack of third-party providers who can deliver comprehensive solutions on a pay-as-you go basis. Hotel technology vendors are mostly small and undercapitalized. While there is much in the way of quality product to meet each area of functional need, each product addresses only a very limited set of the total application requirements. Interoperability of systems, with a few notable exceptions, has been an elusive goal.

Annual global hotel technology spending has been estimated by various studies to be as high as US$25 billion, although the truth is that, as technology expenses are buried in so many parts of hotel budgets, such estimates are at best educated guesses. By any measure, however, hospitality represents one of the largest industries in terms of technology spend, perhaps surpassed only by the retail industry and the technology industry itself. The largest software providers and technology service delivery companies in the hotel industry each command less than 1% of the market.

The vast majority of vendors have market shares of less than 0.1%. Many major software and service providers that dominate other industries have left this huge market largely untouched. Others recognized the opportunity and tried to stake out positions, but have been largely unsuccessful. Several have abandoned the industry completely, often after years of frustration and losses. Among the existing set of hotel technology vendors, only a few have achieved any significant success with consolidation or partnership strategies, whether by acquisition, through alliances, or through internal development.

The resulting fragmentation of systems and vendors has imposed significant costs and inefficiencies on hotels. At the property level, it requires high levels of management effort to manage the multi-system, multi-vendor environment. For multi-hotel organizations it complicates the consolidation of accurate, comprehensive data on guests' profiles, preferences and activities—the lifeblood of any hospitality organization. Similarly, the industry structure has imposed costs on technology vendors. The frequent need for capital budget approval of multiple parties just to sell to a single hotel (much less a multi-hotel organization) have led to high selling costs, long sales cycles, and lagging financial performance among vendors.

Experience of Other Industries

Today, the vast majority of U.S. branch banks receive all of their technology, delivered to them as a service by one of three independent commercial vendors. It is only because of this structure that the technology suppliers to the banking industry have been able to deliver a reasonably customer-centric, consistent technology ... one that facilitates the financial side of world trade, enables customers to use their ATM cards around the world, allows banks to cross-sell a range of financial products, and frees bank managers to focus on customer retention and profitability rather than technology.

Like the hotel industry, the retail industry is dominated by small outlets with mixed ownership, management, and franchise relationships. Yet retail has achieved quite a high degree of supply chain integration, point-of-sale consistency across a wide variety of merchants, and merchandise management strategies. Those accomplishments would have been impossible without the emergence of technology standards, vendors who supported them, and products that were interoperable even, when required, with competitive systems.

Without these developments, credit cards would only work if the cardholder's issuing bank was the same as the merchant's, and ATM cards would only work with the issuing bank's own cash machines. In each case, the emergence of single-source, full-solution vendors, who can offer turnkey technology on a pay-as-you-go basis, frees the business unit to focus on meeting the needs of its customers, without having to worry about managing complex technology.

— These single-source vendors can focus on ease of use and simplicity of management for the end user.

— In many cases the underlying applications may consist of a patchwork of legacy solutions and newer technologies, but the end user sees a single, consistent, evolving application.

— Software upgrades occur seamlessly, the equipment and networks are reliable, and the applications are nearly bug-free.

— Application suites meet nearly every need of the business unit, and can be configured to meet the competitive requirements of widely varying strategies.

— The cost to the business unit is known in advance and can be budgeted as an operating expense, often directly tied to revenue-generating transactions.

— Over time, the vendors can reduce operating and maintenance costs by rewriting legacy applications into a consistent, modern technology platform.

Simply put, today's branch bank or retail store manager worries no more about technology than he or she worries about the electricity, water supply, or telephone. They pay the "utility" bill each month, and the technology arrives. In the rare instances where it fails, they call the "utility" company and have it repaired.

Structure and Future of HTNG

Hotel Technology—Next Generation was founded as a noncommercial organization by individuals who see change as essential to releasing the constraints of the current situation and to producing a quantum increase in efficiency to the benefit of owners, operators and vendors alike.

HTNG was founded on June 23, 2002 by a group of nine leading hotel industry technology experts, with global representation of hotel technology management, consulting, and academia.The group members' experiences, developed over many decades of work with hundreds of hotel companies and vendors, represented the broadest possible spectrum of the industry.

HTNG is intended as a vehicle to foster the adoption of standards and practices that can help the hotel industry achieve generational change in technology that will provide both a technical architecture and integrated software environment to address the needs of the hotel industry in the years to come. The keys to this vision are application integration, interoperability, stability, flexibility, scalability, and adaptability.

The group also identified the steps that need to be taken in order to raise the hotel industry to a level of technology performance comparable to that achieved in other industries. The group's conclusions were less the result of negotiating different perspectives than they were a process of putting common words around shared experiences and observations. HTNG is actively seeking endorsement from industry participants for the general concepts.

Potential Benefits: The potential benefits to the industry are substantial, although they will differ from hotel company to hotel company and from vendor to vendor. Vendors can achieve many of the benefits through reduced obstacles to selling. The conversion and system integration costs, capital budgeting processes, and "partial solution" nature of existing product and service offerings make it far more difficult for hotels to recognize the full financial return of technology projects. As a result, vendor sales cycles are long, and "large" sales, across an entire management company or brand, are often difficult or impossible.

Current Status of Technology in the Hotel Industry

Dissatisfaction with Technology

The hotel industry is fundamentally dissatisfied with the effectiveness of its current technology options and their ability to satisfy future business needs. This dissatisfaction is amplified by the need of many companies to replace aging systems within the next few years due to hardware and software obsolescence. In many cases, support services have been withdrawn by vendors for their oldest legacy products—for entirely understandable reasons, given that some are more than a decade old and run on platforms that are themselves unsupportable.

Most hotel companies face huge capital spending requirements over the next few years to replace legacy systems such as property management systems, telephone switches and software, and central reservations systems. Even for smaller hotel companies, the costs for these replacements can easily total tens of millions of dollars. Yet in most cases, the available replacement systems fail to offer significant business benefit versus the legacy systems they would replace.

This dissatisfaction is widespread despite the view that there are many technology products on the market that offer more than adequate features and functionality, at least within their defined scopes. Yet with few exceptions, these same products fail to meet the true business needs. Equally, the hotel industry has failed to state those needs to the vendor community clearly, or has stated them in ways that applied only to a subset of the problem. There are four key reasons for dissatisfaction.

Complexity of deployment: Most technology products are physically installed at individual hotels but utilize core technologies that are too complex to be supported cost-effectively by hotel staff. Remote management and support of software, either by a corporate technology group or a third party, is often infeasible due to the choice of technologies used to build the software, the lack of understanding of the need by vendors, and the absence of credible third party service providers. The evolution of products from standalone, turnkey systems into products that operate on the hotel's local area network has created configuration and interoperability issues that neither the vendor nor the hotel staff can easily diagnose or correct.

To effectively manage the current generation of technologies in an average full-service hotel, without support from a central technology organization, can easily require IT skill levels commanding a salary that can rival or exceed that of the general manager. Obviously, it is neither realistic nor cost-effective for hotels to contemplate this approach. Even among the major management companies and brands that provide centralized support and maintenance of core systems, the requirements of the non-core systems that are purchased and managed locally often overwhelm the capabilities of the on-site IT staff, if indeed there are any. The technical evolution that has created these challenges continues unabated. Absent fundamental change in the systems architecture and delivery model, this situation will continue to get worse.

Inability to integrate: Hotels have become intense information producers and users, yet still cannot view required information when and where they need it. No common integration method allows the installed systems to work together to effectively create, store, retrieve, and present information that may exist across them. Proprietary interfaces are seen as expensive and in constant need of upgrade as the respective applications evolve to meet new industry requirements. Furthermore, the growing need for integrated information has resulted in the need for more interfaces and for greater functionality from existing interfaces.

The situation has been exacerbated by the need to integrate information not only within the hotel, but at multiple levels of organizations (management company, brand, ownership company, regional cluster). These entities frequently have differing needs and priorities, and competing and incompatible standards. Standards bodies such as the HITIS and the Open Travel Alliance have focused on a narrow (if critical) range of systems, principally within the distribution chain. While these efforts are important and worthy of strong hotel industry support, the fact remains that very few hotel technology vendors have embraced them and even fewer have implemented them (and in fairness, few of their customers have demanded them).

Role of hotel management: Hotel managers cannot, do not want to, and should not be expected to manage complex technology systems. Yet, in the current environment, many are forced to take on this role. Arguably, both the experience of most incumbent general managers, and the success drivers of the business, suggest that general managers should be responsible for filling beds, satisfying guests, and controlling costs. It is naïve to believe that they are capable of making valid purchasing decisions for complex systems, or of managing their technology operation effectively. This problem is particularly acute for smaller hotel companies, independent hotels, and globally diverse hotel companies, who often lack the financial resources to provide even limited levels of centralized technology management or support.

Unrealized benefits: Hotel technology investments often fail to deliver the expected benefits. Even when a product meets its functional expectations completely within its intended range, it may prove difficult, costly, or even impossible to integrate it with other components of the hotel's technology. These limitations often become evident only during the implementation of a new system. The vendor frequently takes the blame when this occurs, but in many cases the limitations may be caused more by the legacy systems than by the replacement.

In many cases too, hotel management fails to re-engineer the underlying business processes, and fails to implement the procedures that may be needed to achieve the desired results. Managing this re-engineering process effectively often requires technical project management skills that most hotels cannot find internally – and should not be expected to.

Lack of Leadership and Vision

There is little strategic leadership or vision from either the hotel industry or the vendor community to define the key attributes required of the technology to meet current and future needs, or the key business issues that fund technology investment. While there have been pockets of leadership and vision within the hotel industry and among its technology vendors, too often that leadership and vision has been functionally limited, geographically narrow, market-segment specific, or financially constrained.

At other times it delivers functionality but fails to address integration, supportability, or scalability. Many other industries have the same broad geographic distribution of front-line operations that creates much of the complexity in hospitality. Some of these, such airlines, banks, and retail, are the very industries hotels deal with every day. Yet unlike these industries, the hotel industry lacks any significant presence of major, broad-based product or service vendors with multi-industry expertise to provide technology leadership and vision. Similarly, many hospitality technology executives have worked only within the hotel industry and are unaware of how other industries have addressed some of the same issues they face.

Many hotel companies have been unwilling to fund technology organizations to the level needed to obtain the breadth of experience, creativity, and knowledge of new technologies that is needed to drive change. Finally, technology-related research and development is virtually non-existent within the hotel industry. The result has been incremental rather than generational change, lack of innovation, and persistent reliance on legacy technologies.

The transaction-centric model originated in the days when systems were used primarily to deliver a guest folio and to account for the revenue. The industry need has evolved well beyond those requirements. Even some of today's more customer-centric technology offerings often lack the ability to store multiple profiles for the same customer depending on his/her nature of travel. They also fail to recognize the many levels and types of customers (guests, sales accounts, distributors, etc.). Furthermore, no product or combination of products is capable of delivering a consistent view of the customer across every point of interaction that the customer may have within a single hotel, let alone across multiple hotels within a brand.

There are more than 100 categories of technology-based systems in use within the hotel industry, and the average full-service hotel employs at least 20 to 30 different systems. The vast majority of those systems interact with customers in some way or enable service staff to do so. Yet typically only a few (sometimes as few as one) are connected to any system that can accurately describe the customer in even a limited fashion, or record the results of the interaction. Even where interfaces exist, they may be too expensive to implement, too difficult to maintain, too limited in scope, or simply incapable of delivering the type of customer experience that the hotel wants to provide.

Nowhere is this issue more evident than within the distribution process. Hotels want to control how their product is presented to the customer throughout the distribution network, to retain control of the customer relationship, and to customize the experience of the customer based on their knowledge of who the customer is, what they want, and how they behave. Yet few of the systems within the distribution chain support a notion of "customer" that goes beyond the most basic identifying information. Even where they do, that notion may be lost before delivery of a reservation to the hotel, for lack of an effective interface to the property management system, or even with an interface, for lack of a consistent data model.

The evolution of user requirements from transaction-centric to customer-centric is largely unrecognized. Most hotel systems were not designed to be interconnected as fully as today's business needs require and will fall even further short in meeting hotel requirements in the future, creating inefficiencies and opportunities for service-delivery failures. Interfaces that do exist are expensive, difficult to maintain, and often offer only limited functionality. Worse yet, their number is growing, and the complexity of managing them grows exponentially as the number of interfaces grows linearly.

Infrastructure

The key elements of infrastructure are the wide and local area data networks (WANs and LANs), the network operating system, the server and workstation operating systems, and the data management platform. Secondary elements include such items as office automation software, firewalls, virus scanners, and custom reporting packages. These requirements are no different than for businesses in other industries. Within the hotel industry, however, the required infrastructure is often non-existent. Where it does exist, it is frequently incompatible with modern system requirements. Too often, it is physically crumbling, unsupportable, improperly managed, or vulnerable to security attacks—and quite possibly all at the same time.

Different technology products deployed within the same hotel or hotel group not infrequently require infrastructures that are incompatible in critical ways, leading to redundancy, performance degradation, and inability to achieve integration—and all of these can adversely affect guest service and the overall guest experience. Critical functions such as user authentication, data management, word processing, e-mail, and printer management are often implemented in inconsistent ways, by multiple applications that need to be deployed within the same environment. These functions can and usually are provided by the base operating environment that has been established by the hotel.

Their inclusion in end-user applications, with different functionality and unique user interfaces, leads to redundancy, user confusion, and integration challenges. Some systems even require their own unique, single-use workstations and networks, despite the fact that the intended users may have (or have the need for) standard PCs, connected to the hotel's local area network, to perform other job functions. Some of these problems are legacy-system related, but many result from absence of industry-wide infrastructure standards and ignorance of the impact at the hotel company level. As an industry, our information assets must be sharable as required across multiple organizations, such as management companies, franchisors, owning companies, suppliers, and distribution partners.

Acquisition and Return-on-Investment (ROI) Measurement

The existing funding model, typically based on capital acquisition and spread across multiple budgets, creates many obstacles to effective selection and deployment. The diverse and sometimes incompatible needs of owners, managers and franchisors need to be reconciled, and multiple constituencies need to be represented in, and often to sign off on, acquisition decisions. Even individual properties often have multiple owners with conflicting views and priorities. Vendors cannot easily conclude organization-wide deals because each organization has so many competing interests and because each hotel (e.g. within a management company or brand) may need to be "sold" individually.

This structure has led many of the largest technology players, who have huge presences across many other industries, to abandon their attempts to establish a significant presence in the hotel industry over frustration with the long sales cycles and the inability to close major, organization-wide deals. Compared with most other industries, the presence of such technology leaders as IBM, EDS, Perot Systems, Cap Gemini, and Accenture (among others) is extremely limited.

The capital acquisition model also makes little allowance for technology refresh. Basic items such as workstations, which other industries routinely replace on a regular cycle (such as every three years), are often purchased and left in place until a newly selected system forces their replacement. The cost of those workstations is then factored in as part of the system that requires their replacement, even if other systems use the same workstations (and even if the next upgrade to those other systems will dictate the same workstation upgrade).

The extra cost burden may well make the project appear to be financially unviable. Alternatively, the hotel may try to deploy the new system without the recommended upgrade, and then fail to achieve the performance they require. The operational cost of unreliable and inadequate systems is almost invariably ignored. Hotel budgeting processes recognize the need for physical infrastructure maintenance by creating reserves for furniture, fixtures and equipment (FF&E). This process recognizes that the physical infrastructure of the hotel—the lobby, carpeting, and furnishings, for example—requires periodic renovation or replacement, either because it wears out, because customer needs change, or because the asset becomes dated.

The very same factors are equally applicable to technology infrastructure, but most hotels treat the replacement or refresh of technology assets as discretionary. Infrastructure projects that are necessary to support future systems are often held to ROI standards, when the benefits are impossible to quantify. Failure to invest over any extended period of time would clearly damage or destroy the hotel's revenue base and limit its ability to adapt to changing business needs, yet the budgeting process treats these investments as discretionary.

One can only imagine what the guest experience might be like if the hotel industry were to hold non-technology infrastructure decisions, such as elevator repair, lobby recarpeting, air conditioning, or roof replacement, to the same ROI standard. Overall, the technology systems and infrastructure are almost never supported in a way commensurate with the fact that they contain the most valuable asset that hotels own – their customer data.

Technical Standards : Many applications in use today are built using aging toolsets and/or are targeted at legacy operating environments. These system environments were at one time relevant, and provided a low-cost base from which to deliver increased functionality. In today's modern, networked and Internet-connected world, however, these systems do not provide the needed connectivity to, or integration with, the many other applications that hotels are required to operate.

For a variety of valid business reasons, hotels need to interconnect complementary products produced by vendors who may be direct competitors, either in the same or in other application areas. Yet these inter-connections are often frustrated by architectural in-compatibilities. Many application vendors, for example, are still in the process of migrating MS-DOS based applications to Windows, at a time when technology has moved through several generations of Windows and is now shifting to the Web.

Given the multi-vendor landscape of the industry, a new approach is needed, one based on the effective use of available, modern technologies, and that allows rapid feature function development and facilitates easier application integration, deployment, management and upgrade. It is important to note that there is no requirement to use (or avoid) the products of any particular technology vendor.

Progress toward any technical standard will be evolutionary, and vendors cannot be expected to convert their legacy systems to meet new standards over-night. These standards are not intended to be flexible, but rather the application of the standards in hotel purchasing decisions will of necessity be flexible, at least in the short term. The desired result can be achieved if technology buyers make their commitment to long-term achievement of the standards a critical element of the evaluation, negotiation, and contracting process.

Business Standards: Many of the limitations of the current situation have evolved from contractual restrictions in software licensing and usage, and in the limited willingness or ability of many technology vendors to support the integration requirements of their hotel customers. While the technical standards create the platform for open systems, business standards are needed to en-sure that hotel companies have the contractual right to license and integrate systems as needed, even where competing vendors are involved, and using whatever means of integration are available and ap-propriate. At the same times, vendors have the right to protect their intellectual property, and to compete in the provision of software and services that assist in or accomplish such integration.

Important Actions the Hotel Industry Needs to Take

In order to achieve success, a substantial number of hotel companies may need to change key elements of how they measure, fund, and purchase technology. In some cases these changes can be effected through the auspices of trade organizations such as HFTP; while in other instances they must be undertaken by each hotel company independently. Many of these actions are outside the CIO's scope of responsibility, and will require the endorsement and adoption by hotel company CEOs, COOs, CFOs, and Boards of Directors.

Establish Technology Cost Measurement

The consultants among the founding members of HTNG are continually asked by major industry players to assist in developing solid estimates of industry technology spending. Despite the level of interest among CEOs and CIOs within the industry, technol-ogy cost measurement has proven extremely elusive. There is a widespread view among many companies that, while service delivery models for technology (ASP services being one example) are attractive, the current offerings on the marketplace seem too expensive in comparison to acquisition costs. While this may be true in some cases, there are fundamental issues with attempts to compare service models with capital spending models.

First, current hotel accounting standards make it virtually impossible to measure technology costs. Most technology costs within the hotel are buried within departmental budgets. Costs for a single technology initiative typically span across departmental borders. Technology that is provisioned by management companies or franchisors is often priced to the hotels at an amount that bears at best a loose relationship to underlying costs (and sometimes no relationship at all).

Second, many of the costs borne within the service model are typically excluded when estimating the total cost of ownership of an alternative capital-acquisition based solution. Internal cost calculations rarely include the time of all of the IT and non-IT management and staff needed to manage the operation on an ongoing basis. Furthermore, hotel companies rarely hold internal service departments to the same service-level agreements that they insist upon with external service providers. Perhaps even more important, the service model typically includes regular technology refresh that would lead to additional downline costs in the capital acquisition model, most (or all) of which are often not considered.

One of the consultants in our group has estimated that these issues can cause the typical capital acquisition funding approach to under-state true costs by 30% or more. The industry as a whole needs to find a better way to capture technology costs within its accounting systems. This role should logically fall within the scope of HFTP's charter. In order to manage technology spending appropriately, the hotel industry's accounting, budgeting and ROI analysis approaches need to:

— Clearly identify technology costs by category (e.g. infrastructure, operational sys-tems, sales/marketing/ distribution, guest room, etc.), regardless of which department funds them.

— Clearly measure or, at a minimum, estimate, in-direct costs of technology projects, including management staff time, burdens on support de-partments such as accounting and human resources, and similar resources.

— Measure technology costs actually incurred by the hotel, management company, and franchi-sor levels, and paid to third-party (unrelated) vendors. Too often, technology projects are mis-analyzed and under-funded because a manager or franchisor imposes a cost on a hotel that covers the provision of both technology-based and non-technology services. The hotel experiences a single price for the service and may not be able to assess the technology com-ponents independently.

— Make explicit assumptions about technology refresh costs, and in particular about the organizational costs when change is generational (as is often the case with the capital acquisition model) vs. incremental (as is more common with the service model).

— Identify costs shared among multiple applications as infrastructure, and evaluate infrastructure costs within the context of all supported applications and operations rather than just the single application that forced an upgrade or replacement

Provide Technology Reserve Funds

The need to spend money on an ongoing basis to ensure a stable but evolving technology environment is not optional, but rather is a cost of staying in business. While it may be possible to defer a given expenditure from one year to the next, technology refresh cannot be put off forever any more than can refurbishment of the physical plant.

The need to measure shared infrastructure costs, discussed above, is generated by the need to budget for it separately from end-user projects. A solid technology foundation within each hotel and hotel company is required to operate any of the more modern hotel systems. Today, the property management system, the sales system, the local presence of the central reservation system, the office automation software, and many other applications often share the network infra-structure and workstations, which taken together can account for half or more of the hardware costs within a hotel.

In the future, PABXs, telephone handsets, in-room entertainment and Internet services, door locking, and energy control systems (among others) will likely share the same infrastructure. The cost of maintaining reasonably current technology for the shared infrastructure elements cannot reasonably be burdened on any one application and justified by the project's ROI. Rather, infrastructure costs should be determined, component by compo-nent, with reasonable lifetimes, and an annual budget established for technology refresh. The particular systems being deployed or upgraded within a given budget year may dictate which infrastructure elements are refreshed first, but should not be expected to provide the financial justification for infrastructure elements that would eventually be needed with or without the project.

The vendor that provisions the PCs (whether internal or external) charges the users a monthly lease rate that enables it to deliver, install, maintain, and replace PCs. This maintenance and replacement cycle allows every technology project to assume that it has the workstations needed, at a current level of technology. The incremental cost of the project is affected only if it creates the need for additional workstations.

Recruitment of Qualified Professionals

The hotel industry as a whole, and individual hotel properties in particular, have failed to embrace the establishment of adequately funded and qualified technical staff. While there are many structural reasons why hotel technology has failed to deliver to its potential, many could have been avoided, or could be compensated for, if an adequate IT skill base were available. Only a few hotel companies, mostly larger ones, have embraced this concept.

As an industry, we would not promote an accountant or front desk clerk to the top position in food and beverage, yet hotels routinely promote unqualified staff into key technology positions. If the food is bad and the restaurant service surly, we find a qualified F&B manager and give him or her what is needed to succeed. When technology fails to deliver to expectation, we find the staff member who seems to know how to use a computer and ask them to solve it.

This is akin to selecting, for the next F&B manager or Executive Chef, someone who likes to eat. For many hotels, and particularly those lacking centralized support from a chain or management company, hiring qualified IT staff can be an immense challenge. An IT professional sufficiently skilled to manage all of the technology in a midsized or large hotel can command a salary equal to or greater than that of the General Manager.

Larger management companies, chains, and third-party service providers are inherently in a better po-sition to attract qualified staff with the necessary range of expertise. It is for this reason that most larger companies and some service vendors have begun pulling technology out of hotels, wherever feasible, operating it in a centralized or regionalized environ-ment, and delivering it as a service to hotels. This is not to say that hotels do not need their own IT staff, or to suggest that it would allow hotels to continue to get by with the current insufficient levels of IT skills. Rather, it will allow a competent IT manager within a hotel to deliver and support a broad range of technol-ogy services cost effectively.

As an industry, we need to upgrade the position of IT manager, in all but the most basic types of hotels, to an executive committee level position, with commensurate pay, so that we can hire IT professionals with the qualifications needed to run the diverse systems we use. Perhaps in the future, if the industry evolves to more standard software delivered by third-parties and management companies, this position can be eliminated, but for the next five to ten years it is likely to be essential for most hotels.

When we hire IT professionals, whether at the corporate or hotel level, we should be looking at their range of technical education and skillsets more than their hotel experience. We need more IT people at all levels who know how problems have been solved in other industries and disciplines, and who have been trained to solve these problems in a professional way. We can teach them what they need to know about hotels; we cannot as an industry teach them what they need to know about technology.

Bibliography

Ankomah, P., and Larson, R. T., 2000, Education tourism: a strategy to sustainable tourism development in sub-Saharan Africa, DPMN Bulletin, 79(1), pp.19-24

Boella, M.J. 'Human Resource Management in the Hospitality Industry', Stanley Thornes: UK, PB, 1996.

Boissevain, J. (ed) 'Coping with Tourists: European Reactions to Mass Tourism', Berghahn Books: UK, 1996.

Boniface, B.G. and Cooper, C. 'Geography of Travel and Tourism', Butterworth Heinemann: UK, 1994.

Boniface, P. 'Managing Quality Cultural Tourism', Routledge: UK, 1995.

Borocz, J. 'Leisure migration: A Sociological Study on Tourism', Pergamon Press: UK, 1996.

Bramham, P., Henry, I., Mommaas, H. and Van der Poel, H. (eds) 'Leisure Policies in Europe', CAB International: UK, 1993.

Bratton, R. D., Go, F., and Ritchie, J. R. B., New Horizons in Tourism and Hospitality Education, *Training and Research, Calgary, World Tourism Education and Research Centre, 1991.*

Briggs, S. 'Successful Tourism Marketing', Kogan Page: UK, 1997.

Buhalis, D. Tjoa, A.M. and Jafari, J. (eds) 'Information and Communication Technologies in Tourism: Enter 98', Springer Verlag: Vienna, PB, ISBN 321183088X £37.50, 1998.

______________, *"Infromation technologies in tourism: implications for the tourism curriculum"*, paper presented at ENTER - International Conference on Information and Communication Technologies in Tourism, *Istanbul, Turkey, 1998.*

Bull, A. 'The Economics of Travel and Tourism', Longman: UK, PB, ISBN 058280731X £19.99, 1995.

Burton, J. and Burton, L. 'Interpersonal Skills for Travel and Tourism', Longman: UK, 1994

Clark, M. 'Interpersonal Skills for Hospitality Management', ITBP: UK, 1995.

______________, Riley, M., Wilkie, E. and Wood, R.C. 'Researching and Writing Dissertations in Hospitality and Tourism', ITBP: UK, 1998.

Collins, M.F. and Cooper, I.S. (eds), 'Leisure Management: Issues and Applications', CAB International: UK, 1997.

Cooper, C.P. and Lockwood, A. (1992) 'Progress in Tourism, Recreation and Hospitality Management Vol 4', Belhaven Press: UK, HB, ISBN 0471945129 £80.00

Foley, M., Lennon, J. and Maxwell, G. (eds) 'Hospitality, Tourism and Leisure Management: Issues in Strategy and Culture', Cassell: UK, 1997.

Foster, D.L. 'An Introduction to Travel and Tourism: First Class', McGraw Hill: UK, 1995.

Goodall, B. and Ashworth, G. (eds) 'Marketing in the Tourism Industry: The Promotion of Destination Regions', ITBP: UK, HB, ISBN 0415045452 £45.00, 1988.

Graham, B. 'Geography and Air Transport', Wiley: UK, HB, ISBN 0471957577 £75.00, 1995.

Grainger-Jones, B. 'Managing Leisure', Butterworth Heinemann: UK, 1998.

Gunn, C.A. 'Tourism Planning: Basics, Concepts and Cases', Taylor and Francis: UK, 1994.

Hall, C.M. 'Tourism and Politics: Policy, Power and Place', Wiley: UK, 1994.

______________. and Jenkins, J.M. 'Tourism and Public Policy', ITBP: UK, 1995.

______________. (ed) 'Sustainable Tourism: A Geographical Perspective', Longman: UK, 1998.

Holloway, C.J. and Robinson, C. 'Marketing for Tourism', 3rd ed, Longman: UK, 1995.